# YEAR **B**

IAN ADAMS
JEFF ASTLEY
ALAN BARTLETT
JOHN BARTON
ROSALIND BROWN
RICHARD A. BURRIDGE
GILLIAN COOPER
STEPHEN COTTRELL
STEVEN CROFT
ANDREW DAVISON
DAVID FORD
ALAN GARROW
BRUCE GILLINGHAM
PAULA GOODER
PETER GRAYSTONE
MARY GREGORY
MAGGIE GUITE
MALCOLM GUITE
HELEN-ANN HARTLEY
LINCOLN HARVEY

CHRISTOPHER HERBERT
SUE HOPE
JOHN INGE
MARK IRELAND
CHRISTOPHER JONES
PAUL KENNEDY
JOHN KIDDLE
LIBBY LANE
JANE LEACH
ANN LEWIN
JAN MCFARLANE
DAVID MARSHALL
JANE MAYCOCK
BARBARA MOSSE
DAVID MOXON
ROSALYN MURPHY
NADIM NASSAR
MARK OAKLEY
HELEN ORCHARD
IAN PAUL

MICHAEL PERHAM
MARTYN PERCY
JOHN PERUMBALATH
SUE PICKERING
JOHN PRITCHARD
BEN QUASH
CHRISTINA REES
SARAH ROWLAND JONES
DAVID RUNCORN
TIM SLEDGE
TOM SMAIL
ANGELA TILBY
GRAHAM TOMLIN
FRANCES WARD
KEITH WARD
MARGARET WHIPP
JANE WILLIAMS
LUCY WINKETT
CHRISTOPHER WOODS
JEREMY WORTHEN

Church House Publishing
Church House
Great Smith Street
London SW1P 3AZ

ISBN 978 1 78140 030 2

Published 2017 by Church House Publishing
Copyright © The Archbishops' Council 2017

The opinions expressed in this book are those of the
authors and do not necessarily reflect the official
policy of the General Synod or The Archbishops'
Council of the Church of England.

Liturgical editor: Peter Moger
Series editor: Hugh Hillyard-Parker
Designed and typeset by Hugh Hillyard-Parker
Copy edited by Ros Connelly
Printed by CPI Bookmarque, Croydon, Surrey

What do you think of *Reflections for Sundays*?

We'd love to hear from you – simply email us at

**publishing@churchofengland.org**

or write to us at

Church House Publishing, Church House,
Great Smith Street, London SW1P 3AZ.

Visit **www.dailyprayer.org.uk** for more information
on the *Reflections* series, ordering and subscriptions.

# Contents

# About the authors

**Ian Adams** is a poet, writer, photographer and artist. An Anglican priest, he is director of StillPoint, co-founder of Beloved Life and Spirituality Adviser for CMS.

**Jeff Astley** is an Anglican priest, and currently Alister Hardy Professor of Religious and Spiritual Experience at the University of Warwick, and an honorary professor at Durham University and York St John University.

**Alan Bartlett** is Vicar of a Durham City parish and two former pit village churches. He was formerly on the staff of Cranmer Hall (teaching church history, Anglicanism, spirituality and practical theology).

**John Barton** retired as Professor of Old Testament at Oxford University in 2014 and is now a Senior Research Fellow of Campion Hall, Oxford. He is an Anglican priest and assists in the parish of Abingdon-on-Thames.

**Rosalind Brown** is Canon Librarian at Durham Cathedral with oversight of the Cathedral's public ministry. A town planner before ordination, she has written books on ministry and several published hymns.

**Richard A. Burridge** is Dean of King's College London and also Professor of Biblical Interpretation. He writes on Jesus and the Gospels, and New Testament ethics.

**Gillian Cooper** is a writer, teacher and Old Testament enthusiast. She has worked as a theological educator, a cathedral verger and an administrator.

**Stephen Cottrell** is the Bishop of Chelmsford. He is a well-known writer and speaker on evangelism, spirituality and catechesis. He is one of the team that produced *Pilgrim*, the popular course for the Christian Journey.

**Steven Croft** is the Bishop of Oxford and writes widely on scripture, leadership and mission.

**Andrew Davison** is the Starbridge Lecturer in Theology and Natural Sciences at Cambridge University, Fellow in Theology at Corpus Christi College and Canon Philosopher of St Albans Abbey.

**David Ford** is Regius Professor of Divinity Emeritus at the University of Cambridge, Fellow of Selwyn College, and author of *The Drama of Living* and *Christian Wisdom*.

**Alan Garrow**, formerly Vicar Theologian of Bath Abbey, is Vicar of St Peter's, Harrogate and an Honorary Academic at the Inter-disciplinary Institute for Biblical Studies at the University of Sheffield.

**Bruce Gillingham** has had considerable experience in mission and pastoral ministry in Oxford, having served as Pastorate Chaplain at St Aldates, Chaplain of Jesus College and most recently as Rector of St Clement's Church for over 20 years.

**Paula Gooder** is Theologian in Residence for the Bible Society. She is a writer and lecturer in biblical studies, author of a number of acclaimed books, and a co-author of the *Pilgrim* course. She is also a Reader in the Church of England.

**Peter Graystone** works for Church Army, developing projects that take Good News to people who have no real experience of Church. He edits the website Christianity.org.uk and reviews theatre for the *Church Times*.

**Mary Gregory** is Team Rector of Ashby de la Zouch and Breedon on the Hill in the Diocese of Leicester. She is an amateur quilter and a passionate retired-greyhound owner.

**Maggie Guite** is Team Rector in the Linton Team Ministry, south-east Cambridgeshire. She has spent most of her ministry in the Diocese of Ely including a stint of eight years teaching Doctrine in theological colleges.

**Malcolm Guite** is Chaplain of Girton College, Cambridge. An acclaimed poet, he lectures widely on theology and literature. His many books include *Sounding the Seasons: Seventy Sonnets for the Christian Year*.

**Helen-Ann Hartley** is the seventh Bishop of Waikato in the Diocese of Waikato and Taranaki, New Zealand. She was ordained priest in the Diocese of Oxford and served as Director of Biblical Studies at Ripon College Cuddesdon.

**Lincoln Harvey** is Assistant Dean and Lecturer in Systematic Theology at St Mellitus College, London. He has written numerous books and articles, including *A Brief Theology of Sport*.

**Christopher Herbert** was ordained in Hereford in 1967, becoming a curate and then Diocesan Director of Education. He was an incumbent in Surrey and, later, Archdeacon of Dorking and then Bishop of St Albans. He retired in 2009.

**Sue Hope** is the Vicar of St Paul's Shipley and an Adviser on Evangelism for the Diocese of Leeds.

**John Inge** is the 113th Bishop of Worcester. He is Lead Bishop on Cathedrals and Church Buildings, and Chair of the College of Evangelists.

**Mark Ireland** is Archdeacon of Blackburn and co-author of six books on mission-related themes, most recently *Making New Disciples: Exploring the paradoxes of evangelism* and *How to do Mission Action Planning*.

**Christopher Jones** was widely respected across the Church of England, spending eight years as Home Affairs policy adviser for the Archbishops' Council until his death in 2012.

**Paul Kennedy** is Rector of East Winchester and Area Dean. He is also a Benedictine oblate at the Anglican Alton Abbey and blogs at http://earofyourheart.com/wp/

**John Kiddle** is Archdeacon of Wandsworth and was previously Director of Mission in St Albans Diocese after parish ministry in Watford and Liverpool. He is passionate about resourcing churches for mission.

**Libby Lane** is Bishop of Stockport in the Diocese of Chester. In 2015 she was consecrated as the Church of England's first woman bishop. She is an elected Suffragan in the House of Bishops and Chair of Cranmer Hall Theological College Committee.

**Jane Leach** is a Methodist Presbyter. She has been the Principal of Wesley House, Cambridge since 2011. Jane teaches practical theology in the Cambridge Theological Federation and contributes regularly to Radio 4's *Thought for the Day.*

**Ann Lewin** is an accomplished poet who is much in demand as a retreat leader. She was a secondary school teacher for 27 years and has also worked tutoring ordinands at Sarum College.

**Jan McFarlane** is the Bishop of Repton in the Diocese of Derby. She has served as Archdeacon of Norwich, Director of Communications, Chaplain to the Bishop of Norwich, Chaplain of Ely Cathedral and Curate in the Stafford Team Ministry.

**David Marshall** became Associate Professor of Anglican Episcopal Studies and Ministry at Duke Divinity School in 2013. He has worked in parish ministry, in university chaplaincy in Oxford, in theological training and as chaplain to the Archbishop of Canterbury.

**Jane Maycock** is a priest in the Diocese of Carlisle, with experience in parish ministry, as a Director of Ordinands, theological educator, writer and retreat centre chaplain.

**Barbara Mosse** is a writer and retired Anglican priest. She has worked in various chaplaincies, and has taught in theological education. Her books include *Welcoming the Way of the Cross* and *The Treasures of Darkness*.

**David Moxon** is the Archbishop of Canterbury's Representative to the Holy See and Director of the Anglican Centre in Rome. He was formerly Archbishop of New Zealand.

**Rosalyn Murphy** is vicar of St Thomas' Church, Blackpool. She is a writer in biblical studies, often bringing a liberation and womanist theological perspective to her research.

**Nadim Nassar** is an Anglican priest, and is the Director and Co-Founder of the Awareness Foundation and co-author of the Awareness Course. He was born and raised in Lattakia, Syria.

**Mark Oakley** is Chancellor of St Paul's Cathedral, London, and a Visiting Lecturer in the Department of Theology and Religious Studies, King's College London. He writes on the relationship between faith, poetry and literature.

**Helen Orchard** is Team Vicar of St Matthew's Church in the Wimbledon Team. She was previously Chaplain-Fellow at Exeter College, Oxford and before ordination worked for the National Health Service.

**Ian Paul** studied maths and worked in business before training for ordination and completing a PhD on the Book of Revelation. After a decade in parish ministry and another in theological education, he now teaches part time, writes, and blogs at www.psephizo.com.

**Michael Perham** was Bishop of Gloucester from 2004 to 2014. He was one of the architects of the Church of England's *Common Worship* and has written extensively about worship and spirituality.

**Martyn Percy** is the Dean of Christ Church, Oxford. From 2004 to 2014 he was Principal of Ripon College Cuddesdon, and prior to that was Director of the Lincoln Theological Institute.

**John Perumbalath** is Archdeacon of Barking in Chelmsford Diocese. He has served as a theological educator and parish priest in the dioceses of Calcutta (Church of North India) and Rochester.

**Sue Pickering** is a spiritual director, retreat leader and writer. A clerical Canon of Taranaki Cathedral, Sue finds inspiration in family, friends, 'ordinary' life, contemplation, creation, gardening and quilting.

**John Pritchard** retired as Bishop of Oxford in 2014. Prior to that he was Bishop of Jarrow, Archdeacon of Canterbury and Warden of Cranmer Hall, Durham.

**Ben Quash** is Professor of Christianity and the Arts at King's College London, the author of the 2013 Lent Book *Abiding*, and Canon Theologian of Coventry and Bradford Cathedrals.

**Christina Rees** is a writer, broadcaster, communications consultant and practical theologian. For many years she was a member of the General Synod and Archbishops' Council and a leading campaigner for women's ordination.

**Sarah Rowland Jones** was a mathematician, then a British diplomat, before ordination in the Church in Wales. After 11 years as researcher to successive Archbishops of Cape Town, she returned to the UK to run Cardiff's city centre church.

**David Runcorn** is a writer, speaker, spiritual director and theological teacher. He is currently Associate Director of Ordinands and Warden of Readers in the diocese of Gloucester.

**Tim Sledge** is vicar of Romsey Abbey and Area Dean. Prior to this he was Mission Enabler in the Peterborough Diocese. He is author of a number of books including *Mission Shaped Parish* and *Youth Emmaus*.

**Tom Smail** was a leading Scottish theologian, preacher and writer. He was Vice-Principal and Lecturer in Doctrine at St John's College, Nottingham.

**Angela Tilby** is a Canon Emeritus of Christ Church Cathedral, Oxford. A former BBC producer she was Tutor and Vice-Principal of Westcott House, Cambridge for ten years and then vicar of St Bene't's Church, Cambridge.

**Graham Tomlin** is Bishop of Kensington and President of St Mellitus College. He was formerly Vice Principal of Wycliffe Hall, Oxford and the first Principal of St Mellitus.

**Frances Ward** is Dean of St Edmundsbury in Suffolk. She is the Diocesan Environmental Officer, on General Synod, and a Trustee of the National Society. Her latest book is *Why Rousseau Was Wrong*.

**Keith Ward** is a Fellow of the British Academy, Emeritus Regius Professor of Divinity, Oxford, a Canon of Christ Church Cathedral, Oxford, and Senior Research Fellow at Heythrop College, London.

**Margaret Whipp** is the Lead Chaplain for the Oxford University Hospitals. She has served in parish ministry, university chaplaincy, and most recently as Senior Tutor at Ripon College Cuddesdon.

**Jane Williams** lectures at St Mellitus College, London and Chelmsford, and is a Visiting Lecturer at King's College London. She taught previously at Trinity Theological College, Bristol.

**Lucy Winkett** is Rector of St James's Piccadilly. Formerly Canon Precentor of St Paul's Cathedral and a professional singer, she writes for the national press and broadcasts regularly on radio.

**Christopher Woods** is a vicar in Stepney, East London, also working in the Stepney Training and Development office. Before that he was Secretary to the Church of England's Liturgical Commission and National Worship Adviser.

**Jeremy Worthen** is the Secretary for Ecumenical Relations and Theology at the Church of England's Council for Christian Unity. His publications include *Responding to God's Call* (Canterbury Press).

## About *Reflections for Sundays*

*Reflections for Daily Prayer* has nourished tens of thousands of Christians with its insightful, informed and inspiring commentary on one of the scripture readings of the day from the Common Worship lectionary for Morning Prayer. Its contributors over the years have included many outstanding writers from across the Anglican tradition who have helped to establish it as one of today's leading daily devotional volumes.

Here, in response to demand, *Reflections for Sundays* offers thoughtful engagement with each of the *Common Worship* principal service readings for Sundays and major holy days. Reflections are provided on:

- each Old Testament reading (both Continuous and Related)
- the Epistle
- the Gospel.

Commentary on the psalm of the day can be found in the companion volume, *Reflections on the Psalms*.

In addition, Paula Gooder provides specially commissioned introductions to the Gospels of Mark and John, while contributions from 60 distinguished writers ensure a breadth of approach.

Combining new writing with selections from the weekday volumes published over the past ten years, *Reflections for Sundays* offers a rich resource for preaching, study and worship preparation.

# An introduction to Mark's Gospel

One of the glories of having a Gospel in a lectionary year is that, over the course of the year, our ear can become attuned to the voice of that year's evangelist. The more we hear their voice, the more we learn to recognize the emphases and motifs that each evangelist provides. The more we recognize their emphasis and motifs, the more we are drawn into the life and ministry of the one they seek to depict: Jesus.

On one level, this is especially the case in Year B. The Jesus of Mark's Gospel springs off the page and into our hearts in a more vivid and dynamic way than in any of the other Gospels. In fact, I would say – and you can decide whether you agree or not – that Mark's telling of the story of Jesus is the most stirring and affecting of all of the Gospels.

## A year of two Gospels

The challenge of Year B, however, is that Mark's voice is not the only evangelist's voice we hear. Mark's voice is spliced with John's voice throughout the year, so that the dynamic, fast-paced telling of Mark's Gospel, sits alongside the more reflective, unhurried style of John's telling. For the most part this is helpful and inspiring; the two contrasting styles work well together, giving lots of food for thought.

There is, however, one problem with it. The telling of Mark's Gospel is structured almost entirely around Jesus' crucifixion. The shadow of the cross looms throughout the whole Gospel, deepening with intensity the closer we get to chapter 15. It is, therefore, slightly odd that, when we get to Holy Week and Easter, much of what we read and hear comes from John (the exceptions to this is are the liturgy of the Passion and the Gospel reading in the Easter Vigil). In other words, we hear the crucial event at the heart of Mark's narrative in John's words not Mark's.

It is worth, therefore, at the start of the year in which we hear, read and meditate on Mark's Gospel, spending time in working out how to hear the Gospel to the very end and with all the emphases that Mark wanted to place on his telling of the story, lest we lose sight of his major emphasis when we switch over to John for Holy Week and Easter.

Anyone who has spent a significant amount of time reading Mark's Gospel will be aware of its fast pace and dynamic style. In Mark, the story of Jesus moves along swiftly, conveying the sense that one event happened on the heels of another: Mark tells us that no sooner had Jesus done one thing than 'immediately' another took place.

Mark also loves depicting his scenes in greater detail than we find in the other Gospels, feeding us, his readers, titbits of information like the colour of the grass upon which the 5, 000 sat to eat the loaves and fishes (Mark 6.39). All of this transforms our relationship with the text. It is hard, when reading Mark, to be a dispassionate observer of events. Mark's style – and indeed his structure – all work on the readers of his Gospel not only to tell us about Jesus, but also to ask how we will respond to Jesus, Son of God.

There are, throughout the Gospel, many subtle ways in which this question is asked and asked again, and it is worth exploring some of the key ways in which this takes place in order to understand the power of Mark's telling of the story.

## The beginning of Mark

Mark's Gospel doesn't so much begin as burst upon us: 'The beginning of the good news of Jesus Christ, the Son of God'. The very first sentence of the whole Gospel declares in no uncertain terms precisely what we are to expect in the pages that follow. We are to prepare ourselves for good news, good news about Jesus, the long awaited Messiah who, at his baptism, God declared to be the Son of God. On one level we could argue that Mark 1.1 is superfluous. We do not need to be told that we are at the beginning of a story (no more than we need to be informed that we are at its end) – surely we can work this out for ourselves.

The purpose of this opening sentence in Mark, however, may have more significance than an announcement of the start of a story. Some see 1.1 not so much as the announcement of the commencement of the Gospel itself but as a title for the whole Gospel. The Gospel itself is the beginning of the good news of Jesus Christ; there is not an ending (a point that becomes even more pertinent when we explore the ending of Mark below). The life, ministry, death and resurrection of Jesus is indeed the beginning of the good news of Jesus Christ, son of God, but the good news does not end there. The good news continues onwards in the lives of those who respond to his call to 'come follow me'. It is this dynamic of the Gospel as only the beginning of the great adventure of good news that sets the tone for the whole of the rest of the Gospel.

## The characters of Mark's Gospel

Another striking feature of Mark's Gospel is the way in which he portrays the characters of the Gospel. More so than in any other Gospel, three groups of characters, and their responses to Jesus, stand out. There are the Jewish leaders – often but not exclusively the scribes and the Pharisees – who always respond negatively to him, finding fault with him and challenging him. Then there is the crowd that jostles around Jesus eager to hear his teaching and to bring him people for healing but never progressing beyond amazement at what he says and does.

The third group – the disciples – appear to be more promising, at least at first. Jesus called them personally (and they responded right away) and he taught them in private (Mark 4.34). It would be reasonable, therefore, to expect them to respond to Jesus, understand him and his message and to be ready to proclaim the good news about him whenever he told them to. The reality of the disciples' response was far removed from this. They misunderstood him time and time again, asked dim questions and – when it mattered most, at his arrest – ran away as fast as they could.

Even on the one occasion when Peter did get it right – at Caesarea Philippi where Jesus asked who they thought he was and Peter said the Messiah (Mark 8.29) – Peter followed his response of recognition with an attempt to prevent Jesus from following his vocation to death on a cross. Even then Peter's recognition was, at best, partial; he saw who Jesus was but failed to understand what this meant.

This is in stark contrast to a motley collection of individuals whom Jesus met in his ministry. Chapters 4 to 8 focus around a number of events in which, to put it mildly, the disciples' response to Jesus was less than ideal. Three events, in particular, focus these encounters, each of which took place in boats: the stilling of the storm (Mark 4.36-41); the walking on water (Mark 6.47-52) and the conversation about the leaven of the Pharisees (Mark 8.13-21). In each of these encounters, the disciples reveal, yet again, the depth of their lack of understanding. Interwoven with these three key events are a number of encounters between Jesus and certain individuals many of whom were, in different ways, outcasts from society: a man with an unclean spirit; a woman with a haemorrhage; a young girl (Jairus' daughter) who had died; a gentile woman; a deaf man and a blind man. These individuals, who had little or nothing to lose, without exception responded wholeheartedly to Jesus, often begging to be allowed to share the good news about him to everyone they knew.

In telling the story as he did, Mark sets up for us multiple stimuli to challenge us to think deeply about what it is that encourages or prevents a response to Jesus and why some people are more confident and at ease with spreading the good news of Jesus than others.

## The structure of Mark

Although Mark's Gospel constantly throws down the challenge of response to Jesus, it does not sugarcoat the consequences of doing so. The structure of the Gospel builds up to the recognition that those who follow Jesus are making the choice to follow him wherever that may lead – even if that path leads right to the cross.

There are many possible ways of analysing the structure of Mark's Gospel, but one that seems particularly helpful is to recognize the importance of the cross in the narrative. The Gospel of Mark can be split into four key sections:

- 1.2 – 4.34    *An Introduction to Jesus and his ministry*

  These four chapters contain healings, teachings, the calling of the disciples, a parable, a first conflict with the Jewish leaders, as well as many other stories. In other words, they introduce us to Jesus and who he was.

- 4.35 – 8.25    *The challenge of discipleship*

  In this section we encounter the disciples (in chapters 4, 6 and 8) in a boat struggling to understand who Jesus really was, despite the many miracles they had seen and teaching that they had heard.

- 8.26 – 10.52 *The cost of discipleship*

  From this point onwards the shadow of the cross looms over the story. We know that Jesus must die and that his calling to his followers is that they should be prepared to follow him to the cross as well.

- 11.1 – 16.8 *The death and resurrection of Jesus*

  The importance of the crucifixion in Mark is marked by the quantity of the material dedicated to the last week of Jesus' life (six chapters in all).

## The ending of Mark

This brings us neatly to the ending of the Gospel. All manuscripts contain the material that runs up to Mark 16.8. Some manuscripts end there, but others have additional endings: either a shorter one (around one verse long) or a longer one (Mark 16.9-20). The problem with both these additional endings is that their style and language are significantly different from the rest of the Gospel, making it unlikely that the same person wrote them as wrote Mark itself.

The question is whether there was another ending that is now lost that these replace or whether Mark 16.8 always ended as it does. It must be said that the ending at 16.8 is unusual: 'So they went out and fled from the tomb, for terror and amazement had seized them; and they said nothing to anyone, for they were afraid.' It hardly classes as a dramatic dénouement. However, I have always found it oddly satisfying and fitting well with the rest of the Gospel.

As we noted above, Mark's Gospel is a Gospel that asks us again and again the question that Jesus asked of Peter in Caesarea Philippi – 'Who do you say that I am?' – and, having asked it, throws down a challenge – 'and what will you, now, do about it?' The frankly unflattering portrayal of the disciples throughout the Gospel leaves a question echoing through the centuries of whether we, like them, will misunderstand who Jesus was and what he came to do. When it really matters, will we run off in the opposite direction or will we pick up the challenge laid down in the 'beginning of the good news of Jesus Christ' and live it out in a different way?

If Mark really does end at 16.8, then its ending feels closer to Matthew's great commission. In Matthew 28.16-20, Jesus famously sent the disciples out to the ends of the earth to make disciples, to baptize and to teach. Although much more implicit in Mark, the same message remains: will we go and tell the good news of Jesus as instructed or will we, like the women, run away afraid.

## The Messianic secret

Mark 16.6-8 is in some ways linked powerfully to the odd secrecy theme that emerges throughout the Gospel. One of the strangest features of the way Mark tells the story of Jesus is that Jesus regularly instructs people to tell no one about him and what he has done. This seems bizarre. Surely the whole point of the Gospel is that it tells the good news about Jesus and who he was? Why then would Jesus go out of his way to prevent them from declaring it? Mark 16.6-8 and 8.29-33 might give us the clue to the mystery.

In Mark 8.29-33, Peter, finally, acknowledged who Jesus really was ('You are the Messiah') but immediately began to chastize Jesus for suggesting that the Messiah must suffer and die. He had some of the jigsaw pieces but not all of them, and with this incomplete set of pieces created the wrong picture of who Jesus was. Until they had all the pieces, even Jesus' closest followers were liable to get the wrong end of the stick and proclaim the wrong kind of Jesus.

The only place in the Gospel where anyone is told to 'go, tell' is in Mark 16.6-8. The pieces are now all in place: Jesus has lived, taught, healed and loved; he has died and risen again. His followers now have all the pieces they need to go, tell the good news of Jesus in the world. The only question remaining, as we noted above, is whether they will find the courage to do so or whether they will run away afraid.

## The dating and authorship of Mark's Gospel

There is very little that gives us any clear sense of who the author of Mark's Gospel was. Within the Gospel there are only two hints about authorship or audience. The first is that Mark explains various features of Jewish custom, such as the custom of cleansing before eating (Mark 7.3-4). Thus suggests that his audience was, at least in part, non-Jewish. The other is that he occasionally gets geographical details wrong: for example, in 5.1 and 13 Mark implies that Gerasa was right on the shores of Galilee, whereas in reality it was a few miles inland. That is all, however, that we can tell from the Gospel itself.

Other evidence for the authorship of the Gospel comes from outside the New Testament. In the second century AD, Papias of Hierapolis attributed the Gospel to Mark who, he said, was an interpreter of Peter and who wrote down carefully, though not in order, all of Peter's memories of Jesus (what Papias said no longer remains but Eusebius quoted him as saying this in his History of the Church 3.39.15). This tradition is supported by a wide number of early writers such as Irenaeus, Origen, Tertullian and Clement of Alexandra. Most of these early Christian writers also claim that Mark wrote the Gospel before

Peter died (Peter is thought to have died in Nero's persecutions in AD 64 or 65); the only exception to this is Irenaeus, who appears to claim that Peter had died by the time Mark wrote the Gospel.

## Concluding reflections

Mark's Gospel could easily be subtitled 'the challenge and cost of discipleship'. It is a Gospel that reflects in depth not only on the nature and character of Jesus himself, but also on the nature and character of those he calls to follow him. It is not just a Gospel that tells you 'about' Jesus; it is a Gospel that invites each of us, its readers, to respond to him: to declare with Peter that he is the Messiah, to join with the centurion in declaring him truly to be God's son, and to listen to the call to 'go, tell' the good news of his life, death and resurrection to the ends of the earth.

Mark's Gospel may be the shortest and, in some ways, the easiest of all the Gospels to read, but – if read in the right way – it will ensure that our lives will never be the same again.

*Introduction by* **Paula Gooder**

# An introduction to John's Gospel

In many ways John's Gospel forms the perfect companion to Mark's Gospel. Where Mark's Gospel is immediate and direct; John's is slow and reflective. Where Mark's moves 'immediately' from event to event; John's takes its time to explore and unpack the significance of what Jesus did and said. Placing these two Gospels side by side provides rich material for our own reflections in Year B.

One of the great challenges of preaching John's Gospel is that the author himself has spent time slowly unpacking the meaning of what was going on – so much so, in fact, that one can occasionally wonder what more there may be to say. I find this particularly true of John 6 and John 17, two chapters that circle their theme (of bread and unity respectively) so reflectively and slowly that it can feel superfluous to add any more to the theme. I can't be the only person to wonder, in the middle of ordinary time when there is a string of readings from John 6, whether we have fallen into a time loop in which the same readings (and sermon) loop around endlessly!

The key to preaching (and hearing John) in Year B is, in my view, to learn to experience his message deep within so that the words sink – even more than usual – from being interesting concepts into realities to live by. John's Gospel is a Gospel to pray, to live and to follow far more than it is a Gospel to comprehend. The challenge of Year B is how to communicate this in words.

## The structure of John's Gospel

In the introduction to Mark's Gospel, I noted the downside of John's Gospel forming the focus of the readings about the death and resurrection of Jesus as detracting from Mark's deep focus on the cross and the cost of discipleship. There is a similar, but opposite, problem for understanding John's

Gospel in Year B of the lectionary. This is that Mark's Gospel provides the structure for the year, with John providing the fillers where Mark has insufficient material to complete the whole. This obscures elements of John's careful structuring.

A very simple structure of John's Gospel looks like this, with three major sections of the book flanked by a prologue and concluding statement:

- 1.1-19        The prologue
- 1.19 – 12.50   The public ministry of Jesus revealing who he was (more focus on narrative than discourse)
- 13.1 – 17.26   Jesus' farewell message revealing how we should live (more focus on discourse than narrative)
- 18.1 – 20.29   Jesus' death and resurrection
- 20.30-31      Concluding statement
- 21.1-25       The epilogue

The first twelve chapters focus around the seven signs that Jesus did:

1. Changing water into wine (2.1-11)
2. Healing the royal official's son in Capernaum (4.46-54)
3. Healing the paralysed man at Bethesda (5.1-18)
4. Feeding the 5,000 (6.5-14)
5. Walking on water (6.16-24)
6. Healing the man born blind (9.1-7)
7. Raising of Lazarus (11.1-45)

These seven key events provide the framework into which the discourses in this section are inserted. John is careful to indicate how we are to understand them – they are signs. In other words, they point to the deep nature of Jesus. The discourses that support them give more detail about who this person really is: themes of generosity, empathy, love and new life swirl around each other in this first half of John's Gospel pointing inexorably to who Jesus really was. Indeed, John 2.11 states that the signs revealed Jesus' glory, i.e. his splendour and that of him that can be known in the world (it is interesting to note that of the 19 occurrences of the word 'glory' in John, 16 of them appear in John 1–12; the other three are in John 17).

The middle section of the Gospel focuses around the message that Jesus wanted to give his followers about how to live their lives in his absence. The final section, as we shall see below, returns to the theme of the revelation of Jesus' glory – this time through his death and resurrection.

This simple structure helps us to hold more clearly in our minds the purpose of each section of the Gospel. Chapters 1–12 point us to who this Jesus was; chapters 13–17 to how we now live in the light of who he was, and chapters 18–20 to where his true nature is most clearly revealed (in the cross and at the resurrection).

## Resurrection in John's Gospel

The resurrection is particularly important in John's Gospel. It is worth noting that John's Gospel has far more resurrection appearances than any other Gospel. Mark has the fewest accounts, with just an empty tomb visited by the women; Matthew has the empty tomb, followed by an encounter between Jesus and the women by the tomb and then the great commission; Luke has the empty tomb, the road to Emmaus and an encounter with Jesus in Jerusalem before his ascension. John has the empty tomb seen by Peter and the beloved disciple; Mary's encounter with Jesus in the garden; the disciples meeting with Jesus in a locked room; Thomas' invitation to touch Jesus' hands and side, plus the extra encounter between Peter and Jesus by the lake. In contrast to the other Gospels, John's is resurrection heavy. It is no wonder that this Gospel is used so extensively during the Easter season.

Why are there so many more accounts of the resurrection in John's Gospel than in the other Gospels? The key seems to be belief and proclamation. At the empty tomb, the beloved disciple 'saw and believed' (John 20.8); in the garden Mary declared that she had 'seen the Lord' (20.18); in the locked room the disciples also stated that they had 'seen the Lord' (John 20.25); and at the end of chapter Thomas too believed (John 20.27-29).

The resurrection appearances, then, seem to be the culmination of the seven signs. The signs revealed Jesus' glory; chapter 20 contains the accounts of the *ultimate* sign – the resurrection as a revelation of Jesus' glory. In the resurrection we see more clearly than in any other sign who he really was. In the light of that, the only response is to believe and declare that 'we have seen the Lord'. In fact, the resurrection was such an important sign for John that he told four (indeed five if you count John 21 as well) different stories about it to ensure that we do not miss his point.

## Structural anomalies

One of the striking features of John's Gospel is that it contains a number of stories or episodes that feel out of place in the overall narrative. One key oddity occurs in John 14.31 where Jesus proposes that they arise and go on their way, something that only takes place much later, at the beginning of chapter 18, but even that pales into insignificance in comparison with the epilogue to the Gospel. John 20.30-31 states:

*'Now Jesus did many other signs in the presence of his disciples, which are not written in this book. But these are written so that you may come to believe that Jesus is the Messiah, the Son of God, and that through believing you may have life in his name.'*

This appears to complete the Gospel satisfactorily. John states that he could have written more of what Jesus did, but that he chose what he did 'so that you may come to believe that Jesus is the Messiah'. Given the way in which the resurrection appearances are recounted in John 20, this brings the Gospel to a perfect end. The ultimate sign – that of Jesus' resurrection – has caused the beloved disciple and Thomas to declare their belief. It now becomes clear that the whole Gospel has been told to evoke a similar response in its readers. There is little need for more, and yet, the Gospel continues for another whole chapter. It seems, to put it mildly, slightly odd.

It is these structural anomalies that have given rise to extensive speculation about how the Gospel of John reached its current form. The prologue (chapter 1), the epilogue (chapter 21), the additional farewell material (between 14.31 and 18.1), to name but a few examples, all suggest that the Gospel was not written from beginning to end in one sitting, or even at the same time. The Gospel feels as though it has developed with well-loved stories being added in or expanded over time.

The best explanation is that the Gospel developed organically as a community reflected on and discussed their favourite stories about Jesus. The most famous proponents of this theory were the biblical scholars J. Louis Martyn and Raymond Brown, who argued that not only did the Gospel develop over time but that it was possible to trace key moments in the community's history through various of the Gospel stories. The best example of this is that they argued that John 5.15-16 ('The man went away and told the Jews that it was Jesus who had made him well. Therefore the Jews started persecuting Jesus, because he was doing such things on the Sabbath.') was written at a time when John's community were experiencing persecution but that 9.22 ('His parents said this because they were afraid of the Jews; for the Jews had already agreed that anyone who confessed Jesus to be the Messiah would be put out of the synagogue.') came from a later time when the Jews had begun to expel Christians from the synagogue.

Modern scholars recognize that this theory went too far and stated too much with too much certainty on too little. This does not mean that the Gospel did not develop over time, simply that it is almost impossible to state with any certainty whether any one story came from a particular time in the life of their community.

## The dating and authorship of John's Gospel

### Dating John's Gospel

This brings us to the dating and authorship of John's Gospel. John has always been considered the latest Gospel to have been written, largely because of its reflective style. The extended reflections on Jesus' words and identity all suggest that the material has been honed over time before being written in this form.

Having said that, however, the Gospel was almost certainly in its final form by the end of first century or very early second century at the latest. Two papyri in particular, which contain fragments of the Gospel, have been dated to the early to mid second century AD. This suggests that the Gospel was already in use at that point and had spread as far as Egypt. As a result, most scholars would give a date to the Gospel in the AD 90s.

## Authorship of John's Gospel

The fourth Gospel was associated with John relatively early (mid to late second century AD). Irenaeus, who claimed to have the tradition from Polycarp, associated the fourth Gospel with 'John, the disciple of the Lord, who leaned on his breast' (*Against Heresies* 3.1.1, in other words in one neat movement John, the beloved disciple and the author of the Gospel were all associated together). As with all the Gospels, however, there is little internal evidence to associate the Gospel with 'John'.

All that is available is that John is not otherwise mentioned in the Gospel and that the author refers to himself as the disciple whom Jesus loved in 21.20-24 and refers to a disciple whom Jesus loved elsewhere throughout the Gospel (see 13.23, 19.26, 19.34-35, 20.2, 21.7, with a possible additional mention in 18.15, where a disciple is called 'another disciple' but not named). Some have noted that this ascription only occurs in the second half of the Gospel (i.e. after the section of the seven signs), though it is hard to evaluate how significant this might be.

This, then, raises questions of the identity of this disciple. As noted above, John, son of Zebedee, is absent from this Gospel, which in turn raises the question of whether he was referring to himself allusively in order to deflect attention from himself. The only problem here is that the disciple described as 'another disciple' in 18.15, whom many think should be associated with the disciple Jesus loved, is said to be well known in the High Priest's household. It is not easy to explain why a fisherman from Galilee would be known in this way.

The uncertainty raised by the suggestion that the Beloved Disciple was John, son of Zebedee, has allowed room for speculation as to other possible candidates – some of them more plausible than others: Lazarus (since Jesus loved him); John Mark (a young man connected to the Jesus movement, see Acts 12.12 and possibly also Mark 14.51); Matthias, a blood brother of Jesus; Thomas; a minor disciple who remains unnamed; Mary Magdalene; John the Baptist or someone else by the common name of John.

The reality is, probably as the author intended, that the identity of the disciple whom Jesus loved and hence the author of this Gospel, remains a mystery. This mystery means that we must instead focus all our attention on Jesus Christ, the Word made flesh.

## Theological themes

John's Gospel contains a large number of theological themes that are interwoven throughout the Gospel, themes such as: light and darkness; good and evil; love; the 'I am' sayings; belief; eternal life – to name but a few. Indeed, there are so many themes that it is better to observe them as they emerge in your reading of the Gospel. However, two particularly contentious themes are worth exploring here. One is the mention of the Jews in the Gospel and the other is Jesus' humanity.

### The Jews in John's Gospel

One of the slightly uncomfortable features of John's Gospel is that the people named as opposing Jesus in John's Gospel are 'the Jews'. In Matthew, Mark and Luke, the people who opposed Jesus were usually named as a group, such as the Pharisees, but in John they are most often called just 'the Jews'.

Scholars have wrestled hard to make sense of this. Some argue that the term ('hoi ioudaioi') is, in fact, a geographical term not a religious one and should be translated as 'the Judeans' not 'the Jews'. This has not, however, received much support.

A more widely held view is that John's Gospel emerged out of a time when the Christian community was in regular conflict with their Jewish neighbours and, as often happens at times of heightened conflict, the whole group (in this instance the Jews) were regarded as responsible for the opposition of what was, in reality, a few people.

*Humanity and divinity*

Another issue often raised in the context of John's Gospel is the question of whether Jesus was portrayed as fully human. Unlike in Matthew, Mark and Luke, Jesus' divinity is stressed on a regular basis in the Gospel. This has led some to propose that, in John, Jesus was depicted solely as 'God striding over the earth' (Ernst Käsemann). In the light of this, it is important to recognize the role of the prologue to John's Gospel (John 1.1-18). The prologue is a beautiful piece of poetry – possibly even an example of an early piece of liturgy or hymnody from the Christian community.

It is, however, more than just that. It also functions as the lens through which to read the rest of the Gospel. One of the remarkable features of the prologue (John 1.1-18) is that it presents a profoundly balanced theology of Jesus: divine and human; announced by John; bringing light in the darkness and changing the world forever. Anyone who is tempted to pull John's Gospel out of kilter in one direction or another should return, again, to the prologue. It stands at the start of the Gospel reminding its readers of the importance of balance, warning them not to pull the Gospel too far in any one direction but to read its stories through the lens of the Word made flesh and dwelling among us. Only when we are reading a narrative or discourse through this lens can we be confident that we are reading as we should.

## Concluding reflections

John's Gospel is a majestic reflection, through story and discourse, on the nature of Jesus Christ. Through signs and, most importantly, through Jesus' resurrection, we learn more and more about who he really was, his relationship with the Father and what impact that must have on the lives of those whom he calls friends (John 15.15).

Woven throughout the Gospel is a key theme that weaves together the nature of Jesus, his relationship with the Father and his expectations of his followers: the theme of love. Love was what caused God to send his son into the world; love was revealed in a different way in each of the signs; Jesus spoke with love to those he met; he commanded love from his followers; and finally, in the epilogue, he revealed that love was the underpinning of new relationships and forgiveness. John's Gospel is a Gospel of love, written by the disciple that Jesus loved, so that we, its readers, might hear, experience and know that love for ourselves.

*Introduction by* **Paula Gooder**

**Isaiah 64.1-9**
Psalm 80.1-8, 18-20 [or 80.1-8]
1 Corinthians 1.3-9
Mark 13.24-end

## Isaiah 64.1-9

*'O that you would tear open the heavens and come down'*
*(v.1)*

Today's passage is part of the lament that started with chapter 63. Its tone is anguished, pleading, longing for God to be God. The prophet is tired of trying to justify God's anger with the people. The people have sinned – of course they have – and the prophet has said so over and over again. They have nothing to offer God, but then they never did, but God loved them anyway.

Now God's continuing silence is beginning to be seen not as punishment but as absence. People are beginning to give up on God. Usually in the prophetic literature, that is seen as culpable, but now our sympathy is with these heart-broken, directionless people. How can they go on believing in God when there is so little evidence that he cares about them?

Come on, God, the prophet shouts! Be God! We know you can do it, or at least that you used to do it. Remember how, when you and Moses used to talk, the mountain used to be covered in smoke, and the whole ground shook? Remember how, when Elijah prayed, you made soaking wood catch fire, so that the heathen prophets knew who was God? Dear God, that's what we so desperately need now, says the prophet.

As Advent starts we, like Isaiah, wait to see what God will do: not smoking mountains and fire, but a baby, God with us.

*Reflection by* **Jane Williams**

Isaiah 64.1-9
Psalm 80.1-8, 18-20 [*or* 80.1-8]
**1 Corinthians 1.3-9**
Mark 13.24-end

**First Sunday of Advent**

### 1 Corinthians 1.3-9

*'I give thanks to my God always for you' (v.4)*

Paul wrote this letter because he needed to lay into a group of Christians for factionalism, arrogance, incest, sexual immorality, gluttony and chaotic worship. It would be understandable if he had begun his letter in a tone of fury. So it's a surprise that his opening words are, 'I give thanks to my God always for you'.

All of us are surrounded by fellow Christians who are far from perfect. I could probably make a similar list of six things about Christians I know that are just as bad. But the first Sunday of Advent is the beginning of a new year for the Church. So instead I plan to spend some time thinking of reasons to thank God for the Christian community to which I belong.

I'm going to need help, so I intend to start by bringing to mind some wonderful things that we share. Undeserved as it is, we are all enriched by the extraordinary grace of God. In our different ways, understated or eye-catching, we all have spiritual gifts to use in God's service. We draw strength from the fact that we will greet Jesus on the day of his return knowing that we are forgiven. God is faithful and the Lord Jesus is among our number.

Those marvellous truths ought to be enough to see me through a few ups and downs with my fellow Christians until the Lord comes.

*Reflection by* **Peter Graystone**

**First Sunday of Advent**

Isaiah 64.1-9
Psalm 80.1-8, 18-20 [*or* 80.1-8]
1 Corinthians 1.3-9
**Mark 13.24-end**

### Mark 13.24-end

*'... stars will be falling from heaven' (v.25)*

With fabulous Middle Eastern hyperbole, using evocative descriptions of the darkened sun and falling stars, Jesus is trying to communicate the urgency of his message to live differently, to be attentive to the presence of God and the intolerable injustices of organized religion and politics.

It has often seemed to me that to be too literal about these pictures, and therefore to worry about whether they are 'true', is, ironically, to rob them of their beauty and power. At Advent, singing Charles Wesley's words 'Lo he comes with clouds descending', quoting directly from this passage, has often given me a greater sense of awe and expectation as the musical picture unfolds than I have received from simply reading the words. The sense of God being 'at the very gates' as Jesus says, just beyond, just out of reach, the other side of the door – all these spiritual truths are recognizable to anyone who wants to take their own spiritual lives seriously.

In the rhythm of night following day, as Spring follows Winter, we learn to expect change and movement at the heart of creation. Jesus is urging his listeners to learn from the fig tree's seasons, to be attentive to its transformation and to know the potential for transformation for us too.

*Reflection by* **Lucy Winkett**

Isaiah 40.1-11
Psalm 85.1-2, 8-end
[*or* 85.8-end]
2 Peter 3.8-15*a*
Mark 1.1-8

## Second Sunday of Advent

### Isaiah 40.1-11

*'Then the glory of the Lord shall be revealed' (v.5)*

One of the greatest of the Old Testament prophets begins his song with his life's message from God: 'Comfort, O comfort my people'. His songs continue (most think) until the end of Isaiah 55. These 15 chapters are the most powerful words of hope in Scripture, addressed to the second generation of exiles to prepare them for salvation.

We do not know this prophet's name. He values gentleness and humility in God and God's servants. Perhaps for that reason he refers to himself only as 'a voice'. I like to call him 'Col' (from the Hebrew q'ol meaning voice).

Col's words throughout are full of contrasts. In this opening song he contrasts past and present: we are at a crisis, a turning point in God's dealings with his people. He contrasts the weightiness and permanence of God's power and glory breaking in with the lightness and fragility of human lives (flowers and grass, vv.6-7). The Hebrew word 'glory' means something heavy, dense and immensely powerful.

The Christian's task and calling in Advent is to prepare the way of the Lord: to so witness to those around us that a way is opened for them to hear God's message of comfort and forgiveness and come home. As we journey through Advent together, what will your life message be? How will it be read?

*Reflection by* **Steven Croft**

## Second Sunday of Advent

Isaiah 40.1-11
Psalm 85.1-2, 8-end
[*or* 85.8-end]
**2 Peter 3.8-15a**
Mark 1.1-8

### 2 Peter 3.8-15a

*'... what sort of people ought you to be?' (v.11)*

One of the pressures on the first Christians was this: the first generation believed, very naturally, that the Lord would return very soon, put an end to suffering and establish the kingdom.

People from the new religions and the old mocked this belief that Christ would return as year after year went by. The apostles counter this mockery with a constant emphasis on true Christian hope: a steadfast assurance that Christ will return, at an hour we do not know and in God's own time.

Peter makes a distinctive contribution to this teaching in verses 8-9 with his assurance that for the Lord of heaven and earth, time moves differently. The delay is not because the Lord is slow but because the Lord is patient. A key element in his patience is love: he is not willing for anyone to perish, but for all to come to repentance.

The answering of one question leads, of course, to another. If the Lord is not to return yet for many years, how then should we wait and live and make the most of the time? A new ethic is needed. This question is answered not with a list of what we should do, but with a description of what kind of people we should be: leading lives of holiness and godliness.

As you continue to walk through Advent, what kind of person have you been?

*Reflection by* **Steven Croft**

Isaiah 40.1-11
Psalm 85.1-2, 8-end
[*or* 85.8-end]
2 Peter 3.8-15*a*
**Mark 1.1-8**

## Mark 1.1-8

### *'The beginning of the good news' (v.1)*

Strange though it may seem, Mark feels compelled to tell us in the opening sentence that this is the beginning. Most translations of Mark render his opening words 'The beginning of the good news ...'. But Mark doesn't even bother to use the word 'the'; he starts with 'Beginning ...'. We are, in other words, straight into it. And, of course, if you turn to the end of Mark's Gospel, you'll also see that it has no proper ending either – it is all a bit ragged.

An abrupt beginning and an abrupt ending point to several themes that occur throughout Mark's Gospel. Readers don't get a gentle introduction to Jesus. The good news is here, now. And it requires your attention, and a response. Here, now. The end is the same. There is no neat finish. You have to write that yourself, with your life as a disciple.

So there is no room for the armchair critic in Mark's opening remarks. You are not offered an easy introduction to Jesus – his genealogy, for example (see Luke and Matthew) – but are invited straight away to deal with the challenging presence of John the Baptist. It is his call to repent, be baptized and follow Jesus that forms the heart of Mark's Gospel. So, the tone of abruptness in the message of Mark is also his theme. There is no time to cogitate and deliberate. Choose Jesus. Drop everything you are doing, and follow him. Now.

*Reflection by* **Martyn Percy**

## Third Sunday of Advent

Isaiah 61.1-4, 8-end
Psalm 126 *or*
*Canticle:* Magnificat
I Thessalonians 5.16-24
John 1.6-8, 19-28

### Isaiah 61.1-4, 8-end

*'... he has clothed me with the garments of salvation' (v.10)*

When Jesus sets out on his ministry, it is to these words in Isaiah that he turns as an announcement of what is to come (Luke 4.18-19). What is it about this song that makes it so apposite for Jesus' purposes?

In spirit, it belongs with what are usually called the 'servant songs' earlier on in Isaiah (see Isaiah 42, for example). These earlier songs suggest that the suffering that the people of God are undergoing is part of their 'service' to the nations, somehow. The nations may despise the 'servant' and write him off, but God is using him, even in his distress.

Here in Isaiah 61, the anointing that was usually reserved for kings, priests and prophets is now poured out on the whole people; all are 'ministers of God', repairing and restoring the devastated land.

Their ministry is part of the 'year of the Lord's favour', a time of jubilee, when the whole earth is given back to its creator, so that it can flourish again. Just as in the first garden at the beginning of time, so in this new garden earth, everything is good, plants and people alike. The results of the 'fall' are undone, so that people wear the garments of righteousness and salvation, not the shoddy leaves that Adam and Eve sewed to hide their disobedience.

Does that give us some clues about Jesus' ministry, his life, his death and his resurrection?

*Reflection by* **Jane Williams**

Isaiah 61.1-4, 8-end
Psalm 126 *or*
*Canticle:* Magnificat
**I Thessalonians 5.16-24**
John 1.6-8, 19-28

**Third Sunday of Advent**

## 1 Thessalonians 5.16-24

*'Rejoice always, pray without ceasing' (vv.16–17)*

The big picture of the Lord's advent does not require us to jettison ordinary life with its structures and responsibilities, but to embrace it. The lightning flash of his coming can only safely be contemplated from an earthed life. So Paul ends his letter first by urging his readers to continue to attend to the demands of relationships at every level. Each one is encouraged to play their part in the full life of the community, taking responsibility for the health and welfare of the whole people of God.

And then Paul hands us this small nugget of gold, a recipe for a daringly joyful life. 'Rejoice always, pray without ceasing, give thanks in all circumstances.' There are no exceptions. *Pantote* – 'always' – really means that – 'always, at all times'. *Adialeiptos* describes a quality of prayer that is constant, faithful, settled. *En panti* means 'in every single thing that happens, in all circumstances'.

Note that Paul is not suggesting we thank God *for* every circumstance – that would be impossible if not downright blasphemous. Not 'for' but 'in'. Whatever the painful or dull or sad or uncertain circumstances of our lives, we are encouraged to thank God in them. And there's more. We are even invited – if we dare – to see in them the outline of his good and perfect intention for us.

*Reflection by* **Sue Hope**

## Third Sunday of Advent

Isaiah 61.1-4, 8-end
Psalm 126 *or*
*Canticle:* Magnificat
I Thessalonians 5.16-24
**John 1.6-8, 19-28**

### John 1.6-8, 19-28

*'What do you say about yourself?' (v.22)*

We learn in verse 8 that John the Baptist is 'not the light'; we now learn of three more things that he is 'not'. Crucially, John is not the Messiah. When asked to clarify his identity, this is stated emphatically so that no mistake may be made: he 'confesses, does not deny, but confesses' that this is not who he is.

If he is not the Messiah, could he perhaps be one of the other end-time figures the Jews were expecting: Elijah or 'the Prophet'? He is neither, he confirms, leaving the priests and Levites with no further options to guess at. Instead, they ask for a positive identification in his own words: 'What do you say about yourself?' In response, John does not use his own words, turning instead to those of fellow prophet, Isaiah (v.23, cf Isaiah 40.3: 'A voice cries out: "In the wilderness prepare the way of the Lord"...'). While Jesus is 'the Word', John is 'a voice'.

John's choice of text is telling. He is the mouthpiece not the message, and his role is to ensure that ears will be open when the Word appears and speaks. Such is his humility that his identity is entirely defined with respect to another: there is nothing noteworthy, or indeed worthy, about John in relation to the one who is to come.

Let us reflect on which verse of Scripture we would choose if asked 'What do you say about yourself?'

*Reflection by* **Helen Orchard**

**2 Samuel 7.1-11, 16**
*Canticle:* Magnificat *or*
Psalm 89.1-4, 19-26 [*or* 89.1-8]
Romans 16.25-end
Luke 1.26-38

**Fourth Sunday of Advent**

## 2 Samuel 7.1-11, 16

*'The Lord will make you a house' (v.11)*

After a long period of war, David finally had peace from his enemies and – ever the man of action who had already built his own house – he turned to the idea of building a permanent house for the ark of God, which he had brought to Jerusalem with such rejoicing. It was perhaps not entirely coincidental that he thereby consolidated his own power by providing this temple for national worship. His good intention was initially endorsed by Nathan. But sometimes it is easier to start a project than wait for God to lead, and God had much greater ideas than David could imagine. While David thought of building physical houses for himself and God, God intended to build David a dynastic house beginning with Solomon (who would build a physical house for God), leading ultimately to the birth of the Son of God to a member of that dynastic house, Mary.

So God intervened to deflect David from his good idea in order to open the way for God's greater one. Centuries later, in a similar way, Peter proposed building dwellings to contain the experience of the Transfiguration (Mark 9.5-7). But God will not be domesticated by us, however sincere our intentions. As Solomon later prayed at the dedication of his temple, even the highest heaven cannot contain God. The wonder is that this uncontainable God had begun to work in David's life and continues to do so in our lives.

*Reflection by* **Rosalind Brown**

| **Fourth Sunday of Advent** | 2 Samuel 7.1-11, 16 |
| | *Canticle:* Magnificat *or* |
| | Psalm 89.1-4, 19-26 [*or* 89.1-8] |
| | **Romans 16.25-end** |
| | Luke 1.26-38 |

## Romans 16.25-end

*'... according to the revelation of the mystery
that was kept secret for long ages' (v.25)*

Biblical scholars largely believe these verses were a later
addition to Paul's letter – perhaps a sort of liturgical flourish,
so that as the letter was read out, it ended by highlighting
once again the central themes of the good news of salvation
found in Jesus Christ, and directed praise and glory through
him to God.

This disclosure of the revelation of the mystery of the secret
has echoes of Churchill's famous description of Russian
intentions at the beginning of World War II: 'a riddle wrapped
in a mystery inside an enigma'. But while Churchill was
describing his inability to predict how Russia might act, these
verses invite us to be caught up in the experience of God's
great purposes, which are now made manifest to all people,
through Jesus Christ.

Perhaps it is a weakness of the English language that we don't
distinguish between the 'knowing' of having an experience,
and the 'knowing' of being able fully to understand
something – hence the potential confusion at first sight in the
prayer that we might 'know the love of Christ that surpasses
knowledge' (Ephesians 3.19).

As we prepare for Christmas, we should remind ourselves that
at least part of our celebration must surely be to stop
overthinking, and to ensure we let ourselves be transported in
sheer wonder and adoration at the incarnation, God in Christ
made manifest.

*Reflection by* **Sarah Rowland Jones**

2 Samuel 7.1-11, 16
*Canticle:* Magnificat *or*
Psalm 89.1-4, 19-26 [*or* 89.1-8]
Romans 16.25-end
**Luke 1.26-38**

## Luke 1.26-38

*'How can this be?' (v.34)*

God's ways are not our ways, nor are his thoughts our thoughts (Isaiah 55.8). We see the truth of this when we consider the people God calls to serve him in specific ways throughout scripture. From David, the youngest (and therefore, humanly, the least considered) son of Jesse (1 Samuel 16), to Saul, the persecutor of Christians (Acts 9), God's choice of those he calls to serve so often challenges our human judgements.

Mary was a young girl betrothed to a carpenter, living in an insignificant backwater of the Roman Empire. There was nothing in her past that could have prepared her for what Gabriel told her was to happen. She has been specially chosen – favoured – by God, but she appears to share nothing of those features that many today associate with that favour: good health, wealth or high social status.

Mary's 'blessing' was to bear a child out of wedlock (which could have seen her stoned to death) – a child who would later be executed as a criminal. The experience of Mary should remind us that God's blessing has no connection with human standards of acceptability, wealth or comfort, and offers no easy reassurances.

In opening ourselves to receive God's blessings, we, like Mary, are encouraged to step out in trust. Like her, we too are challenged to 'Go out into the darkness and put [our] hand into the Hand of God' (Minnie Louise Haskins, *The Gate of the Year*).

*Reflection by* **Barbara Mosse**

Christmas Eve

24 December

[1] 2 Samuel 7.1-5, 8-11, 16
Psalm 89.2, 19-27
Acts 13.16-26
Luke 1.67-79

### Acts 13.16-26

*'Paul stood up and with a gesture began to speak' (v.16)*

We read elsewhere that Paul (unlike Peter) is not an impressive public speaker (2 Corinthians 10.10), and in imagining this scene, it is intriguing to picture him beginning to speak to the crowd in the synagogue, 'with a gesture'. He then, as the urbane, educated speaker he is, sets out what he hopes will be received as incontrovertible proof, tracing the action of God in the lives of the Israelites from their liberation from Egyptian slavery through the reigns of Saul and David right up to the message of John the Baptist pointing towards Jesus of Nazareth as the Messiah promised by God. Paul uses the very phrase made famous by John the Baptist which by now no doubt is a saying familiar and repeated by the faithful. 'One is coming after me. I am not worthy to untie the thong of his sandals'.

Paul's learning and ability to set out arguments are evident here. He is painstaking in building the case for Jesus. This is the man who is capable of the most extraordinary poetry about love (in his letter to the Corinthians) while at the same time providing cool-headed quasi-legal arguments to convince anyone who will listen that he was wrong and that Jesus is the Christ. Such a talented and able person is marshalling his considerable ability in the service of Christ, who, he tells us elsewhere, is simply everything to him. It's inspiring that he brings all that he is to this task – his emotion, his intellect, his energy – leaving nothing in reserve. He pours himself out, as we are asked to pour out ourselves, imitating God's self-emptying love that erupts into the world in the birth of Jesus, celebrated tonight.

*Reflection by* **Lucy Winkett**

[1] *For a reflection on 2 Samuel 7.1-5, 8-11, 16, see page 39.*

2 Samuel 7.1-5, 8-11, 16
Psalm 89.2, 19-27
Acts 13.16-26
**Luke 1.67-79**

### Luke 1.67-79

*'... you will go before the Lord to prepare his ways' (v.76)*

The priest Zechariah speaks these words after the naming of his son, John, born according to the promise of the angel of the Lord after years of childless marriage. At first, we might wonder whether this child is the 'mighty saviour' God is raising up. But no, he is to 'go before the Lord to prepare his ways'. We probably know him better from his adult ministry, as John the Baptist.

We are called to put on Christ (Romans 13.14), have the mind of Christ (1 Corinthians 2.16), imitate Christ (1 Corinthians 11.1) and together be the body of Christ (1 Corinthians 12.27). Yet, while we should often ask ourselves 'What would Jesus do?', in important ways we are *not* Jesus Christ. He alone is the Lamb of God who takes away the sin of the world. Therefore it may often be more helpful to ask what John the Baptist might do. How do we prepare the way of the Lord, so others may better find that pathway to knowledge of his salvation?

As we anticipate celebrating Christ's birth anew, we might also ask ourselves how we should prepare for his fuller coming in our own lives. The promises of God's holy covenant are for us also. Do we serve him without fear, living in holiness or righteousness? Or do we need to acknowledge our dark shadows, and ask for his light to guide us into greater life and peace?

*Reflection by* **Sarah Rowland Jones**

[Set I readings:
**Isaiah 9.2-7**
Psalm 96
Titus 2.11-14
Luke 2.1-14[15-20]

### Isaiah 9.2-7

*'The people who walked in darkness
have seen a great light' (v.2)*

Isaiah is constantly exercised by those who trust in something other than God. In chapter 8, it is first the Assyrians and then the spirits of the dead, whom Israelites were forbidden to consult. God's final word, however, is not one of punishment even for this offence, but one of hope and salvation.

The famous passage in today's reading celebrates God's glorification of his people by giving them a king. For the first hearers of this prophecy, it will have been understood as predicting or celebrating the birth of a royal heir; Christians have heard in it a promise that would be ultimately fulfilled only in Jesus Christ, whose incarnation we celebrate today.

How do we understand the kingdom of God in Jesus? Not as a political system, a kind of theocracy as in many Islamic hopes for the world, but as an influence that can permeate a society, inspiring but not controlling. Overtly Christian political parties have usually proved to be a snare and delusion, because they are parties first and Christian second. But, in the political as in the personal sphere, it is possible for the values Christians stand for to find expression in the practical living of our common life, so that 'justice and righteousness' are the foundation for a stable and creative society.

*Reflection by* **John Barton**

[There are three sets of readings for use on Christmas Night and Christmas Day. Set III should be used at some service during the celebration.

Set I readings:
Isaiah 9.2-7
Psalm 96
**Titus 2.11-14**
Luke 2.1-14[15-20]

## Christmas Day
### 25 December
*Principal Feast*

### Titus 2.11-14

*'... a people of his own' (v.14)*

Every TV drama uses a combination of shots to tell its story, throwing our attention onto different characters using close-ups, catching intimate moments and giveaway details, then pulling back to take in a whole scene in long shot. The Christmas story is told to us in a series of tableaux – scenes that introduce the major characters, Jesus, Mary and Joseph, Gabriel, and their interactions with a host of supporting characters, including cousins, shepherds, angels, foreign visitors and, of course, a villain.

This short passage is from a 'pastoral letter' written probably some 60 years after the events described in the gospel nativity narratives. It is like a pull-back of the camera to give an overview of the story from a new perspective, reminding us of its wider significance, before zooming in to include new events and characters.

Those new characters, of course, include not only the early Church and its struggles to maintain 'sound doctrine', but all of us today who are drawn towards worshipping the infant Jesus. Our own lives are drawn into this story – it matters how we respond to the appearance of grace in the world through the birth and redemptive death of Jesus. It is as if, having been attracted to the story, we discover that part of the script has not yet been completed and that we are invited to join the cast and play out a role before the glorious final ending.

*Reflection by* **Libby Lane**

## Christmas Day

**25 December**
*Principal Feast*

*Set I readings:*
Isaiah 9.2-7
Psalm 96
Titus 2.11-14
**Luke 2.1-14[15-20]**

### Luke 2.1-14[15-20]

*'This will be a sign for you' (v.12)*

The angel is speaking to frightened shepherds. They need reassuring. This is entirely understandable. Shepherds were among the most marginalized and mistrusted people in their world. They would not dream of being included in any important social event, still less responding to a personal invitation from angels. To the contrary, if they strayed near such events, they would expect to be chased off.

And what is the sign they are offered? More spectacular, heavenly visions? The star above? A compelling supernatural presence? It is none of these. The sign is simply what the baby is wrapped in. Swaddling clothes are what the poorest of society, like shepherds, used to wrap their babies.

So it is their sign. This baby is in their world. Whatever the exalted language used of this child, 'he is one of us'. No wonder they come running.

Mary, at her annunciation, sang of the new order in which the lowly would be raised up and given special place, and the familiar hierarchy of the privileged and powerful would be dismantled. The gospel begins here, as it will continue. The welcome of the kingdom will continually fall into the 'wrong' hands. Its annunciation will be entrusted to unsuitable messengers. Theology is declared from the mouths of the untaught. Faith will be found among the marginalized. The forgotten are remembered. The despised beloved.

It is still the sign.

*Reflection by* **David Runcorn**

¹ *Set II readings:*
**Isaiah 62.6-end**
Psalm 97
Titus 3.4-7
Luke 2.[1-7]8-20

## Christmas Day
**25 December**
*Principal Feast*

### Isaiah 62.6-end

*'Say to daughter Zion, "See, your salvation comes ..."' (v.11)*

It's all to do with geology. When you are looking for a good threshing floor, you need a large, flat, hard stone surface, preferably high up so that the wind can blow the chaff away, leaving only the grains of wheat.

It was a threshing floor bought by King David from a Jebusite citizen called Araunah (see 2 Samuel 24.18) that, according to tradition, became the spot on which Solomon constructed the temple and therefore the centre of the Jewish sacrificial system. It was that simple stone threshing floor that gave rise to a cluster of powerful ideas resulting in Jerusalem being regarded as God's chosen city. Those ideas helped to shape the identity and the hopes of both Judaism and Christianity.

Isaiah, reflecting on the exile of the Jews in Babylon, saw Jerusalem as the place to which those who had been redeemed by God would come back, not as a forlorn and tragic group of refugees but as victorious and joy-filled citizens. They would be there as of right and would be a living sign of God's covenant, his solemn promise to be with his people always. In God's city lived God's children; that was the ideal.

Isaiah's words were pored over by the early followers of Jesus who saw in the prophet's poetry a foretelling of the coming of Christ. He, they believed, was like a grain of wheat ground on the threshing floor that would become the Bread of Life for all.

*Reflection by* **Christopher Herbert**

¹ *There are three sets of readings for use on Christmas Night and Christmas Day. Set III should be used at some service during the celebration*

**Christmas Day**

**25 December**
*Principal Feast*

*Set II readings:*
Isaiah 62.6-end
Psalm 97
**Titus 3.4-7**
Luke 2.[1-7]8-20

## Titus 3.4-7

*'... not because of any works of righteousness that we had done' (v.5)*

Small children have no inhibitions in expressing delight when unexpected, undeserved presents come their way, no matter how extravagant. Not so, as we get older, when gift-giving can become an exercise in exact reciprocity in the value of gifts given and received, with a fear of being burdened by the weight of any outstanding balance.

While not all of us may share this anxiety, we can still struggle to receive graciously the gifts of others' generosity. The perennial problem of pride can get us into all sorts of tangles about whether the giver is in the position of being superior, trapping the recipient in future obligation. We may feel safer if we are in the donor's driving seat, taking refuge in quoting 'the words of the Lord Jesus, for he himself said "It is more blessed to give than to receive."' (Acts 20.35)

At Christmas, however, pride must take a back seat. There is no getting away from the glorious truth that there is absolutely nothing we could possibly do to earn or deserve the fullness of God's mercy. Nonetheless, in love he delights to pour it out on us richly, extravagantly, unreservedly, through Jesus Christ, by his Spirit.

At Christmas, there is nothing else to do, but to become as little children once again, and share uninhibitedly in the delight with which God gives us his own true self.

*Reflection by* **Sarah Rowland Jones**

Set II readings:
Isaiah 62.6-end
Psalm 97
Titus 3.4-7
**Luke 2.[1-7]8-20**

## Christmas Day

**25 December**
*Principal Feast*

### Luke 2.[1-7]8-20

*'Mary treasured all these words and pondered them
in her heart' (v.19)*

Luke's nativity narrative is familiar and well loved. However, this very familiarity tends to blunt its shock value, as we hear it related again year after year. But shocking it was, and its impact on Mary and Joseph must have been disorienting and full of mystery. This account brings to a conclusion what was promised to Mary by the angel Gabriel, but it does more than this: it also gives us a real insight into Mary's character. When the shepherds came, she listened to their experience, treasured their words 'and pondered them in her heart'.

Not content to be simply a passive vessel, Mary engages deeply with her experience, meditating on the meaning of the wonderful thing that has happened. As Jesus' life continues to gather momentum, we will learn that understanding, for Mary, does not come easily. When she and Joseph take Jesus to the temple at eight days old, they were 'amazed' at what was said about their son (Luke 2.33), and there were to be later incidents in Jesus' life when Mary's bafflement was equally apparent (Luke 2.48).

Today, the pressure is for everything to be done instantly, with no real time for thought or reflection. God's ways are mysterious (Isaiah 55.8), but if we are willing to 'ponder' our life-experiences in his presence, we will discover that we are somehow 'plugged in' to the flow of his life and work in our world.

*Reflection by* **Barbara Mosse**

## Christmas Day

**25 December**
*Principal Feast*

*¹ Set III readings:*
**Isaiah 52.7-10**
Psalm 98
Hebrews 1.1-4[5-12]
John 1.1-14

### Isaiah 52.7-10

*'How beautiful upon the mountains
are the feet of the messenger who announces peace' (v.7)*

Standing on the ramparts, the watchman gazes across the landscape, golden in the morning sunlight. At first, the figure he sees coming towards the city is indistinct. The shimmering haze obscures the details. Is the runner bringing bad news or good? As the figure draws closer, the watchman can see that the runner's head is up, his arms swing easily and his feet touch the ground with a light and lissom energy. The watchman screws up his eyes to get an even sharper view. Now he can see the details of the runner's face, his deep brown eyes, his hair plastered to his forehead with sweat ...

An order is shouted to the sentries; the heavy wooden gates are swung open, and the watchman clatters down the steps from the wall to greet the runner. Some early-morning labourers about to go out to work in the fields shout with delight and a little boy standing nearby claps his hands.

The message, however, is not about a far-off victory in a battle; it is instead a message about the very nature of God. The runner announces that God who had appeared so far away is now very close. 'God reigns,' proclaims the runner, 'and is coming to rebuild the ruins of Jerusalem'. The news is brilliant, beyond the watchman's wildest imaginings. And the message, of course, was fulfilled – but not in a restored city; rather, it became reality in the humility and beauty of a babe in a manger.

*Reflection by* **Christopher Herbert**

¹ *There are three sets of readings for use on Christmas Night and Christmas Day. Set III should be used at some service during the celebration.*

50

*Set III readings:*
Isaiah 52.7-10
Psalm 98
**Hebrews 1.1-4[5-12]**
John 1.1-14

## Christmas Day

**25 December**
*Principal Feast*

### Hebrews 1.1-4[5-12]

*'He is the reflection of God's glory and the exact imprint of God's very being' (v.3)*

The opening of the Epistle to the Hebrews reads like a miniature creed, focused on the person of the Son. In four verses, it discusses revelation, the creation and preservation of the universe, the atonement and the ascension. At the heart lies a statement about both God and the incarnation. The Son, we read, is 'the reflection of God's glory and the exact imprint of God's very being'.

The Son redoubles the Father, as his exact reflection, and yet there is only one God, because that reflection is perfect. Only add the Holy Spirit, and we have the doctrine of the Trinity. With the incarnation, exactly the same principle applies: Jesus is the perfect image of the Father, made flesh. Jesus could therefore say of himself 'Whoever has seen me has seen the Father' (John 14.9).

If this seems rather abstract – although also important and true – then we might note that the word at the centre of these four verses has much to say about the Christian life. The Son is the 'exact imprint' of the Father. The Greek word is *charactēr*: the word for the stamp left in sealing wax. It is the origin of our English word 'character', meaning both our moral quality and the mark left by an inscription. The early Church linked these two meanings. Christians are to display the (moral) character of Christ and can do so because in baptism they are embossed with his life, as his brothers and sisters.

*Reflection by* **Andrew Davison**

51

**Christmas Day**

**25 December**

*Principal Feast*

Set III readings:
Isaiah 52.7-10
Psalm 98
Hebrews 1.1-4[5-12]
**John 1.1-14**

### John 1.1-14

*'... we have seen his glory' (v. 14)*

In this magisterial introduction to his Gospel, the Evangelist gathers together the significant themes he is going to use to tell his story of the enfleshed Word of God. Light and darkness, life and rebirth, truth, witness, seeing and believing all make an appearance as terms that will be employed in his interpretation of the life and death of the person of Jesus Christ. Crucially, despite the fact that no one has ever seen God, what we have seen, and will see, is his glory. This is, in fact, what the only-begotten has made known to us.

Our focus during the Christmas season is on the beloved Son as the baby in the manger, who is 'of the Father's heart begotten'. But when John writes of glory, he is projecting us forward to the man on the cross, who shows us the depth of God's love in a climactic act of self-giving. This glory is not something that the Father and the Son possess in some kind of exclusive arrangement, but is also shared with those to whom Jesus has been given. Not only do they see his glory, but he is also glorified in them (John 17.10ff) – and, astonishingly, as believers, we are called to make this glory our own.

That glory is our destiny for all eternity, but we know, from the pattern set before us, that there is no way to glory except via the cross.

*Reflection by* **Helen Orchard**

Isaiah 61.10 – 62.3
Psalm 148 [*or* 148.7-end]
Galatians 4.4-7
Luke 2.15-21

**First Sunday of Christmas**

## Isaiah 61.10 – 62.3

*'For as the earth brings forth its shoots ...' (61.11)*

It is still the dead heart of winter. Branches are bare; the earth locked in by frost. But somewhere, just below the surface, life is already preparing to stir. It will take several weeks yet before those underground disturbances break the surface. For the moment, in spite of all appearances, we have to take on trust that the glorious shoots of spring are on their way.

So we wait. It is not something we are good at. We are too restless, too anxious, too driven. But, pause for a moment and consider this. If, as funeral services make clear, we humans are earth, ashes and dust, might our spiritual selves have to follow the same deep processes of nature as our frail bodies? Perhaps there will be times when we have to endure the deadness of spiritual winter so that a new spring may erupt.

It sounds easy. The reality is altogether different. The absence of God, the absence of hope is terrible, an anguish that is almost unbearable. We cannot sense any underground stirrings: all colour, shape and form are drained from our inner spiritual landscape. Death itself seems to inhabit our very souls.

And yet ... and yet. The poetic cry from Isaiah is one of a glorious spring waiting to break the surface. The radiance and prodigal glory of new life is almost upon us. Paradise gardens will overwhelm us with their beauty, and God himself will walk with us in the cool of the day.

*Reflection by* **Christopher Herbert**

**First Sunday of Christmas**

Isaiah 61.10 – 62.3
Psalm 148 [*or* 148.7-end]
**Galatians 4.4-7**
¹Luke 2.15-21

### Galatians 4.4-7

*'So you are no longer a slave but ... an heir' (4.7)*

Paul wants his listeners to have a grown-up faith. He wants them to move on from being a slave to being an heir, from minor to major, and he uses all sorts of images and arguments in Galatians to make the point. Paul did his theology on the run, but what rings through his writing all the time is the theme of freedom. He has experienced the power of religion to imprison us in small spaces under the control of rulebooks, and he aches for his converts to know the liberation of a Christ-centred life.

Distorted religion can still clip our wings. The big move forward for me was the realization that faith was not about regulating my life but about relishing a relationship. I had many of the pieces of the Christian jigsaw lying around but they had seemed obscure and opaque. What was this piece for, and that one? (I thought the same about maths). When I found the liberating piece of the jigsaw that described a relationship with Christ, everything began to make sense – and what's more, every other relationship was transformed as well. 'There is no longer Jew or Greek ... slave or free ... male and female ...' (Galatians 3.28). We've been working on that ever since.

How, I wonder, will we claim and live that freedom today?

*Reflection by* **John Pritchard**

¹*For a reflection on Luke 2.15-21, see page 49.*

Jeremiah 31.7-14
Psalm 147.13-end
Ephesians 1.3-14
John 1.[1-9]10-18

## Second Sunday of Christmas

### Jeremiah 31.7-14

*'I am going to ... gather them from the farthest parts of the earth' (v.8)*

The motif evoked by this oracle from Jeremiah's Book of Consolation is that of journeying. God will bring the remnant of Israel back to the Promised Land after decades in exile. Gathered from the farthest parts of the earth, they will be led by God as a great company, walking without stumbling on straight paths by flowing streams. Great will be the rejoicing and they will be radiant (literally 'shine') at God's goodness.

This diverse throng of old and young, blind and lame, mothers and children travelling joyfully and noisily along contrasts with the three intrepid figures of the magi, making their way to Bethlehem, whom we will soon remember at Epiphany. They come, not as the remnant of God's firstborn returning from exile, but as the first fruits of the gentile nations seeking the only-begotten, and they too are illuminated by God's goodness and overwhelmed with joy.

Whatever the journey, be it to familiar or unknown parts, be it unexpected or carefully planned, dangerous or by flowing streams, God goes ahead of us to guide us and gather us. In the final analysis we are all – exiles, magi, ourselves – travelling to the same destination, which is home to the Father, whose love has made that possible for all people through the Son. As we worship this morning, let us kneel next to the magi at the crib.

*Reflection by* **Helen Orchard**

55

**Second Sunday of Christmas**

Jeremiah 31.7-14
Psalm 147.13-end
**Ephesians 1.3-14**
John 1.[1-9]10-18

### Ephesians 1.3-14

*'Blessed ... in Christ with every spiritual blessing' (v.3)*

Paul's letter to the Ephesians begins with a 'blessing', or act of praise expressed to God. This was, and is, a very common Jewish expression of prayer, whether at home over the bread or in the more formal setting of the synagogue. It is a response to what God has done in creation and redemption (for example, 'Blessed be the Lord, the God of Israel, who with his hand has fulfilled what he promised with his mouth to my father David' in 1 Kings 8.15; see also Psalm 103.1-5; Psalm 104.1-4). It is therefore a response to who God is and (in hope) to what God will do.

For Christian writers, like the author of Ephesians and 1 Peter (1.3-5), this Jewish prayer has become centred on Christ. God is no longer just 'O Lord our God, King of the Universe', but 'the God and Father of our Lord Jesus Christ'. And the blessings for which God is blessed are those that Christians have received through the words and works of Jesus: 'adoption as his children', redemption, forgiveness, grace, knowledge of 'the mystery of his will'. And – supremely – 'an inheritance', which is pledged by his mark, the 'seal' of his Spirit.

Everyone sees God from somewhere. For the Jews, God is seen mainly from the vantage point provided by the shape of their history; Christians, however, claim that the best views are to be had when they stand within the pattern of their Christ.

*Reflection by* **Jeff Astley**

[1] *For a reflection on John 1.[1-9]10-18, see page 52.*

Isaiah 60.1-6
Psalm 72.[1-9]10-15
Ephesians 3.1-12
Matthew 2.1-12

## The Epiphany

**6 January**
*Principal Feast*

### Isaiah 60.1-6

*'Arise, shine; for your light has come,
and the glory of the Lord has risen upon you' (v.1)*

On Christmas Day 1622, Lancelot Andrewes preached a remarkable sermon at the Court of King James. It was about the Magi: *'It was no summer progress. A cold coming they had of it at this time of the year, just the worst time of the year to take a journey, and specially a long journey. The ways deep, the weather sharp, the days short, the sun farthest off, in* solsitio brumali, *the very dead of winter.'*

Some of those phrases were borrowed and made famous by the twentieth-century poet T.S. Eliot in his poem *The Journey of the Magi*. Eliot was only doing what all artists and writers of the Epiphany story have done through the centuries. They have taken certain motifs in the story and developed them in their own style to suit their own purposes.

There is something about the story of the journey of the Magi that has haunted human imagining ever since St Matthew first created it. Perhaps it's the contrast between the splendour of the Oriental figures and the humility of a child in a manger. Perhaps it is their mysterious arrival and equally mysterious departure. Perhaps it's the symbolism of their gifts. Whatever the reason, the story continues to intrigue and delight us.

Andrewes concluded his sermon with these words: *'And as they offered to Me, so I am come to bestow on them, and to reward them with endless joy and bliss on My heavenly Kingdom.'* It says it all.

*Reflection by* **Christopher Herbert**

**The Epiphany**

**6 January**

*Principal Feast*

Isaiah 60.1-6
Psalm 72.[1-9]10-15
**Ephesians 3.1-12**
Matthew 2.1-12

### Ephesians 3.1-12

*'... the mystery hidden for ages in God' (v.9)*

In common parlance, we are most likely to encounter the word 'mystery' in connection with detective fiction. What makes the murder mysteries of Agatha Christie so enjoyable is the way they engage our minds as we try to guess 'whodunnit' before Poirot summons everyone into the drawing room for the dénouement ...

The concept of mystery is important to Ephesians: the term occurs six times in the epistle, which is more than in any other New Testament book. However, this is not the type of mystery that can be solved by brainpower as we follow a trail of clues in the wake of some calamity; rather, it is revealed by God through an incredible act of love. The mystery can be found in Christ, who implements God's secret plan to unite all in his body. For Ephesians, it is an astonishing mystery that Jews and Gentiles are now one in Christ. Unable to be understood by human ingenuity, it has been revealed to the apostles by the Spirit and is now open to everyone to comprehend. 'To you', says Jesus to his uneducated disciples, 'it has been given to know the mysteries of the kingdom of God' (Luke 8.10).

This mystery of profound unity with other Christians is ours to wonder at and live out.

*Reflection by* **Helen Orchard**

Isaiah 60.1-6
Psalm 72.[1-9]10-15
Ephesians 3.1-12
**Matthew 2.1-12**

## The Epiphany

**6 January**
*Principal Feast*

### Matthew 2.1-12

*'Where is the ... king of the Jews?' (v.2)*

As shown in his trial before Pilate (Matthew 27.11), Jesus' destiny revolves around the notion of true kingship. The 'kingdom of heaven' is Matthew's somewhat roundabout way of referring to God's rule: God's will done on earth, 'as it is in heaven'.

The magi, 'wise men' or 'astrologers', are only identified as three kings in later Christian tradition. (References to foreign kings paying homage to Israel doubtless aided this transformation, e.g. Isaiah 60.3, 5-6 and Psalm 72.10-11.) Our magi are concerned with kings, though, unwisely asking a ruling king about the whereabouts of his successor. Ironically, it was the Romans who applied the title 'king of the Jews' to Herod, who was neither a son of David nor anyone with a right to the throne.

Israel yearned for a righteous 'ruler' and 'shepherd' (a term routinely used of kings). As a king, he would be anointed, and that verb is the root meaning of the Hebrew 'messiah', 'Christ' in its Greek translation. Such a king would inevitably be a rival to Herod, who was in no sense a shepherd to Israel but a cruel, paranoid tyrant.

Yet the king who finally comes is not exactly what was hoped for – or feared. The contrast between foreign dignitaries prostrating themselves before a baby, and Herod plotting and fuming over his status and security, shows us all we need to know about where true kingship lies.

*Reflection by* **Jeff Astley**

## The Baptism of Christ

**First Sunday of Epiphany**

**Genesis 1.1-5**
Psalm 29
Acts 19.1-7
Mark 1.4-11

### Genesis 1.1-5

*'Let there be light' (v.3)*

When and why do we tell stories of origins?

I was once helped to appreciate the story of creation by imagining Noah telling it to his family in the dark confines of the ark, when their world had been all but completely destroyed. It's a story that speaks to us most powerfully of all when we doubt our world and ourselves, when darkness and chaos seem in the ascendant.

In the season of Epiphany, at the darkest time of the year, it makes sense to hear once again the story of how light came out of darkness, and of how the waters of chaos were made to yield every kind of life by the infinitely creative power of God.

As we are told in that other great story of beginnings, the Prologue to John's Gospel, Jesus, the light of the world, entered into the world's deepest darkness and yet kept on shining. As the yearly recollection of Jesus' baptism reminds us, the Son of God went into the water of the Jordan in solidarity with our sin and emerged to an open heaven that showered promise and delight. The new creation was afoot.

No chaos is greater than God's power to make. If God can make the world even *ex nihilo* – from nothing – then God can heal the world, however catastrophically it seems to be falling back into chaos.

*Reflection by* **Ben Quash**

Genesis 1.1-5
Psalm 29
**Acts 19.1-7**
Mark 1.4-11

## The Baptism of Christ
**First Sunday of Epiphany**

### Acts 19.1-7

*'When Paul had laid his hands on them,
the Holy Spirit came upon them' (v.6)*

Paul acts with episcopal authority and apostolic faith to new Christian believers in Ephesus. We witness people who have been exposed by followers of John the Baptist to some basic aspects of the Christian faith, but whose faith, education and experience are not yet mature. The most vital experience they lack is that of the Holy Spirit, but through Paul's laying on of hands and teaching, they experience the fullness of God's Holy Spirit.

This is an example of how the early Church regularized a variety of independent streams of Christianity. Baptism very clearly in the name of the Lord Jesus followed by the laying on of hands are the litmus tests of apostolic Christianity as Paul understands it. Paul's laying on of hands might be regarded as an early form of 'confirmation', where the seal of the Spirit is conferred on the newly baptized.

For the joy of faith to be fully alive in us, we are invited to receive the Holy Spirit into our hearts. This is effected in many ways in the contemporary Church, most obviously in the form of the sacraments, which are offered as a free and open access to the Holy Spirit for every one of us who wishes to accept this gift. On this day when we celebrate Jesus' own baptism, let us rejoice in this gift and receive it happily.

*Reflection by* **Christopher Woods**

## The Baptism of Christ
### First Sunday of Epiphany

Genesis 1.1-5
Psalm 29
Acts 19.1-7
**Mark 1.4-11**

### Mark 1.4-11
*'... in the wilderness' (v.4)*

This passage begins with John the Baptist in the wilderness and ends with Jesus' baptism, after which Jesus himself is driven by the Spirit out into the wilderness.

These two kinsmen had a lot in common in terms of their message – even though the Baptist cuts a more rough-and-ready figure. They wanted to give people a sense of the primordial goods of life, and a suspicion of some of the constructions of human society that make life more complicated than it should be. Locusts and wild honey were probably not some sort of penitential diet for John – they were quite rich and nourishing fare. The real point was that they weren't farmed or sold at market; they were part of God's bounty in nature. Jesus would later celebrate that same bounty when he invited his followers not to be over-anxious about how they would clothe or feed themselves, and asked them to consider the example of lilies and birds (Matthew 6.26, 28).

Even the wilderness immediately around the Jordan where John preached and baptized wasn't (and isn't) arid and desert-like either; it is quite lush and verdant.

So perhaps John and Jesus offer us reminders of Eden – the fundamental goodness of creation – in which humans, wild beasts and angels all coexist well with one another. We can live well on what God provides, if we do not live with too much fear or with too much greed.

*Reflection by* **Ben Quash**

**I Samuel 3.1-10[11-20]**
Psalm 139.1-5, 12-18
[*or* 139.1-9]
Revelation 5.1-10
John 1.43-end

## Second Sunday of Epiphany

### 1 Samuel 3.1-10[11-20]

*'Here I am, for you called me' (vv.5, 6, 8)*

We catch a glimpse of Samuel's strange and lonely childhood with Eli, an ageing man, with failing sight, which could almost be his chosen defence mechanism: out of sight, out of mind. At night, the little boy sleeps in the temple, amidst the smell and smoke of the burnt offerings, the flickering light of the lamp, and with the terrifying presence of the ark of God for company.

Yet, in the midst of all of these reminders, Samuel does not immediately understand his call. It's hard not to see this as Eli's failing: he failed to give his own sons any sense of the reality of God, and in the same way he has apparently not given Samuel any expectation of the presence of God in the sacred space where he lives, works and sleeps.

The first message God gives to Samuel is a brutal one, a hard test of whether Samuel is willing to be a truthful speaker of the word of God. Samuel is not to know that Eli has already heard this news, but we, the readers, know and wait to see what Samuel will do. Samuel chooses, and sets the pattern of faithful response that is to shape the rest of his days.

With awe, God's people, who have come to despise Shiloh under the ministry of Eli and his sons, come back, to hear and meet their God again, at last.

*Reflection by* **Jane Williams**

**Second Sunday of Epiphany**

I Samuel 3.1-10[11-20]
Psalm 139.1-5, 12-18
[*or* 139.1-9]
**Revelation 5.1-10**
John 1.43-end

### Revelation 5.1-10

*'I saw ... a Lamb standing as if it had been slaughtered' (v.6)*

The Greek word for Revelation, apocalypse, implies the uncovering of secrets. The secrets of God are contained in the scroll – that is, in human history as told through Scripture. The only one worthy to reveal the secrets of the Scriptures is the one who is their subject, Jesus Christ. In spite of the multitude of angels around the throne, God bestows his secrets and his promises only to a human figure. Christ stands here for the whole human race. Christ is both the Son of David – which is why he is named as the conquering Lion of Judah – and the sacrificed Lamb of God who still bears the wounds of his passion. The fruit of his sacrifice is shown by the presence of the saints who have been ransomed by his death from every tribe and nation. It is because the Lamb/Lion is uniquely qualified to open the scroll and reveal the depth of God's judgement and love that the angels and the elders fall down and worship (Revelation 5.14).

Today's reading invites us to remember that our personal faith is a small part of a big canvas: all human history is there – all hope, all suffering, all destiny. All this is potentially judged and redeemed by Christ. Nothing that is human is alien to him.

*Reflection by* **Angela Tilby**

I Samuel 3.1-10[11-20]
Psalm 139.1-5, 12-18
[*or* 139.1-9]
Revelation 5.1-10
**John 1.43-end**

## Second Sunday of Epiphany

### John 1.43-end

*'Rabbi, you are the Son of God! You are the King of Israel!'*
*(v.49)*

John makes it clear that the first disciples followed Jesus because they believed him to be the Messiah – in Greek 'the Christ'. The Torah, the law of Moses, looked forward to the ending of conflict and injustice, and to the establishment of a society in which all could live in peace. The prophets looked for a time when all the scattered people of the twelve tribes would be reunited and would live joyfully and without deceit. The Messiah would usher in this time.

Jesus' words to Nathanael echo the prophet Zephaniah (3.13), and Nathanael recognizes that Jesus knows him as one who waits for the messianic kingdom. He acknowledges Jesus in the words of Zephaniah: 'The king of Israel, the Lord, is in your midst' (Zephaniah 3.15). At Bethel, the patriarch Jacob dreamed of the gate of heaven where angels ascend and descend upon the earth (Genesis 28.10-22). Now, Jesus implies, the Messiah is the gate of heaven, the prophet who unites heaven and earth in his own person.

Nathanael followed Jesus from that moment, though it must often have been hard to see how and when God's kingdom would come. John records that Nathanael saw the risen Christ at daybreak in Galilee. That is where the kingdom begins, as the risen Christ is made known in the breaking of bread.

*Reflection by* **Keith Ward**

**Third Sunday of Epiphany**

Genesis 14.17-20
Psalm 128
Revelation 19.6-10
John 2.1-11

## Genesis 14.17-20

*'Blessed be Abram by God Most High,
maker of heaven and earth' (v.19)*

Since Abram's first appearance in Genesis 11.31, the focus on him has been quite narrow. He has been leading a nomadic life, enjoying the considerable wealth that his obedience to God seems to have brought him. He does have a bit of a skirmish with Pharaoh in chapter 12 but, on the whole, the other inhabitants of the land through which Abram is driving his flocks stay very much in the background.

But now Abram enters the world stage in a big way. The kings who are fighting it out over the land of Israel don't initially take any notice of Abram – he has nothing to do with the struggle they are involved in. To protect his family, Abram gets involved, but he quickly proves to be a heroic warrior and a cunning strategist. King Melchizedek of Salem pays Abram the compliment of saying that Abram's God must be 'God Most High', the name usually reserved for the most important of the Canaanite gods. Melchizedek now makes the imaginative leap to recognition that this is Abram's God. Abram reinforces this (Genesis 14.22) as he describes God: he is not only the 'Most High'; he is also the creator of all.

Melchizedek must have imagined that his statesman-like gesture would go down in history. He does not realize that he and his kingdom of 'Salem' will actually be remembered because of the descendants of this nomadic fighter, and that he, Melchizedek, will barely count when history remembers Jerusalem's kings.

*Reflection by* **Jane Williams**

Genesis 14.17-20
Psalm 128
**Revelation 19.6-10**
John 2.1-11

## Revelation 19.6-10

*'Blessed are those who are invited ...' (v.9)*

Nowadays, wedding invitations come in ever more inventive form, being surpassed only by the 'Save the date' cards, bookmarks, fridge magnets or even tea-towels that precede them, pointing to the big day ahead.

John's Gospel describes events at the wedding at Cana as 'the first of Jesus' signs', which 'revealed his glory' (John 2.11). Much of the Revelation to John is also a signpost, in its grasping for imagery adequate to the vision of the glory of God in Jesus Christ that is in store for all who put their trust in him.

One powerful image is 'the marriage of the Lamb' and the feasting that follows. It pictures the consummation of Christ's love for his bride – understood as the Church. And, as we all know, what comes next for God and God's people is that we 'all live happily ever after'.

It's a vision that is almost too wonderful to grasp. And so John of Patmos warns against being distracted by the invitation and its delivery. For him, the temptation was to worship the angel. For us, distraction may mean trying to pin down, into everyday categories, the apocalyptic language that strives to signal the transcendent. As with the sign at Cana, what matters is that we, like Jesus Christ's disciples, recognize his glory and believe – and direct our lives of faith towards the big day to come.

*Reflection by* **Sarah Rowland Jones**

**Third Sunday of Epiphany**

Genesis 14.17-20
Psalm 128
Revelation 19.6-10
**John 2.1-11**

### John 2.1-11

*'Do whatever he tells you' (v.5)*

Mary is a woman of few words in the Fourth Gospel, but the ones she utters are authoritative and effective. She states the problem and identifies the solution. The solution, as always, is her son Jesus. Hesitant though he may be to intervene in this situation, Mary has made it difficult for Jesus not to act, advising the servants to await his instruction.

We know more of Mary's character from Luke, who shows us that she is not afraid to ask questions of archangels, or to risk scandal and death by accepting her vocation. Presenting a practical human need to her son is not the hardest thing she has had to do. When we see how her request is answered, we are thankful for her initiative, which has prompted Jesus' first sign in this Gospel, revealing something of his identity. It speaks of abundance to the point of excess, of quality beyond anything that has previously been experienced and of the glorious celebration at the messianic banquet of the bridegroom and his bride the church.

Would that we were more like Mary, the first to welcome Jesus into her life and, in this sense, the first Christian. Her every action points us to Jesus and highlights his words and deeds. To those in need she says: 'Do whatever he tells you.' As for herself, her desire is always the same: 'Be it unto me according to thy word' (Luke 1.38).

*Reflection by* **Helen Orchard**

**Deuteronomy 18.15-20**
Psalm 111
Revelation 12.1-5*a*
Mark 1.21-28

## Fourth Sunday of Epiphany

### Deuteronomy 18.15-20

*'... you shall heed such a prophet' (v.15)*

How do you know whether to trust something that someone says or not? This is a question that remains as relevant today as ever and was certainly something that troubled the author of Deuteronomy. Indeed, it is a theme that ran not only through this book but through the whole of the literature associated with this tradition (Judges, Joshua, 1 and 2 Samuel, and 1 and 2 Kings, sometimes known as a whole collection under the title the Deuteronomistic histories).

The answer provided here was an important one within this tradition – you know that something that someone says is trustworthy when it comes true; if it does not come true, it cannot be trusted. The unfolding of this tradition is one of the striking features of Deuteronomy: every single prophecy made by a 'reputable' prophet within any book of this tradition (from Deuteronomy to 2 Kings) came true, even if only three or four books later.

Although, to our modern mindset, this might appear to be an over-simplistic test, it warrants further reflection. If we lay aside the 'soothsaying' aspect of prophecy and instead remind ourselves that prophecy is primarily about speaking out about the things of God, then this test becomes more and more valuable. The veracity of someone's words must surely become a test of what they say – their trustworthiness lies in a direct correlation with how true what they say can be seen to be.

*Reflection by* **Paula Gooder**

**Fourth Sunday of Epiphany**

Deuteronomy 18.15-20
Psalm 111
**Revelation 12.1-5a**
Mark 1.21-28

### Revelation 12.1-5a

*'... crying out in birth pangs' (v.2)*

With the resurgence of vocal atheism, the challenge of other faiths, continued questioning of traditional morality and ever-faster changes in technology, we can sometimes feel as though we are being drawn into a trial of strength with the cultural forces of our day. Only those who are strong enough will survive, let alone prosper.

Yet in this part of Revelation we see layer upon layer of weakness and vulnerability as the means of God's power and victory. God's expectant people are depicted, using imagery from Isaiah 66 and Micah 4, as a woman in the very pains of labour – you could hardly find an image of greater vulnerability. Then the promise of God's deliverance of his people takes the form of a child, snatched away to safety with unseemly haste. What follows this is the war in heaven and the angels' victory over the dragon (Revelation 12.7-9).

It is as we offer our weakness and vulnerability that God's power and victory breaks through. Just as the decisive victory over the 'deceiver' was won through weakness, so we live in that victory as we offer our weaknesses and allow God the space to do his work.

Perhaps, then, the most important question is not 'Why am I weak?' but 'Where am I weak?' This is the place where God's victory will be revealed; this is the place where we can stand in the power that God alone can provide.

*Reflection by* **Ian Paul**

Deuteronomy 18.15-20
Psalm 111
Revelation 12.1-5a
**Mark 1.21-28**

### Fourth Sunday of Epiphany

### Mark 1.21-28

*'I know who you are ...' (v.24)*

The first chapter of Mark's Gospel is so condensed, so rich, so full of allusions and suggestions, it's breathtaking. We hurtle, via some Old Testament prophecies, to Jesus' baptism and his time in the wilderness, followed by John's arrest, then the calling of the disciples, and now, in verse 21, we come to a temporary halt in Capernaum, inside the small synagogue, where Jesus confronts a man possessed. The man screams out: 'What have you to do with us, Jesus of Nazareth? Have you come to destroy us? I know who you are, the Holy One of God'.

Here we touch a deeper level: an encounter with a spiritual, eternal dimension; evil confronted by goodness, darkness by light. This is the battle between God and the rebellious angels and powers. It isn't only about people's wellbeing, it's about the truth of their thinking, the reality of their perceptions.

While it is useful and important to consider what is meant by 'possession' and interpret it in modern terms, all illness is to a certain extent defined and conditioned by culture. What we need to grasp is that overwhelming sense of the beginnings of a titanic struggle between Jesus of Nazareth and the forces opposed to him.

And Mark takes us even further, to a question of identity – who is Jesus? It is a question we have to wrestle with, all our lives.

*Reflection by* **Christopher Herbert**

71

## The Presentation of Christ

**in the Temple (Candlemas)**
**2 February** *Principal Feast*

**Malachi 3.1-5**
Psalm 24.[1-6]7-end
Hebrews 2.14-end
Luke 2.22-40

### Malachi 3.1-5

*'He is like ... fullers' soap' (v.2)*

A popular Bible version translates this verse 'he will come like strong soap'. Fire and refining are familiar images of God's judgement and purifying. But soap? Are we to imagine enduring a vigorous scrubbing in the bath?

God's people are in exile far from home and temple – and far from God. The announcement of God's coming in this passage is surely all they long for? But the warning here is not to assume it will be comfortable. The work of a fuller was an essential part of the treatment of freshly woven cloth to make it supple, pure and ready for use. Fuller's soap was an alkali made from plant ashes used to clean and swell new cloth. This vigorous process involved washing, bleaching, soaking and beating the fibres into a consistent and desirable condition. Cloth was not ready for use until the fuller had cleaned and thickened the cloth (thus making it 'full').

So God works on his people as a fuller on new cloth – vigorously working our spiritual fibres into a consistent and desirable condition, to be a full and effective offering in his service. Like all purifying work, it is rough and rugged at the time, but it has to be to do its work. If nothing else, this image warns us against domesticating the life of faith and obedience.

*Reflection by* **David Runcorn**

Malachi 3.1-5
Psalm 24.[1-6]7-end
**Hebrews 2.14-end**
Luke 2.22-40

## The Presentation of Christ

### in the Temple (Candlemas)
**2 February** *Principal Feast*

### Hebrews 2.14-end

*'... he himself likewise shared the same things' (v.14)*

God's purpose is to bring 'many children to glory', according to verse 10 of this chapter. We are called to share in the family likeness of Jesus Christ. The author of Hebrews urges us to contemplate the coronation of Jesus, recognizing that it is the consequence of his willingness to share our humanity to the very end, to death itself.

Hebrews is noted for its stress on the humanity of Christ. That humanity is celebrated in the story of the baby Jesus being brought into the temple by Mary and Joseph, offered to God as the first fruits of God's new creation. We can trust him as he has become just like us, his brothers and sisters. As long as we keep focused on him, we will keep going towards the goal of salvation. When we lose heart, we need to recall what he has achieved for us by sharing our flesh and blood. He has made us holy, liberating us from the fear of death and so destroying the hold that death has over us.

The author uses the image of 'a merciful and faithful high priest' to help us understand what Christ can mean to us. His mediating role is a priestly role. Just as he was brought to the temple as a child, so he offers the sacrifice of himself that sets us free. As a faithful priest, he knows what it is to be tested and tempted. His encouragement to us comes from his own experience.

*Reflection by* **Angela Tilby**

## The Presentation of Christ
### in the Temple (Candlemas)
**2 February** *Principal Feast*

Malachi 3.1-5
Psalm 24.[1-6]7-end
Hebrews 2.14-end
**Luke 2.22-40**

### Luke 2.22-40

*'Guided by the Spirit, Simeon came into the temple' (v.27)*

In today's world there is constant pressure on us to respond instantly to situations and demands, with no time allowed for thought or reflection. Such reflection was a feature of Mary's life and character, as Luke tells us in verse 19 ('Mary treasured all these words and pondered them in her heart') and we see that feature also at work in the two people Mary and Joseph meet when they take the baby Jesus to the temple: Simeon and Anna.

Closely akin to this quality in both was another: the willingness to wait on God patiently, day after day, in hope and expectation. Simeon had been promised that he would not die 'before he had seen the Lord's Messiah'. He could not have known precisely what that meant, but his long, patient time of obedient waiting on God meant that he was instantly able to see in the baby Jesus the Messiah he had been waiting for. And the aged Anna, who never left the temple 'but worshipped there with fasting and prayer night and day' also recognized the Christ, and immediately began to speak of him 'to all who were looking for the redemption of Jerusalem'.

The encouragement to wait on God was already centuries old (Psalm 27.14), and remains equally valid for us today. It is not usually a way of instant understanding, but of a slow, imperceptible growth in spiritual insight.

In hope and trust, how much time are you prepared to give today to waiting on God?

*Reflection by* **Barbara Mosse**

**Isaiah 40.21-end**
Psalm 147.1-12, 21c [or 147.1-12]
1 Corinthians 9.16-23
Mark 1.29-39

**Sunday between 3 & 9 February
inclusive** *(if earlier than the
Second Sunday before Lent)*

## Isaiah 40.21-end

*'Have you not known? Have you not heard?' (vv.21, 28)*

Put yourself, for a moment, in the shoes of a second-generation exile. Babylon is all you have ever known. Those who remember Jerusalem and its mighty temple have passed away. You've heard the prophets telling you of something better, but life really isn't too bad in Babylon. You've put down roots, set up business. Why would you even consider setting out on an arduous and uncertain journey – all on the say-so of a rumour of a promise from God?

'Wake up!' cries the prophet, and his cry echoes down the centuries to us today. Have you forgotten just how great is our God? No one and nothing is his equal. Second best simply won't do for God or for God's people. There are to be no excuses for remaining in Babylon. They have a destiny to fulfil.

In the same way, those same words challenge us, God's weak and weary children, never to be content with living second-rate lives. We may be very comfortable where we are. But is it where God wants us to be? If, in our heart of hearts, we know it is not, God will have an answer to every excuse we care to invent, if we will sit in his presence long enough to listen.

We're frightened of change? Then our God is too small. We don't think we have the energy to do something different? Then God will give us something of his inexhaustible energy and strength. With God beside us we can 'mount up with wings like eagles … run and not be weary … walk and not faint.'

So what is today's excuse for remaining comfortable?

*Reflection by **Jan McFarlane***

**Proper 1**

Isaiah 40.21-end
Psalm 147.1-12, 21c [or 147.1-12]
**1 Corinthians 9.16-23**
Mark 1.29-39

## 1 Corinthians 9.16-23

*'... that I might be partaker thereof with you' (v.23, AV)*

Imagine a culture where people are fixated on their rights, on making sure they receive everything they are entitled to. Imagine a culture where competition is celebrated as the great driver for human achievement, symbolized by sporting events that command huge audiences and extravagant expenditure. How can the gospel be shared and discipleship fostered in such a culture? It is a question we might ask today, and a question with which Paul was grappling 2, 000 years ago as he wrote to the Christians in Corinth.

In responding to the specific issues on which they had asked for his opinion, Paul is also seeking to reshape their attitudes. While it is not always easy to track his thinking in this chapter, it seems clear enough that verse 23 summarizes his overriding point: 'And this I do for the gospel's sake, that I might be partaker thereof with you' (AV). Paul wants the Corinthians to understand that life in Christ means living for the sake of the gospel, and the gospel is not something I can possess as an object or achievement for myself. Rather, I can only have it by participating in it – by letting it become part of me, and letting my whole life become part of it – and I can only do that by sharing it with others, by giving it away. Here is the real prize, but to win it means learning to let go of the need to demand, compare and compete, and instead following the servant of all.

*Reflection by* **Jeremy Worthen**

Isaiah 40.21-end
Psalm 147.1-12, 21c [*or* 147.1-12]
1 Corinthians 9.16-23
**Mark 1.29-39**

### Mark 1.29-39

*'He came and took her by the hand and lifted her up.
Then the fever left her' (v.31)*

The healings of Jesus are radical for at least two reasons. First, they are miraculous. And second, they almost always go to people with no name, status, power or obvious religious reputation. Moreover, Jesus was interested not just in healing, but also in how people had been classed as 'ill' in the first place, and what or who kept them there. He was, I suppose, in the modern idiom, tough on illness, and tough on the causes of illness.

We also need to remember that when Jesus heals those 'sick with various diseases', he makes himself unclean by touching these sources of impurity. The radical demand of Jesus is that the Church is required to assume the pain and impurity of the excluded, the demonized and the (allegedly) impure. That's why the Church often works with the most marginalized in our communities – in hospitals, prisons and asylum centres, for example. It is just carrying on the job of Jesus, namely looking for the lost, rejected, marginalized and fallen, and trying, with the love of God, to bring them back into the fold of society and the arms of God.

Jesus, the friend of tax-collectors, prostitutes and other undesirables – but that's not how the Church portrays Christ. And I guess that's the trouble with Christians; we regard only ourselves as honorary sinners, and the Church as a haven for the saved and secure. Yet, it is for the lost and the loveless, the place for the unplaced, the home for the homeless.

*Reflection by* **Martyn Percy**

**Proper 2**

**Sunday between 10 & 16 February
inclusive** *(if earlier than the Second
Sunday before Lent)*

2 Kings 5.1-14
Psalm 30
1 Corinthians 9.24-end
Mark 1.40-end

### 2 Kings 5.1-14

*'Let him come to me, that he may learn that there is a
prophet in Israel' (v.8)*

Getting into God's healing zone often means getting out of
our own comfort zone, as this story shows. A slave girl has to
lift her head from cleaning floors to refer her sick master to
the right consultant, 'the prophet who is in Samaria'. A king
has to turn from politics to ask one of his vassals to facilitate
the healing of his leading general.

It is hardest of all for Naaman and Elisha. Elisha has to learn
how to be inclusive and generous to a threatening stranger
without compromising his own faith and calling. He will
indeed heal Naaman, but he has to seek that healing by a
baptism in Israel's river and at the hand of Israel's God.

For Naaman himself, it is hardest of all. He has to go into an
alien culture and submit himself to the ministry of a man
whom he would have considered his natural enemy. He
certainly does not like the prescription that is offered to him,
with its claim that the rivers and the God of Israel have a
saving power far beyond those of Syria. But the reward of
such humiliation is more than healing – it is conversion to the
living God.

*Reflection by* **Tom Smail**

2 Kings 5.1-14
Psalm 30
**I Corinthians 9.24-end**
Mark 1.40-end

### 1 Corinthians 9.24-end

*'Exercise self-control in all things' (v.25)*

When this letter was written in the first century, the Olympic Games took place every four years, as today. A centuries-old tradition had been revived because war was on the increase, which was believed to be a result of declining worship of the Greek gods. During the run-up to the Games, there was a truce between warring nations so that soldier-athletes could train, both physically and spiritually. Paul was living in Ephesus in the mid-50s. He would certainly have seen the rigours of preparation going on during an Olympic year. When he wrote to the Christians in Corinth, he must have known that athletics was a talking point in that city too. Considering the association of the Games with sacrifice to the gods, he was surprisingly positive.

Now as then, the gymnasium can be a punishing place. It is immediately obvious who is there because they take exercise seriously and who is 'running aimlessly'. I have often observed this – usually from the sauna.

In contrast, a church is a place where it is easier to dissemble. There are many who exercise their spirituality rigorously, treating prayer like a muscle and service of God like a discipline. However, others have a relationship with God that is more like a spectator than a participant. Paul knew which he wanted to be. We are all beneficiaries of that. If we emulate him, others too will have reason to be grateful.

*Reflection by* **Peter Graystone**

**Proper 2**

2 Kings 5.1-14
Psalm 30
1 Corinthians 9.24-end
**Mark 1.40-end**

### Mark 1.40-end

*'See that you say nothing to anyone' (v.44)*

Who told Mark what happened at Capernaum? (He apparently wasn't there.) The early Church Father Papias, in the second century, suggests that Mark wrote down the stories Peter had told him 'accurately, as far as he remembered them, the things said or done by the Lord, but not however in order'. Scholars have debated this for years, some arguing that the material may be derived from Church communities that had already shaped it for their own purposes.

And look at what happens: after the turbulent events of the previous evening – Jesus casting out demons and healing the sick – described in verses 21-34, Jesus gets up early and finds a deserted place to pray. Peter and the others pursue Jesus and hunt him out. There is a sense of anxiety and urgency. Peter tells Jesus, 'Everyone is searching for you' (Mark 1.37), and so Jesus launches out into the surrounding area. He teaches, preaches and heals.

But now in today's reading we come to the twist: a man struck down with leprosy is healed by Jesus, but is commanded not to speak about what has happened. The man disobeys, and, as a result, crowds pour out into the countryside to find Jesus.

Mark has a tension between the openness of the message and Jesus' deep reticence about revealing his own true identity – true historically, but also humanly true for all of us who 'pursue' Jesus. The beauty, awe, holiness and deep enigmas of the Christ are always there, yet always beyond our full understanding.

*Reflection by* **Christopher Herbert**

Isaiah 43.18-25
Psalm 41
2 Corinthians 1.18-22
Mark 2.1-12

**Sunday between 17 & 23 February
inclusive** *(if earlier than the Second
Sunday before Lent)*

## Isaiah 43.18-25

*'I will make a way in the wilderness' (v.19)*

Unlike the carefully manicured lawns of Oxbridge colleges, which have alert porters to guard them from straying tourists and undergraduates, the lawns of university campuses in the US are regularly criss-crossed by students. And there is a name for the beaten paths that emerge most clearly and consistently as the grass is worn away: 'paths of convenience'. These paths tell you important things about the routes that those who live in the place most want and need to travel.

The university authorities have two options at the end of each academic year. They can re-seed them, in the hope that a new generation will find a different way to travel from A to B. Or they can acknowledge the value of the paths of convenience, give in, and pave them!

The route that God most wants and needs to travel takes him across surprising terrain that few would normally cross: not precious grass, but the terrifying waters of ocean chaos, and the deadly expanses of desert wilderness. He chooses this way in order to reach the prison where his children are being kept, so as to set them free. It is, you might say, a path of *in*convenience, but for God it is travelled in love.

At the end of the reading, we are invited, by contrast, to think about how poorly the paths we take compare with God's: our love of *convenience* makes us poor travellers whose footsteps need re-seeding.

*Reflection by* **Ben Quash**

**Proper 3**

Isaiah 43.18-25
Psalm 41
**2 Corinthians 1.18-22**
Mark 2.1-12

## 2 Corinthians 1.18-22

*'For in [Jesus] every one of God's promises is a "Yes."' (v.20)*

Paul had twice changed his plans to visit Corinth a second time. He therefore has to answer the charge of fickleness brought against him by some in the Church. His denial that he was a 'Yes and No' man is filled out by a meditation on the faithfulness of God. The divine 'Yes' is confirmed in Jesus Christ as the fulfilment of the divine promises, and conveyed to his people by the anointing of the Spirit. This gives the firm hope that salvation will finally be completed.

Paul's object is to defend the trustworthiness of his ministry and message by identifying himself, and his companions Silvanus and Timothy, with the constant grace of God towards the Corinthians. He goes on to assert that his purpose in not visiting was for their sake, to spare them sorrow, and was in truth a mark of his love.

Appealing to the reliability of God as the basis of our Christian service is probably unavoidable, but it carries dangers. The temptation to excuse our transgressions and mistakes by appeal to good intentions or the larger purpose of God is to be resisted. Yet we must expect failures and misunderstandings to occur, and we must be forbearing towards others in order to carry on the work of God.

*Reflection by* **Christopher Jones**

Isaiah 43.18-25
Psalm 41
2 Corinthians 1.18-22
**Mark 2.1-12**

### Mark 2.1-12

*'… some people came, bringing to him a paralysed man, carried by four of them' (v.3)*

It's often said by Christianity's despisers that Christianity, like all religion, is a 'crutch'. Religious people, it's said, cannot stand on their own two feet. They cannot cope with life's demands like mature people who have learnt to take responsibility for themselves: to think and act by their own lights.

So what model of being a human well do these crutch-haters have in mind? It is a model that owes a great deal to the Enlightenment, and to give it a little more thought is to begin to realize that it has disturbing undertones. It presupposes that the normal state of the human being is to be healthy, self-sufficient and independent of others. Children, the elderly, the sick, the disabled are all departures from this norm, and patterns of life can ensue that make few concessions to them.

Actually, none of us can be this norm consistently, at every point in our lives – and the Christian model of being a human well makes this a cause for celebration. Christians find blessing not by denying their need of others, but by being members of a Church where all, at different times, carry one another, and in which this interdependence is the norm. The bringing of the paralysed man to Jesus by his friends is a scene of exceptional tenderness and tenacity that shows something profound about the best that humans can be.

*Reflection by* **Ben Quash**

**Second Sunday before Lent**

Proverbs 8.1, 22-31
Psalm 104.26-end
Colossians 1.15-20
John 1.1-14

### Proverbs 8.1, 22-31

*'When he established the heavens, I was there' (v.27)*

Wisdom is pretty sure of herself in today's reading. She takes to herself the most exalted role in creation, having been created right at the beginning and then being right alongside the Lord as creation continued. The language is rich and evocative: 'When he drew a circle on the face of the deep, when he made firm the skies above ... then I was beside him.' Wisdom's confidence is enchanting: 'I was daily his delight'. So what do we make of such extravagant claims?

The Bible has been likened to the debris that's left over after a huge explosion. The results of the explosion lie around in all directions. If that explosion is Jesus Christ, then we can see the particular debris in Proverbs as speaking of the same mediator who centuries later, by a river, heard a voice from heaven saying: 'With you I am well pleased' (Luke 3.22). Jesus was daily the delight of his Father.

It is from that confidence that we set out each day on the adventure of being a disciple. We may not have been there when the Lord started creating the earth, but we have been a twinkle in God's eye for a very long time. Our identity lies in the loving heart of God. We, too, are loved beyond reason.

Can we recognize today that we are the delight of our heavenly Father?

*Reflection by* **John Pritchard**

Proverbs 8.1, 22-31
Psalm 104.26-end
**Colossians 1.15-20**
¹John 1.1-14

### Colossians 1.15-20

*'... through the blood of his cross' (v.20)*

The lilting language of these verses indicates that this is an early Christian hymn. Unlike much that passes for praise in our churches, it is not focused upon the believer's experience; rather it draws worshippers into adoration through focusing on Christ's glorious nature until they are 'lost in wonder, love and praise'. Christ is described as true image of God – the restoration of the image given to humanity in creation); the beginning – as both the firstborn of creation and the firstborn from the dead. It is in Christ that all things and the Church hold together.

But what is this hymn doing in this letter? Its purpose is to remind the Colossians of two things. First, that despite his cosmic significance, Christ had a body made of flesh and blood. Secondly, that right belief is important.

For us today, these two reminders are important. Many of the growing Churches in the world tend to spiritualize Christian faith and make it other-worldly focused as if Christ had not been made flesh, had not healed the sick, had not been interested in issues of justice and community. At the same time, post-Christian society relies on Christian-derived values as if their basis in the doctrines of the faith were irrelevant.

The language of this passage reminds us of the connection between praising the one who bears the image of God and recognizing God's image in our fellow human beings.

*Reflection by* **Jane Leach**

¹ *For a reflection on John 1.1-14, see page 52.*

**Sunday next before Lent**

**2 Kings 2.1-12**
Psalm 50.1-6
2 Corinthians 4.3-6
Mark 9.2-9

### 2 Kings 2.1-12

*'Tell me what I may do for you, before I am taken
from you?' (v.9)*

In the Jewish Scriptures, people tend to view death as the natural conclusion to a life rather than as some feared enemy. This story, from which a faith in resurrection later develops, gives the sense that Yahweh is a God of life and that there is existence with him beyond the confines of our earthly living. For those who looked for the Messiah in the time of Jesus, it was to be Elijah returned from heaven who would announce his arrival – hence John the Baptist's Elijah overtones.

Elisha is appointed as Elijah's successor, inheriting his spirit and powerful mantle. We get another important theme here – that faith in God is something that is inherited and handed down. We have a duty to pass on the truths that have inspired us and helped us through life to another generation. We cannot expect them to discover the riches of the soul for themselves. This is a day to recall all those who nurtured and encouraged your own Christian discipleship – and then to ask whom you must now help.

As faithful vocation is handed on in this passage, so the whole impression is of life, glory and expectancy. To the jaundiced of the world, everything will look rather yellow, but to the faithful, life will be constantly opened up as we are carried by grace and enabled to do good things in the time given to us.

*Reflection by* **Mark Oakley**

2 Kings 2.1-12
Psalm 50.1-6
**2 Corinthians 4.3-6**
Mark 9.2-9

**Sunday next before Lent**

### 2 Corinthians 4.3-6

*'... in the face of Jesus Christ' (v.6)*

Have you ever found yourself looking at someone across a room and thinking, 'I'm sure I know that face'? We search our memory for where it might have been. C. S. Lewis suggested that when we finally see the face of Jesus, we will have the same feeling: 'You look so familiar. I know I've seen you before somewhere.' We will recognize him. How? Because, says Lewis, in his face will be all our faces – the likeness and image of all our faltering, flawed attempts at loving and being loved by others. He was there in it all because he is love itself.

There is a key movement in Christian faith and discipleship – a turning. A relationship is not possible until there is a turning towards another. The vital choice is *who* we turn our face to. In the baptism service we do not assent to an idea or doctrine; we promise an action. 'I turn to Christ.' St Paul speaks of it as an unveiling, and that captures both the beauty and the vulnerable exposure this brings. But it is all mutual. We turn, and we meet Jesus already turned to us. In his face we meet ourselves in our true likeness. And there too shines the glory and love of God. Our true likeness restored, creation can begin again.

*Reflection by* **David Runcorn**

**Sunday next before Lent**

2 Kings 2.1-12
Psalm 50.1-6
2 Corinthians 4.3-6
**Mark 9.2-9**

### Mark 9.2-9

*'This is my Son, the Beloved; listen to him!' (v.7)*

What did the chosen disciples expect as they tramped up the mountainside, pausing to catch their breath, looking out over the wide plains to Galilee? Surely not the sight of two foundational figures evoking the law and the prophets standing alongside Jesus, the fulfilment of both? Nor Christ, lit as if from within, his purity and holiness shimmering out in uncommon brilliance around them? Nor the sudden cloud cover and the voice from nowhere echoing around their startled ears, the words of God affirming his Son?

This profound religious experience comes without warning, revealing Jesus as the Light, as the Beloved, and leaving the observers stunned. We can understand Peter's impulsive attempt to capture the moment, to hold it still long enough to make some sense of what was happening before their astonished eyes.

But soon they have to come down from the mountain – and Jesus, knowing that this event will only make real sense after the resurrection, warns the disciples not to dissipate the intensity and wonder of their experience by conjecture, nor to incite envy among the other disciples, but to keep it to themselves.

This will not be the end of their – or our – encounters with the fullness of Christ.

All they, and we, need to do for now is listen. Listen to Jesus.

*Reflection by* **Sue Pickering**

Joel 2.1-2, 12-17 *or* Isaiah 58.1-12
Psalm 51.1-18
2 Corinthians 5.20b – 6.10
Matthew 6.1-6, 16-21 *or* John 8.1-11

**Ash Wednesday**

*Principal Holy Day*

### Joel 2.1-2, 12-17

*'... with fasting, with weeping, and with mourning' (v.12)*

Tears are our first language. We announced ourselves to the world with a cry. Until we have words, tears express our every mood. In the Bible, tears have an honoured and unembarrassed place, deeper than words.

But many of us have an uncomfortable relationship with tears. The way we talk about them gives us away. They are a malfunction – we 'break down', or 'crack up', or 'lose it'. Books on Christian living and prayer tend to ignore tears. They are discussed in the context of bereavement and suffering, but are hardly mentioned elsewhere. By contrast, the pastoral guides on discipleship in the early centuries of the Church contain chapter after chapter on the discerning of tears. Indeed a person was not taken seriously unless they had begun to weep. These guides write of tears as an extension of our baptism, a sign of the presence of the Spirit at work.

It is a puzzle that a faith that proclaims both the gift of unconditional love and the terrible reality of human fallenness should need reminding of tears at all. But it does. When Jesus blesses those who mourn, he gives special place in his kingdom for what is too often repressed as 'negative' emotion. We must weep. No other language expresses more truly what we must ever bring before the love and mercy of God.

*Reflection by* **David Runcorn**

## Ash Wednesday

*Principal Holy Day*

Joel 2.1-2, 12-17 *or* **Isaiah 58.1-12**
Psalm 51.1-18
2 Corinthians 5.20*b* – 6.10
Matthew 6.1-6, 16-21 *or* John 8.1-11

### Isaiah 58.1-12

*'Look, you fast only to quarrel and to fight
and to strike with a wicked fist' (v.4)*

Lynch mobs are ugly. The lynch mob has a collective face that is distorted by rage; and so the 'wicked fist' pummels mercilessly, focusing its anger on the victim's face, leaving it pulped and unrecognizable. The mob becomes inhuman and the victim is deprived of their unique identifying features.

Fortunately, lynch mobs are rarely seen in civilized societies, but this does not mean that our impulse as humans to disfigure others has ceased to exist. Look at newspaper headlines when editors bay metaphorically for blood; read the savagery of cyber-bullying; see what happens when the trolls on social media platforms vent their vicious spleen. Ugliness is not just a visible manifestation of a herd instinct; it is a dark energy hidden deeply within our souls.

What is to be done? Isaiah offers us a strong counterblast. It's a vision of the moral heart of God: God, says Isaiah, is not concerned with the religiosity of fasting; he wants to see true justice on earth; he wants a place where oppressive yokes are lifted from people's shoulders, where the hungry are fed, where the poor are clothed, where the homeless are housed, where our human moral duties towards each other are fulfilled in compassionate care.

Isaiah's solution is rooted in the being of God, and therefore rooted in a redeeming possibility: that the dark energy of our souls can be transformed when we recognize the potential victim as a human being like ourselves.

*Reflection by* **Christopher Herbert**

Joel 2.1-2, 12-17 *or* Isaiah 58.1-12
Psalm 51.1-18
**2 Corinthians 5.20b – 6.10**
Matthew 6.1-6, 16-21 *or* John 8.1-11

**Ash Wednesday**

*Principal Holy Day*

## 2 Corinthians 5.20b – 6.10

*'... having nothing, and yet possessing everything' (6.10)*

'It's not about me!' – Paul's plea to the Corinthians to accept the grace of God as he has proclaimed it draws him into a round of vigorous self-justification. In a rhetorical flood, he first recalls what he has endured physically. Next, he lists the personal qualities he has shown in his ministry. He ends with a series of oppositions showing the conflicting responses he has evoked and the paradoxical character of the apostolic life.

These oppositions turn on the difference between evaluation by human standards (2 Corinthians 5.16) and recognition of God at work. The tensions of Paul's ministry are in many ways similar to the Beatitudes pronounced by Jesus in Matthew 5.3-10 – persecuted but not defeated, striving for righteousness, sorrowful but rejoicing, having nothing but possessing everything. The upside-down quality of life in the kingdom translates into the cross-shaped life of the apostle.

Paul's catalogue should make us ask what is truly worth having and what actually motivates our decisions and actions. These are questions well worth pondering during the coming weeks of Lent.

The uncomfortable truth is that we only discover the character of authentic living with God when we take risks and let go of our normal securities – and, when we have done so, only God can show us whether we have got it right.

*Reflection by* **Christopher Jones**

## Ash Wednesday

*Principal Holy Day*

Joel 2.1-2, 12-17 *or* Isaiah 58.1-12
Psalm 51.1-18
2 Corinthians 5.20*b* – 6.10
**Matthew 6.1-6, 16-21** *or* John 8.1-11

### Matthew 6.1-6, 16-21

*'... where your treasure is, there your heart will be also' (v.21)*

In this part of the Sermon on the Mount, Jesus preaches about the spirituality of religious practices. We are first told how *not* to pray, indeed how *not* to be religious. If our piety is not a true expression of ourselves before God, as when it is done for show, it is disfigured. The reward of the hypocritical ('play-acting') pray-ers is the respect of others. If that is what they want from prayer, well that is what they will get.

The rewards of which Jesus speaks, however, can only come when the relationship the true disciple has with God is made clearly visible. And that cannot happen until this relationship has been forged – like every other successful relationship – in a spiritual furnace fuelled by humble honesty and love.

In contrast to these rewards, earthly treasures are apt to fail; they flicker out like dodgy bulbs. We must look for the stuff that lasts. Valuing is a way of seeing that is affected by the sort of person we are, and (as New Testament scholar Craig Evans argues) 'the type of treasure that one accumulates is a reliable indication of what one values'.

We must learn to look beyond all these good, valuable things and loves, and even beyond ourselves. For to see the kingdom and righteousness of God, we must be able to glimpse – in and through and beyond them all – the Giver who transcends these gifts, and the Love that exceeds all loving.

*Reflection by* **Jeff Astley**

Joel 2.1-2, 12-17 *or* Isaiah 58.1-12
Psalm 51.1-18
2 Corinthians 5.20*b* – 6.10
Matthew 6.1-6, 16-21 *or* **John 8.1-11**

**Ash Wednesday**

*Principal Holy Day*

## John 8.1-11

*'Has no one condemned you?' (8.10)*

There is a terrible disregard for this woman caught in adultery. There is no indication that she has been falsely accused, but that seems incidental. This is about catching Jesus out, and she is collateral damage in that bigger fight. She is, to the scribes and Pharisees, it seems, a pawn easily sacrificed in a larger game plan.

Jesus is forced to face the dilemma we so often face too: how to remain clear on points of principle without losing sight of the individuals who live with the consequences. Jesus does not answer the question put to him on the point of principle. He cuts through the posturing and self-righteousness with a response that places the responsibility for the outworking of the dilemma back with those who raised it.

The scribes and Pharisees had separated themselves from the woman but Jesus reunited them with her. They had isolated her by the sin they had caught her in. Jesus' response required them to realize they stood with her. Not one of them could cast a stone because no one of them was without sin.

So often we judge ourselves against others; sometimes counting ourselves better, sometimes diminishing ourselves in comparison. This, though, is to miss the point. This story reminds us that 'all have sinned and fall short of the glory of God' (Romans 3.23). Jesus is without sin, but he chose mercy for this woman and offers mercy to us.

*Reflection by* **Libby Lane**

**First Sunday of Lent**

**Genesis 9.8-17**
Psalm 25.1-9
1 Peter 3.18-end
Mark 1.9-15

## Genesis 9.8-17

*'... never again shall all flesh be cut off' (v.11)*

The so-called Noahic Covenant is the first great covenant of God with human beings. It is of huge importance for understanding what will become the characteristic pattern of God's dealings with his world, and especially with humanity. It establishes the very foundations of the world in which all subsequent covenants will unfold – the Abrahamic, the Mosaic and the Davidic, and then eventually the Christian 'new covenant' in Christ's blood. It says: 'I will not give up on this world, whatever wrong turns it takes. I will work within this world, paying whatever price is necessary in order to sustain, redeem, and transform it for a better future.'

A Christian account of history may want to begin with the idea of covenant, reading history as punctuated by a series of covenantal moments in which some sense of 'significant form' in historical process is affirmed. The revelation of God takes place through intensive disclosures of the divine presence at certain points in the temporal series.

We might say that covenants are like 'Amens'. Amen derives from a Hebrew root that signifies reliability. Like the covenant with Noah and all its various successors through time, Amens are strung out through history as points of intensity and recognition. Even if it may sound like a conclusion, Amen is never just said once – not, at least, by us creatures in history. Yet it points to a conclusive truth: that God is faithful.

*Reflection by* **Ben Quash**

Genesis 9.8-17
Psalm 25.1-9
**1 Peter 3.18-end**
Mark 1.9-15

## 1 Peter 3.18-end

*'... he went and made a proclamation to the spirits in prison'*
*(v.19)*

Medieval imagination loved to picture this scene. Jesus has died on the cross and descended, after the way of all flesh, to the world of the dead. There at the gates of the underworld, Satan, whose kingdom this is, waits to receive what he assumes to be the routine delivery of another human body due to him – for the penalty for sin is death. But he finds, to his utter horror, that he has signed for and received into his domain, the sinless Lord of Glory. The exchange economy collapses and its theology with it. At a stroke his kingdom is laid waste, hell is harrowed, evil is vanquished and death itself is defeated.

And there Christ preaches resurrection to the startled shadowy congregation of Adam and Eve, our lost humanity, takes their hands, and calls them into new life.

Peter's text affirms two things. First, that in the reach of his incarnate love, there is nowhere Christ is not. There is nowhere he does not seek us and nowhere we will not find him. Second, it is precisely in our wilfulness, our resistances, our exile and prisons that we meet him, not in our notions of what goodness or perfection earns. In the words of the former Bishop of Edinburgh, Richard Holloway: 'Only the sinner understands the gospel, for only the sinner knows their need of it.'

*Reflection by* **David Runcorn**

**First Sunday of Lent**

Genesis 9.8-17
Psalm 25.1-9
1 Peter 3.18-end
**Mark 1.9-15**

### Mark 1.9-15

*'Now after John was arrested' (v.14)*

At what speed did Mark write? He gives the initial impression of pressing on: it's all urgent. He is fond of phrases such as 'and immediately'. But, on second reading, it all seems much more careful. Take the phrase, 'Now after John was arrested' – it could not be more brief. We have been given no warning that John the Baptist is under threat, but perhaps the original readers would already have known the background to the arrest.

Mark uses a special word for what has been translated into English as 'arrested', which comes from the Greek word *paradidomi* – 'to hand over'. It's a word that Mark later uses about Jesus himself: he was 'handed over' to the chief priests and scribes, and Jesus also predicts that the disciples will themselves be 'handed over' to councils and synagogues (Mark 13.9).

There are times for each of us, perhaps, in illness, accident or tragedy, when we are no longer in control, when we are, as it were, 'handed over' – in the grip of forces that are beyond our control and, possibly, beyond our understanding. Yet, inside our own experience of being handed over, we may discover the presence of Christ – who stays with us and who shares totally in our helplessness. And out of that, by God's grace, new possibilities and new life emerge.

*Reflection by* **Christopher Herbert**

**Genesis 17.1-7, 15, 16**
Psalm 22.23-end
Romans 4.13-end
Mark 8.31-end

## Second Sunday of Lent

### Genesis 17.1-7, 15, 16

*'I will bless her, and she shall give rise to nations' (v.16)*

Names in the Bible carry meaning. The person who names something has authority over it. So, when God renames Abram ('exalted father'), 'Abraham' ('father of a multitude') and Sarai becomes Sarah (in both cases this means 'princess'), this tells us that God is about to do something through them. In the thirteen years since the birth of Ishmael, Abraham's son with the slave-girl Hagar, Abraham has staked his hopes on him as his heir. So, when God reiterates that Sarah will have a son, Abraham questions it. In chapter 15, God's promise comes in the middle of Abraham's daily life and he has a conversation with God about it; here, God announces the covenant unilaterally and Abraham hardly says a word, but instead falls over laughing, as you will read if you carry on past today's reading (v.17).

So, Abraham, worn out by waiting for God's word to be fulfilled, is ready to settle for blessing through Ishmael. But God has other ideas: Ishmael will indeed be blessed, but there is still more blessing for Abraham and Sarah, because their child, whom God names Isaac ('laughter'), will be the one with whom the covenant is established.

When we are under pressure and growing weary, it is easy to settle for what we have got rather than remain open to God's promise of even more blessing in the future. Mercifully, God does not give up. So we can pray to be renewed by God's grace and sustained by God's power in our times of weakness.

*Reflection by* **Rosalind Brown**

**Second Sunday of Lent**

Genesis 17.1-7, 15, 16
Psalm 22.23-end
**Romans 4.13-end**
Mark 8.31-end

### Romans 4.13-end

*'Abraham ... the father of all of us' (v.16)*

There is at present a growing fascination with genealogy. More and more families are tracing their ancestors, digging back into the past to see what has made them the people they are. Often this search leads to some interesting surprises and the discovery of long-lost relatives – and their sometimes shady past.

Today we consider that we are children of Abraham. This is an astonishing and bold claim: that our genealogy as Christians is shared by many and goes back many generations. Our bloodline – as the first chapter of Matthew lists in the genealogy of Jesus – is a rich and varied one. But Paul focuses on Abraham and reminds us of just what a wonderful example he is.

Here is Paul at his most generous and inclusive – as a follower of Jesus Christ, but also recognizing that his inheritance goes back much further and wider. He cites Abraham as a model and an example to follow. During his long wait, Abraham's faith must have been severely tested and challenged, but he remained faithful to God. He must have wondered if there would be any fruit and purpose to his life. For Abraham there were no quick results, but deep faithfulness.

We share this inheritance. Today we thank God for the rich and diverse family of which we are a part, for those who are not like us, for those who are surprisingly different yet connected through this incredible picture of unwavering faithfulness.

*Reflection by* **Tim Sledge**

Genesis 17.1-7, 15, 16
Psalm 22.23-end
Romans 4.13-end
**Mark 8.31-end**

### Mark 8.31-end

*'Peter took him aside and began to rebuke him' (v.32)*

Don't you just love Peter? Even though he has just grasped that Jesus is God's anointed, he can't help himself taking Jesus on one side and presuming to correct his theology! And what does this story tell us about Jesus, that he created the kind of dynamic within his disciples that enabled them to be completely honest with him, even when they thought he was wrong?

These days, more and more people find themselves having to work as part of a team, and many of us will have worked in teams where the boss would not have been able to cope with such honest and open criticism. In his bestselling book, *The Five Dysfunctions of a Team*, business guru Patrick Lencioni identifies the first dysfunction as the absence of trust – unwillingness to be vulnerable within the group. And when Peter says something that is clearly off-message, Jesus is not afraid to confront him, for the sake of the team. Too often the effectiveness of teams is hampered when a leader shies away from confronting behaviour which they know is harmful – as Lencioni also notes.

And what does it say about Jesus that he created the type of team where the members were willing to be open about their mistakes so that others could learn from them? One of Mark's primary sources for his Gospel was probably the personal reminiscences of Peter, which makes me love Peter all the more.

*Reflection by* **Mark Ireland**

**Third Sunday of Lent**

Exodus 20.1-17
Psalm 19 [or 19.7-end]
1 Corinthians 1.18-25
John 2.13-22

### Exodus 20.1-17

*'... you shall have no other gods before me' (v.3)*

I don't suppose that the majority of people in Great Britain could quote the Ten Commandments if asked to do so. Those who do have a vague remembrance of the commandments would probably describe them as negative, a series of 'don'ts'.

In fact, they are not prohibitions but a characterization of the life of a person in relationship with God. God has offered his people a covenant of love, and he now tells them what their lives will look like when they accept his offer.

The commandments consist of a wonderful balance of emphasis upon right relationship with God and right relationship with one another – sensible life balance, getting adequate rest, respect for other people's possessions and other people's relationships. As such, they constitute as relevant a description of the good and godly life today as they did when they were given. That is an astonishing thing, considering how long ago that was – but God has not changed, and nor has human nature.

Now, more than ever, we need to be reminded not only of the perils of neglecting God but also that nothing else but God – and certainly not the sexual promiscuity and covetousness extolled by our consumerist society – can bring us the happiness we so crave and which, for all our material prosperity, increasingly evades us.

We need the Ten Commandments.

*Reflection by* **John Inge**

Exodus 20.1-17
Psalm 19 [*or* 19.7-end]
**1 Corinthians 1.18-25**
John 2.13-22

## 1 Corinthians 1.18-25

*'For God's foolishness is wiser than human wisdom, and God's weakness is stronger than human strength' (v.25)*

We wouldn't wear a hangman's noose around our neck. We wouldn't put an electric chair in our church. But we do put on a cross.

The trouble is, the cross has become too beautiful and too bland. We may flinch from the physical pain depicted in films such as Mel Gibson's *The Passion of the Christ*, but we recognize the horror of crucifixion. It was designed to end all hope, for the victim and crowd alike. In this, it was successful. Jewish hope demanded a messianic miracle, or a religious revolution. Greek curiosity would be satisfied only in novel ethics or the latest theory on life, the universe and everything.

The cross of Christ put an end to all that. Instead of the signs of God's power, it revealed tragic weakness. Instead of the clue to God's wisdom, it revealed human folly.

Or so they thought in Corinth, until Paul preached the cross. Then the discerning Jew could see that the cross inspires a powerful revolution of love and transformation, and the reflective Greek could discover in the cross the wise grace of forgiveness and reconciliation.

As you kneel before the cross in prayer, find the strength and wisdom to stand for Christ and his cross before the crowd.

*Reflection by* **Bruce Gillingham**

**Third Sunday of Lent**

Exodus 20.1-17
Psalm 19 [*or* 19.7-end]
1 Corinthians 1.18-25
**John 2.13-22**

### John 2.13-22

*'Stop making my Father's house a market-place!' (v.16)*

Jesus ate with social outcasts, healed the sick, gave hope to the poor and forgave sinners. The only people he treated harshly were the religious. He drove the animals out of the temple with a whip, overturned the tables of the money-changers, and poured out their coins. He lashed the Pharisees and lawyers with his tongue, accusing them of breaking their own law by their hypocrisy, pride and manipulation of the poor. He said that he had come not to save the righteous but those who were regarded with contempt and indifference.

It is rather ironic that we have constructed a religion around Jesus, that many have become financially rich through religion, and that we have hierarchies of clergy in prominent seats and costly clothing. What can we do about it? Jesus did not want to destroy the temple, but he subtly pointed out that his body was a temple that would be destroyed and raised again. When it was raised, the body of Christ would be the community of those who feed the hungry, heal the sick and comfort the bereaved, the hands and heart of the risen Christ.

Whatever the outward reality, it is when we are Christ's body, living as he lived, living in him, that we are truly the house of God.

*Reflection by* **Keith Ward**

**Numbers 21.4-9**
Psalm 107.1-3, 17-22 [*or* 107.1-9]
Ephesians 2.1-10
John 3.14-21

### Numbers 21.4-9

*'... that person would look at the serpent of bronze and live' (v.9)*

Robert Louis Stevenson asserted that 'to travel hopefully is a better thing than to arrive', though it is hardly a sentiment the ancient Israelites in the wilderness would have shared. Our Lenten journey too has a clear objective – that we should arrive at the foot of the cross on Good Friday fully prepared.

How do we get ready to engage in fresh and deeper ways in all the mysteries of Christ's passion and resurrection? The truth that we are united with Christ in his death, and so also with him in the fullness of his risen life, is not just 'once for all time', but one we may discover again and again, and more and more throughout our Christian life.

Each Lent invites us on a journey of reflection: who are we now? How have we grown in Christ in the past 12 months? More to the point, what do we still lack? Where do we need to go on learning, go on being healed, redeemed, transformed? What do we need to bring to the cross this year?

Perhaps, like the Israelites, we need to be painfully brought up short by the failings of our faith.

But the good news is that what God puts on our agenda is already on his. The more we dare bring to Christ on the cross, lifted up like the serpent, the more we will find transformed by his resurrection life.

*Reflection by* **Sarah Rowland Jones**

Numbers 21.4-9
Psalm 107.1-3, 17-22 [*or* 107.1-9]
**Ephesians 2.1-10**
John 3.14-21

### Ephesians 2.1-10

*'... by grace you have been saved' (v.5)*

The Christian faith has a number of competitive theories as to what its main priorities should be. There is a common thread that runs through them all, however, and it is this. Out of the ashes of Good Friday – of failure, defeat and tragedy – hope and new life are born. The disciples are to be the ambassadors of the new hope and transformation wrought in the person of Jesus. And this role is one that is primarily rooted in developing a dynamic, loving vocation for humanity.

The resurrection, in other words, is something that does not so much *draw* disciples *into* a new sect, as *send* them *out* into the world, with joy, conviction and a desire to serve the world and the needs of others in the name of the living Christ. And critically, this is done in love. It is not a task; it is an entire reconfiguration of one's life. Yet you cannot really command people to love. That's the catch. Love is for falling into; it is a state of being, as well as doing.

Paul reminds the Ephesians that they have been brought from death to life, and from darkness to light. This does not make Christians, per se, superior to others, because none of this was earned. It is only by grace – God's Riches At Christ's Expense, as the old Sunday School mnemonic goes. Understanding this and living it means Christians are free and enlightened. But it also bonds each and every one of us to be bearers of kindness and good works. Yes, even Paul, the champion of unmerited grace, reminds us: '... we are what he has made us, created in Christ Jesus for good works'.

*Reflection by* **Martyn Percy**

Numbers 21.4-9
Psalm 107.1-3, 17-22 [or 107.1-9]
Ephesians 2.1-10
**John 3.14-21**

**Fourth Sunday of Lent**

## John 3.14-21

*'... that whoever believes in him may have eternal life' (v.15)*

As we enter the fourth week of Lent, it's worth reflecting on how well we are using it to prepare ourselves for Easter.

Jesus's words in today's reading are spoken to Nicodemus, a Jewish leader and 'teacher of Israel', who comes to see Jesus 'by night' (John 3.1-2). There follows a conversation typical of John's Gospel, involving (mis-)understandings that move us on from physical ideas to the spiritual level.

By the start of today's verses, Nicodemus has faded away and Jesus is speaking over his head to us all. The contrast he conveys is not just physical and spiritual, but also between 'earthly' and 'heavenly' things (John 3.12). As Moses told the Israelites poisoned by snakes in the wilderness to look at a bronze serpent 'lifted up', so we are to look at the body of Jesus, also 'lifted up' but on a cross, the final destination of our Lenten discipline, and find in him 'eternal life'. This is the ultimate demonstration of how 'God so loved the world' in his giving of himself in his Son.

So, Lent provides 40 days of fasting in the wilderness to help us get our focus back on Jesus – for only by looking to him can we find healing, new birth and eternal life. Take some time today to consider how you will observe Lent to restore your focus on Jesus.

*Reflection by* **Richard A. Burridge**

**Mothering Sunday**

Exodus 2.1-10 *or* I Samuel 1.20-end
Psalm 34.11-20 *or* Psalm 127.1-4
2 Corinthians 1.3-7 *or* Colossians 3.12-17
Luke 2.33-35 *or* John 19.25-27

### Exodus 2.1-10

*'The woman conceived and bore a son' (v.2)*

This passage depicts one of the most famous scenes in all of history: the poignant, riveting drama of a vulnerable baby set adrift on a river by his mother in a desperate bid to try to save his life. The precariousness of the baby's destiny and very survival has captured the imagination of millions for over two and a half millennia.

The drama develops as three women, through a daring act of unexpected compassion, make visible the hidden providence of God and assure the baby's future. Liberation theologian Jorge V. Pixley has noted that this Egyptian 'den of death' is still a place where God may find 'allies of life'. This is an astonishing liberation, which later makes possible the liberation of all Israel as Moses grows up to become their pathway to freedom out of the bondage of the Egyptians. The story has echoes of an 'ark' of life, ensuring the survival and liberation of Noah and his family together with their livestock. Somehow the deep taproots of Israel's story contain possibilities of justice and freedom no matter what. The people of Israel, as with the baby, have always been vulnerable themselves and, so often on the brink of being overcome by the waters of chaos, they still experience unexpected redemption from the hidden hand of an invisible God. There is always hope because there is always God – even when there is no divine sign, only a sense of faith in a God who mysteriously works within whatever happens.

*Reflection by* **David Moxon**

Exodus 2.1-10 *or* **1 Samuel 1.20-end**
Psalm 34.11-20 *or* Psalm 127.1-4
2 Corinthians 1.3-7 *or* Colossians 3.12-17
Luke 2.33-35 *or* John 19.25-27

## Mothering Sunday

### 1 Samuel 1.20-end

*'She left him there for the Lord' (v.28)*

We are not told much in 1 Samuel about Elkanah and Hannah, except where they lived and that Elkanah had two wives, Hannah and Peninnah. However, 1 Chronicles 6 reveals that Elkanah 'ministered with song before the tabernacle of the tent of meeting', so going year by year to worship at the shrine at Shiloh was his religious duty. In a culture where sons were considered to be a reflection of God's blessing on a righteous person, we – especially childless women – can sympathize with Hannah's anguish as year by year Peninnah rubbed in her childlessness (1 Samuel 1.3-7), which cast doubts on Elkanah's righteousness, just as, centuries later, Elizabeth's childlessness did for Zechariah.

Once Hannah's prayer at the shrine was answered, she displayed remarkable devotion and faith: in what must have been a heartbreaking act for her, she left her precious Samuel at the shrine for God, promising him as a Nazirite, someone totally devoted to God. For Hannah, this was an expression of thanksgiving and love, but also one of immense trust in God, coupled with risky trust in Eli, who had failed to raise his own sons in a godly way.

So Hannah challenges us to have radical trust in God who has answered prayer. But, reading this story through Eli's eyes, it is also a reminder that God offered him a second chance, as God does for us. And, as an afterthought, what did Elkanah learn from his wife about trusting God?

*Reflection by* **Rosalind Brown**

**Mothering Sunday**

Exodus 2.1-10 *or* I Samuel 1.20-end
Psalm 34.11-20 *or* Psalm 127.1-4
**2 Corinthians 1.3-7** *or* Colossians 3.12-17
Luke 2.33-35 *or* John 19.25-27

### 2 Corinthians 1.3-7

*'For just as the sufferings of Christ are abundant for us, so also our consolation is abundant through Christ' (v.5)*

Paul doesn't avoid writing about his sufferings, as he recognizes affliction and persecution as crucial elements of his Christian journey. However, total dependence on Christ – to console every pain, sorrow and affliction – can be challenging for us today, mainly because modern medicine readily offers remedies to counteract physical or emotional pain. Sometimes we may even find ourselves 'desensitized' to the daily sufferings of our Christian brothers and sisters around the world. If we're not careful, they become mere images on mission leaflets or media appeals for money. Alternatively, our concern for the suffering of others in distant places can consume us, making us 'insensitive' to those suffering in our local churches or communities.

Paul's sees his relationship with Christ as his primary curative and relief. As Christians, we share in this sacred connectedness. Even as all are united through a common faith in Jesus, all look to him during periods of rejection, affliction and suffering. And, he empowers us to comfort one another.

When we extend God's divine consolation to others during seasons of great suffering, these encounters produce faith-building testimonies – personal stories – that, when shared, bring consolation to others during times of their greatest need. In our prayers today, we ask the Holy Spirit to make us into anointed vessels of comfort, bringing healing and restoration to others.

*Reflection by* **Rosalyn Murphy**

Exodus 2.1-10 *or* I Samuel 1.20-end
Psalm 34.11-20 *or* Psalm 127.1-4
2 Corinthians 1.3-7 *or* **Colossians 3.12-17**
Luke 2.33-35 *or* John 19.25-27

**Mothering Sunday**

### Colossians 3.12-17

*'Clothe yourselves with compassion, kindness, humility, meekness, and patience' (v.12)*

New clothes are a great event in many families. In parts of Yorkshire and elsewhere there is still a memory of the annual Whit walks at Pentecost when children would be given their annual new sets of clothes and come together in great festivals.

Paul continues here the image of the new clothes of our baptism. Here is a list of things we should put on, similar to the picture of the whole armour of God in Ephesians 6. Here there are six virtues: compassion, kindness, humility, meekness, patience and love. The sense of the Greek is that we should put on this character in our inmost being: our foundation garments, as it were. These qualities, the qualities of Christ, should be underneath and flow through all we do.

As we read this passage we should remember that they are addressed primarily not to you or me as individuals but to the whole Church. These virtues lead immediately to forbearance and forgiveness in the body of Christ. From these in turn come peace and thanksgiving, wisdom, worship and glory.

The practical outworking of these qualities will be different in every household and at every life stage. But for today, whatever you are facing, reflect on these six core virtues. How are you called to put them on and live them out where you live and where you work?

*Reflection by* **Steven Croft**

## Mothering Sunday

Exodus 2.1-10 *or* 1 Samuel 1.20-end
Psalm 34.11-20 *or* Psalm 127.1-4
2 Corinthians 1.3-7 *or* Colossians 3.12-17
**Luke 2.33-35** *or* John 19.25-27

### Luke 2.33-35

*'A sword will pierce your own soul too' (v.35)*

Traditionally, these words have been taken as prophecy of the pain of Jesus' mother in witnessing his execution. Some commentators, however, link them instead to the rest of Simeon's words to Mary, about the division that this child will cause within Israel (in the Greek, they come at the start of verse 35, not at the end as in the NRSV). She will feel within herself the distress of the conflicting responses to her son's ministry: a sign that will be opposed.

One line of interpretation is that, in these first two chapters of Luke, Mary represents Israel as a whole. She receives God's word to dwell within her. She celebrates that God has done great things for her, his servant. She brings into the world the one anointed by God to call the nations to know him. These are the acts of Israel. And Mary will also bear the confusion and opposition that this Messiah will evoke within Israel.

The new thing that began with Gabriel's greeting of Mary in Galilee comes for the first time to the centre of Israel's continuing life, the temple in Jerusalem. And, in the midst of the light of recognition, a shadow of darker anticipation is glimpsed. Does it also stretch out to us?

*Reflection by* **Jeremy Worthen**

Exodus 2.1-10 *or* I Samuel 1.20-end
Psalm 34.11-20 *or* Psalm 127.1-4
2 Corinthians 1.3-7 *or* Colossians 3.12-17
Luke 2.33-35 *or* **John 19.25-27**

**Mothering Sunday**

### John 19.25-27

*'When Jesus saw his mother ...' (v.26)*

I am deeply moved by what seems to me the stark contrast between this moment of tenderness as Jesus responds to his mother and friend, and the cold, brutal dividing up of the spoils of the dead which precedes it.

The latter speaks of the closure of history, the finality of death and the turning of intimate, personal garments into objects to be contested for. The women standing near the cross, together with the beloved disciple, desolate as they are, retain that intimacy with Jesus. They had known the goodness of God's love in Jesus, and seen that love made real in his intimacy with others. They honoured Jesus, reflected his love, in the physical caring for his body when they return to the tomb after the sabbath. It is Mary Magdalene who first sees that the stone has been removed from the tomb, and runs back to summon help from Simon Peter and the 'disciple whom Jesus loved'.

The little 'community of the cross' will soon become a 'community of the resurrection'. That community restores to us a sense of his compassionate humanity and of his capacity to hold for us a future hope.

On the cross, Jesus honours his mother as he takes his leave of her. She is not to lose her status as mother. Just as she is given into the care of the 'beloved' disciple, so he is given into hers. Mutual, loving, intimate support is re-established at the heart of the new community.

*Reflection by* **Libby Lane**

**Fifth Sunday of Lent**

Jeremiah 31.31-34
Psalm 51.1-13 *or*
Psalm 119.9-16
Hebrews 5.5-10
John 12.20-33

### Jeremiah 31.31-34

*'I will put my law within them, and I will write it on their hearts' (v.33)*

Jeremiah contains quite a few references to the human heart, most of them unfavourable. Specifically, 'the heart is devious above all else; it is perverse – who can understand it?' (Jeremiah 17.9). In biblical thought, the heart was not simply the seat of emotion but also of volition: it knows and wills as well as feels. When we learn that 'The sin of Judah is written with an iron pen; with a diamond point it is engraved on the tablet of their hearts' (Jeremiah 17.1), we realize that a significant cardiac intervention will be required for health to be restored.

In today's passage we learn of the treatment plan: it is nothing less than a new covenant. Instead of a law chipped out on tablets of stone, a more delicate keyhole procedure is proposed. The law will be skilfully inscribed on the heart of each of God's people. As a result they will all 'know' God, a word that indicates the intimate personal knowledge shared by two parties who are committed wholly to one another in relationship.

How is your heart bearing up this morning: robust or fragile; tender or sclerotic? Sometimes it can be difficult to remember that God has written his law of love on our own hearts, but just remembering that can help to soften it. In Book IV of Against Heresies, the early Church Father St Irenaeus advises, 'Offer to him your heart in a soft and tractable state ... lest you lose the impression of his fingers'.

*Reflection by* **Helen Orchard**

Jeremiah 31.31-34
Psalm 51.1-13 *or*
Psalm 119.9-16
**Hebrews 5.5-10**
John 12.20-33

**Fifth Sunday of Lent**

### Hebrews 5.5-10

*'... the source of eternal salvation for all who obey him' (v.9)*

Jesus is a dynamic figure in these verses: a moving target, the one who travels, who passes through the heavens (Hebrews 4.14), the one who transgresses boundaries, who is agile, mobile, indefinable by heaven or earth.

Jesus is not a remote figure, an extra-worldly bronze statue of a God; he is the one who tramples over previously accepted boundaries between life and death; he is responsive, compassionate, understanding of the frailty of the human condition because he himself offered prayer with loud cries and tears (5.7).

This description of Jesus the high priest is infused with an iconoclastic energy and refusal to be ossified by our human need for clarity or safety. This is God out of the box. Jesus Christ is a dangerous presence, an unfettered, rampaging and suffering divinity who recognizes no limitation except the limitation, willingly chosen, of being human. Even the son 'learned obedience' while on earth and, through this temporary confinement, returned to the eternal realm somehow more authentic than he had come.

All of our lives are lived as a response to this viscerally compassionate and wild God. We are called to learn this freedom, we who are made in the image of this disregarder of barriers or boundaries. It's vibrant imagery, that, if we let it touch us, will set us free.

*Reflection by* **Lucy Winkett**

## Fifth Sunday of Lent

Jeremiah 31.31-34
Psalm 51.1-13 *or*
Psalm 119.9-16
Hebrews 5.5-10
**John 12.20-33**

### John 12.20-33

*'I, when I am lifted up from the earth,
will draw all people to myself' (v.32)*

In today's passage, Jesus interprets his death and begins to reveal the cost of his kingship. He teaches that a grain dies in order to be fruitful, suggesting that his death will bring life to the world. This can seem as dark and impenetrable as the ground the seed is sown in. Jesus talks of how those who hate their life will keep it for eternal life. What does it mean to hate one's life? Is it to be able to deny one's own self for the sake of a greater good? Is it then a Christian truth that the human self is most itself when not being selfish? Certainly, teaches this Gospel, a Christian would be following their Lord if this truth were lived out: 'Whoever serves me must follow me'.

As Jesus talks in this passage, the Gospel becomes shadowed as Jesus' forthcoming death comes into focus. For whom will the sacrifice be made? When he preached in Pasadena in 2005, the Anglican archbishop Desmond Tutu gave the answer:

'When Jesus said, "I, when I am lifted up, will draw..." Did he say, "I will draw some"? "I will draw some, and tough luck for the others"? No. He said, "I, when I am lifted up, will draw all." All! All! All! – Black, white, yellow; rich, poor; clever, not so clever; beautiful, not so beautiful. All! All! It is radical. All! Saddam Hussein, Osama bin Laden, Bush – All! All! All are to be held in this incredible embrace. Gay, lesbian, so-called "straight". All! All! All are to be held in the incredible embrace of the love that won't let us go.'

*Reflection by* **Mark Oakley**

*Liturgy of the Palms:*
**Mark 11.1-11** *or*
John 12.12-16
Psalm 118.1-2, 19-24 [*or* 118.19-24]

**Palm Sunday**

### Mark 11.1-11

*'Blessed is the one who comes in the name of the Lord!' (v.9)*

In his Palm Sunday procession, Jesus is deliberately exerting the imperial claims of God's redeeming love. What happened that day was, as this passage shows, intended and planned down to the last detail. Publicly, boldly, knowing exactly what he is doing, whom he is challenging and what he is risking, Jesus here makes at last a public and open assertion of his right to reign as God's appointed king. He accepts the Hosannas of the multitudes, not because of their depth or their sincerity, but because they are his due and they are true.

He *does* indeed come in the name of the Lord, and he does indeed come to save God's people from the oppressive religious imperialism of the organized religion of the temple and the military imperialism of rampant Rome.

In the estimation of his enemies, he looks weak and vulnerable, but – make no mistake about it – his is a love so strong that it will not yield to anybody or anything, that will go to all lengths and all depths to have its way with humanity.

This king does not oppress; he liberates, his love takes him to the cross, but from that cross he reigns!

*Reflection by* **Tom Smail**

**Palm Sunday**

*Liturgy of the Palms:*
Mark 11.1-11 *or*
**John 12.12-16**
Psalm 118.1-2, 19-24 [*or* 118.19-24]

## John 12.12-16

*'His disciples did not understand these things at first' (v.16)*

Jerusalem, though hailed as the city of God, had a bad reputation for being part of a domination system that encouraged political oppression and economic exploitation that was too often legitimized with religious language. Many prophets had tried to challenge the city with the justice of God, but now, as Jesus rides into the city, so a new reign begins. God's anointed breaks through into the heart of corruption and is greeted with hope and praise.

What the crowd does not yet understand is the cost of this regime change where, in order to draw all people to himself (John 12.32), Christ is raised on a cross. Indeed, we are told that the disciples are a bit confused. They will soon learn more of the nature of Christ's vocation and the intensity of God's love for his people seen in his sacrifice. At the moment, they are happy to wave a branch with everyone else.

The community of Christian people known as the Church has been called a 'school for relating' in which, over time and through their prayer, each begins to learn how to relate more deeply to their self, to each other and to God. It requires patience and the ability to admit to the need for growth and some necessary un-learning. The Gospels are not afraid to tell us that the disciples were often baffled, squabbling and imperfect in their faith and faithfulness. It may be a new kingdom on earth that Christians work for, but this does not mean that they are not in need of constant revision themselves.

*Reflection by* **Mark Oakley**

**Liturgy of the Passion:**
**Isaiah 50.4-9a**
Psalm 31.9-16 [*or* 31.9-18]
Philippians 2.5-11
Mark 14.1 – end of 15 *or*
Mark 15.1-39[40-end]

## Palm Sunday

### Isaiah 50.4-9*a*

*'It is the Lord God who helps me' (v.9)*

Isaiah knew both the power of the tongue of a good teacher who chooses words to sustain weary listeners and his own calling to teach. With this knowledge he first took his place as a disciple and placed himself in the position of a listener woken every day by God. It was not just Isaiah who was wakened: specifically God wakened his ear so he could listen as one who is taught. That image suggests we can have sleepy ears that are unable to listen and prevent us from learning.

Because of his opened ear, Isaiah was not rebellious but could set his face like flint in the face of opposition. This deliberateness, even stubbornness, reflects Isaiah's experience that God's calling not only made him a disciple but also threw him on God's mercy and protection in the face of adversaries out to shame him. Even if he faced accusation in court, he could assert that God helped him, asking rhetorically 'who will declare me guilty?'

Yet, as Jesus knew, this does not result in instant deliverance, because God's ways are not like our ways. Hence the paradox that there can be insult and spitting as well as not being put to shame: one day accusation will simply wear out and, in the ultimate indignity, a tiny moth will eat up the accusers. To comprehend that requires open, non-rebellious listening to the God who wakes us each morning.

*Reflection by* **Rosalind Brown**

## Palm Sunday

*Liturgy of the Passion:*
Isaiah 50.4-9*a*
Psalm 31.9-16 [*or* 31.9-18]
**Philippians 2.5-11**
Mark 14.1 – end of 15 *or*
Mark 15.1-39[40-end]

### Philippians 2.5-11

*'Let the same mind be in you' (v.5)*

A full response to Jesus Christ involves the worship of our hearts, the enagagement of our minds and the obedience of our lives. In this glorious passage, all three cohere.

Most scholars think that here Paul is either quoting or adapting a hymn that would be familiar to his readers as part of the worship of the earliest Church. This is a theology that cannot but set us singing. It acclaims one who shared God's being but in love humbled himself to share ours, and who, for our sakes, shouldered the whole burden and consequence of our suffering and sin. As a result, he has been exalted to share God's name and God's worship so that the whole human future is in his hands.

To worship such a Christ must mean that the shape of his life should become the shape of ours. We are not to be like the first Adam who grabbed at an equality with God he could never attain, but like this second Adam who possessed this equality but used it not to exalt himself but to love us.

'Let the same mind be in you.'

*Reflection by* **Tom Smail**

**Liturgy of the Passion:**
Isaiah 50.4-9*a*
Psalm 31.9-16 [*or* 31.9-18]
Philippians 2.5-11
**Mark 14.1 – end of 15** *or*
Mark 15.1-39[40-end]

## Mark 14.1 – end of 15

*'... in remembrance of her' (14.9)*

In chapter 4 of Mark's Gospel, Jesus talked about those outside as looking but not perceiving and listening but not understanding (Mark 4.12). It set up a theme that rumbles away beneath Mark's telling of the story of Jesus all the way up to the crucifixion and resurrection. Mark presents both those who do see and perceive, listen and understand (the insiders) and those who don't (the outsiders).

As the Gospel unfolds, the surprising element to which Mark draws our attention time and again is that those whom we presume to be 'insiders' (especially the Jewish leaders and even the disciples) demonstrate themselves to be outsiders by their inability to perceive and understand who Jesus was and what he had come to do. By great contrast, those who might otherwise be defined as outsiders (the poor, the ill, the gentiles, the sick and dying, the women) reveal themselves to be insiders because of their ability to see and perceive, listen and understand.

This passage is framed by two such unlikely 'insiders': the woman of Mark 14.1-9, who profligately wasted an extremely valuable jar of pure nard, an expensive perfume, in anointing Jesus' feet and the centurion of 15.39 who recognized Jesus, hanging on a tree between two bandits, to be the Son of God.

Then, as now, the insiders in the kingdom are those who respond to Jesus wholeheartedly; then, as now, they are as likely to be those we view as outsiders.

*Reflection by* **Paula Gooder**

**Palm Sunday**

***Liturgy of the Passion:***
Isaiah 50.4-9*a*
Psalm 31.9-16 [*or* 31.9-18]
Philippians 2.5-11
Mark 14.1 – end of 15 *or*
**Mark 15.1-39[40-end]**

## Mark 15.1-39[40-end]

*'My God, my God, why have you forsaken me?' (v.34)*

Jesus' cry from the cross is one of the most desolate cries in the whole of the Bible. It resonates deeply within anyone who has experienced the kind of despair and desolation that Jesus is giving utterance to.

Jesus' phrase is, in fact, a quotation from the opening verses of Psalm 22, a psalm that also expresses a similar level of despair. Even the briefest of readings of this psalm, however, reveals that verse 1 is not the only part of the psalm alluded to in Mark's crucifixion narrative. Psalm 22 also refers to people mocking, 'making mouths' at me and shaking their heads (Psalm 22.7) and to my enemies dividing my clothes among them (Psalm 22.18). These are both to a greater or lesser extent features of Mark's crucifixion narrative (see especially Mark 15.20, 24, 29, 31).

This raises the question of whether Mark's crucifixion is making a subtle theological point. Psalm 22 strikingly ends very differently from how it began. The psalm's end talks about future generations serving and passing on the message of the Lord. In other words, the ending of the psalm looks to the future with hope. The despair of the opening verses has turned into confidence. It is possible that Mark's subtle telling of the crucifixion is introducing a glimmer of hope even at the darkest moment of Jesus' life; in doing so, he reminds us that in the midst of despair, with God there is hope.

*Reflection by* **Paula Gooder**

Exodus 12.1-4[5-10] 11-14
Psalm 116.1, 10-end [or 116.9-end]
1 Corinthians 11.23-26
John 13.1-17, 31b-35

**Maundy Thursday**

*Principal Holy Day*

## Exodus 12.1-4[5-10] 11-14

*'... eat it hurriedly. It is the passover of the Lord' (v.11)*

The people of Israel are on the threshold of departure. They desire escape from the land where they have known immense suffering. Surely this time, with the threat of death now hanging over his own people, Pharaoh must let them go? Yet as they muster, God gives to their leader an epoch-making, nation-founding ordinance. A meal is to be eaten, which will mark for future generations this moment of liberation.

When Jesus gathers in the upper room with his disciples on the eve of Passover, the sense of threat and need for haste is similar. Jesus also finds time to institute a meal, a way of celebrating a world-changing, new creation-founding moment signifying the liberation of all people from the power of death.

The people of Israel were about to cross a threshold into a liminal space. In the wilderness, the process of their transformation from a slave nation into a holy people would take many years. Their communal faith and sense of identity would be fiercely tested before the final crossing into the promised land.

Christians also live in liminal space – the space between the resurrection of Christ and his coming again. Called to live lightly, as a pilgrim people, in simplicity and purity, we too must live out our faith in testing circumstances. We too celebrate deliverance by eating a meal that looks forward to the final crossing into the full glory of God's kingdom.

*Reflection by* **Libby Lane**

**Maundy Thursday**

*Principal Holy Day*

Exodus 12.1-4[5-10] 11-14
Psalm 116.1, 10-end [*or* 116.9-end]
**1 Corinthians 11.23-26**
John 13.1-17, 31*b*-35

## 1 Corinthians 11.23-26

*'Do this in remembrance of me' (v.24)*

Jesus didn't write a book, and he didn't have children. He knew that the things by which people are usually remembered would not happen. Instead he asked his followers to remember him by eating and drinking. Not by saying a particular prayer or adopting a distinctive moral code, but by doing something so simple that everyone has done it since the day they were born. It doesn't require the ability to read or any great expense. It merely requires a living human body.

Bread and wine were the basic foods of Jesus' day, eaten by both rich and poor, so he used those. By saying that the bread symbolized his body and the wine symbolized his blood, Jesus made sure that it was his death, as well as his life, that stayed in people's minds as they worshipped him.

Originally, eating bread and wine in memory of Jesus formed part of a shared meal. Church leaders developed prayers to ensure it all happened in a dignified way. The prayers grew longer and the meal got shorter, until nowadays there is usually only a tiny portion of bread and wine, but a long service. However, at its heart is the same determination that Jesus will never be forgotten; the ritual gives us both a direct link back to him and a direct connection with every other Christian in the world.

*Reflection by* **Peter Graystone**

Exodus 12.1-4[5-10] 11-14
Psalm 116.1, 10-end [*or* 116.9-end]
1 Corinthians 11.23-26
**John 13.1-17, 31*b*-35**

### John 13.1-17, 31*b*-35

*'Lord, not my feet only but also my hands and my head!'*
*(v.9)*

John doesn't give an account of the institution of the Holy Communion as the other Gospel-writers do. Instead he describes how Jesus gave himself to his followers at the last meal he and his disciples had together before the crucifixion.

It was a natural expression of hospitality in their culture and climate for people to have their feet washed. When Jesus began to perform this servant's work for the disciples, Peter found it difficult. Surely it should have been the other way round, with Peter kneeling before Jesus to wash his feet? Peter's instinct was to refuse to let Jesus do it. But Jesus told him that if he wouldn't let him minister to him, Peter wouldn't really belong to him. Peter, with his endearing impetuosity, immediately went to the other extreme – 'Not just my feet, Lord, but my hands and my head too – I want to belong to you completely'. We can almost hear the laughter in Jesus' voice as he told Peter that he didn't have to go over the top: 'Just let me minister to you, you don't need to do anything more, you belong.'

There is a sombre subtext in this passage, though. Judas had his feet washed too. But there was no acceptance of the love that Jesus was offering. Judas submitted to the act but made no loving commitment in response.

The question we are left with is: how wholehearted is our response?

*Reflection by* **Ann Lewin**

## Good Friday

*Principal Holy Day*

Isaiah 52.13 – end of 53
Psalm 22 [*or* 22.1-11 *or* 1-21]
Hebrews 10.16-25 *or*
Hebrews 4.14-16; 5.7-9
John 18.1 – end of 19

### Isaiah 52.13 – end of 53

*'Surely he has borne our infirmities and carried our diseases'*
*(53.4)*

This is one of the most familiar passages in the Old Testament, not least because Handel used some of these verses so effectively in his Messiah. The picture of the suffering servant is bleak and powerful; it stops us in our tracks no matter how often we read it. What proves especially effective is the conflation of the people of Israel into the single despised figure that Christians are used to seeing scraped over a cross. It's interesting also to see how moving is the picture of the lamb being led to the slaughter. I have stood before Zurbarán's painting 'The Lamb of God' and been reduced to silence and tears.

There's no need to enter arguments about theories of the atonement and the morality or otherwise of a substitutionary understanding of such phrases as 'upon him was the punishment that made us whole' or 'the Lord has laid on him the iniquity of us all'. We're in the realm here of spiritual poetry, metaphors that carry a huge punch but mustn't be tested to destruction. More important is to stop and wonder. This, somehow, is all about love, a love that releases us from the dark tyrannies of moral failure and the fears that cripple our lives. A love, moreover, that embraces embittered societies and quarrelling nations.

This isn't a place for analysis but for prayer and silence.

*Reflection by* **John Pritchard**

Isaiah 52.13 – end of 53
Psalm 22 [*or* 22.1-11 *or* 1-21]
**Hebrews 10.16-25** *or*
[1] Hebrews 4.14-16; 5.7-9
John 18.1 – end of 19

### Good Friday

*Principal Holy Day*

### Hebrews 10.16-25

*'Therefore, my friends, since we have confidence ...' (v.19)*

How can we possibly have confidence? The word means 'to trust boldly'. Can we trust God in this way? The writer of the Hebrews is in no doubt. All we need to do is turn to God, and then realize that having turned, it will turn out fine if we are turned over to God. All we need to do is give back some of the love that has already been shown to us. Love is the lesson – the lesson that God teaches us, and asks us to practise with our fellow believers and the whole of humanity. We are to 'provoke' (!) one another to love and good deeds. As William Langland puts it in Piers Plowman (c. 1370):

*'Counseilleth me, Kynde', quod I, 'what craft be best to lerne?'*

*'Lerne to love,' quod Kynde, 'and leef alle othere.'*

So, the writer of Hebrews encourages us: we need not waver, but rather can hold fast to the one who holds fast to us. The God who has promised is faithful. There is nothing we can do that will make God love us any less or any more. God's love for us is full and complete, abundant and overwhelming. The mystics say that even God has one flaw – a frailty from which grace flows, which will teach us all we need to know about power made perfect in weakness. God's heart: it is too soft. And it is from God's open heart that we learn about God's open hands and embrace. So let us love one another, as God loves us.

*Reflection by* **Martyn Percy**

[1] *For a reflection on Hebrews 4.14-16; 5.7-9, see page 250.*

**Good Friday**

Isaiah 52.13 – end of 53
Psalm 22 [or 22.1-11 or 1-21]
Hebrews 10.16-25 or
Hebrews 4.14-16; 5.7-9
**John 18.1 – end of 19**

## John 18.1 – end of 19

*'What is truth?' (18.38)*

One of the most striking features of John's account of Jesus' trial is the lengthy exchange between Pilate and Jesus. In Matthew, Mark and Luke, Jesus' trial is much more cursory. In John's Gospel, however, the exchange is more lengthy and made so by Pilate's need to go in and out to the Jews.

This to-ing and fro-ing draws attention to the two lengthier exchanges that went on between Pilate and Jesus. In the first exchange (18.33-38) the discussion focused around the nature of truth and in the second (19.9-11) around power. In these two passages John demonstrated both his love of contrasts and his love of irony: Pilate – whose job it was to discern and adjudicate the truth of the claims about Jesus – was forced to ask what truth is, while later on Pilate – who was the fount of all Roman power – was revealed to have very little true power in the face of the hatred of the Jewish leaders for Jesus, the source of all power.

John's account of the crucifixion challenges us to think again about the truth and power we so easily take for granted in our world. It is easy to assume that what is presented to us as truth is indeed true, and that what looks like unassailable world power is deeply powerful. Here John asks us to think again and, in the light of Jesus the source of all truth and power, to find the courage to name reality as it really is.

*Reflection by* **Paula Gooder**

## Easter Vigil

*A minimum of three Old Testament readings should be chosen.*
*The reading from Exodus 14 should always be used.*

| | |
|---|---|
| ¹Genesis 1.1 – 2.4a | Psalm 136.1-9, 23-end |
| Genesis 7.1-5, 11-18; 8.6-18; 9.8-13 | Psalm 46 |
| ²Genesis 22.1-18 | Psalm 16 |
| **Exodus 14.10-end; 15.20, 21** | *Canticle:* **Exodus 15.1b-13, 17, 18** |
| ³Isaiah 55.1-11 | *Canticle:* Isaiah 12.2-end |
| Baruch 3.9-15, 32 – 4.4 | |
| or Proverbs 8.1-8, 19-21; 9.4b-6 | Psalm 19 |
| ⁴Ezekiel 36.24-28 | Psalms 42, 43 |
| ⁵Ezekiel 37.1-14 | Psalm 143 |
| ⁶Zephaniah 3.14-end | Psalm 98 |

| | |
|---|---|
| **Romans 6.3-11** | **Psalm 114** |
| **Mark 16.1-8** | |

¹ *For a reflection on Genesis 1.1 – 2.4a, see page 60.*
² *For a reflection on Genesis 22.1-18, see page 149.*
³ *For a reflection on Isaiah 55.1-11, see page 153.*
⁴ *For a reflection on Ezekiel 36.24-28, see page 161.*
⁵ *For a reflection on Ezekiel 37.1-14, see page 166.*
⁶ *For a reflection on Zephaniah 3.14-end, see page 142.*

**Easter Vigil**

*See page 127 for a list of
the Easter Vigil readings*

### Genesis 7.1-5, 11-18; 8.6-18; 9.8-13

*'I am establishing my covenant with you and
your descendants' (9.9)*

The current and potential chaos of climate change, including
rising sea-levels, soil erosion and atmospheric pollution, gives
the story of Noah and the Great Flood a modern resonance.

In the midst of the uncertainty of our present environmental
dilemmas I am struck by the orderliness of this unfolding
narrative. The pattern reveals a reversal of God's original act
of Creation, a disordering of God's imposition of order on
primordial chaos. The division between land and sea is
dissolved as the waters from the ocean's depths meet the
deluge from the sky. The later ordered retreat of the waters
is another reversal, as creation is restored, and the surviving
remnant go out to 'be fruitful and multiply' again.

The drama in this account is entirely controlled by God. Noah's
role, as the one righteous man in a world turned to
wickedness, is to be hopefully obedient. The ark contains the
whole diversity of creation, everything that has breath: this
floating remnant a faint echo of the breath of God hovering
over the waters in Genesis 1. Noah's obedience is the channel
for a new work of God's spirit.

Underneath this orderly proceeding has been untold
destruction and suffering. As we recognize such suffering still,
we rejoice at God's promise, fulfilled in Christ, that whatever
the continuing evil of the human heart, another way will be
found to redeem the world.

*Reflection by* **Libby Lane**

See page 127 for a list of
the Easter Vigil readings

**Easter Vigil**

### Exodus 14.10-end; 15.20, 21

*'... stand firm, and see the deliverance that the Lord
will accomplish' (v.13)*

Is it really the darkest hour just before the dawn? Well, there's no scientific justification for this claim. But in our own inner experiences, it can certainly feel that the light's arrival shows up the darkness in starkest contrast. More than that, it may seem God's redeeming light bursts in when we are at our lowest ebb, doubting whether we can hold on any longer.

At such a point, when the Hebrew slaves' escape has left them trapped between the sea water and the advancing Egyptians, Moses has the courage to say, 'Do not be afraid' and promise the Lord's deliverance, provided they 'keep still'. Just hang on in there, he seems to say, even if it is by no means clear, even to Moses, what form divine deliverance may take. Perhaps he too is on the point of wavering, given the edge of rebuke in the Lord's words, 'Why do you cry out to me?'.

All he has to do is hold fast, and be conscientious in his trusting. All the people must do is continue their path. God asks such little things – 'Stretch out your hand' or 'go forward' – and then God acts.

As the dark of Holy Saturday is shattered by Easter's light, how are we called to stand firm, or continue forward, conscientious in faith's little things, so that God's great redeeming love may find and change us?

*Reflection by* **Sarah Rowland Jones**

129

## Easter Vigil

*See page 127 for a list of
the Easter Vigil readings*

### Exodus 15.1*b*-13, 17, 18

*'I will sing to the Lord, for he has triumphed gloriously' (v.1)*

Moses leads the people in a jubilant song of celebration. They have escaped from the Pharaoh's army by the skin of their teeth, scrambling across sand briefly uncovered as the strong wind parted the waves of the sea. They have seen the wind drop, the water return and the army swamped. After centuries of slavery, they are free.

*And they sing.*

This night, as we keep the Easter Vigil, we sing that song of thankfulness and joy with all God's rescued people. As the light of resurrection grows brighter, flooding churches and hearts, our voices grow louder and fuller and, with Moses, we sing to the Lord who has triumphed gloriously.

For the resurrection of Christ is rescue and escape; it is triumph and it is victory. Despair and anger, fear and selfishness are destroyed. Death is defeated. Bonds are broken. Life is restored. Hope, love, forgiveness released for all.

*And we sing.*

We sing not just for ourselves, but for the world. Moses rejoiced as he saw his enemies destroyed. We rejoice because we know that Christ's resurrection is the promise of life and restoration for all.

So tonight we sing a song of thanks to God for his gift of life and freedom, and we sing a song of hope for those who live still in the humiliation and frustration of slavery, in all its forms.

*And, tonight, as the world hears our song, it too will sing.*

*Reflection by* **John Kiddle**

*See page 127 for a list of
the Easter Vigil readings*

**Easter Vigil**

## Isaiah 12.2-end

*'With joy you will draw water from the wells of salvation'*
*(v.3)*

Through the early chapters of the Book of Isaiah, we become ever more aware of a sharp tension between the bleak prospect of judgement and the glorious hope of salvation. So, we are left wondering what will be the final word on God's rebellious people.

Some resolution of this tension is offered in chapter 12, a beautiful hymn concluding the book's first section. Verse 12.1 is reminiscent of Hosea's breathtaking vision of an agonizing conflict between wrath and compassion within God, a conflict ultimately 'won' by compassion, for it is compassion, not wrath, that is finally definitive of God: 'My heart recoils within me; my compassion grows warm and tender.' (Hosea 11.8-9). So also for Isaiah, although a rebellious world inevitably experiences God's judgement, this is not the deepest truth about God. Fundamentally, God is salvation. The wells of this salvation are inexhaustible, and the joy drawn from them must be shared 'among the nations', 'in all the earth'.

Christians may well discern a trail from such prophetic texts to the revelation in Christ both of the cost to God of loving a wayward world and also of the salvation given by God in Christ. For to be 'in Christ' is to know that God 'is' salvation; salvation is not a blessing distinct from God's self but participation in the life of God, poured out for the world.

*Reflection by* **David Marshall**

See page 127 for a list of
the Easter Vigil readings

## Proverbs 8.1-8, 19-21; 9.4*b*-6

*'Does not wisdom call?' (8.1)*

Wisdom is personified in this reading, calling out to us, grabbing our attention. There is no escaping her message. And what does she cry? Learn prudence, acquire intelligence and learn from my teaching and example. Wisdom is expressed in action as well as insight.

Although much is unclear about this personification of wisdom, what is clear is that her fruit is to be prized more than gold and silver. Wisdom's gifts have to be received and appropriated and lived in our lives as we abandon immaturity for the insight that comes from walking in wisdom's ways. So what sounds at first hearing like a eulogy in favour of wisdom is actually a challenging call to follow her example and live accordingly. No wonder she, in anthropomorphic terms, raises her voice to make sure we hear: she demands a response.

As we recall salvation history at the Easter Vigil, this reminds us of all that God has done for the human race he created and redeemed when we went astray. Surely our response of gratitude and love to God must be to walk in the ways of God's wisdom, righteousness and justice. And that begins when, as we recall from Maundy Thursday's gospel and our repeated action at the Eucharist, we come to eat of God's bread and drink of God's wine, which Jesus shared with his friends on the night before he died. That is the way to life.

*Reflection by* **Rosalind Brown**

*See page 127 for a list of
the Easter Vigil readings*

**Easter Vigil**

### Romans 6.3-11

*'... we too might walk in newness of life' (v.4)*

The relationship of life to death is not clear-cut. Establishing the moment of death is not straightforward. There are medical criteria for making such a decision – the permanent cessation of cell functions, brain activity, breathing – their application in particular instances can be complex.

The same is true when it comes to the question of 'sin' and 'death' in the life of a Christian. Martin Luther expressed the paradox of being 'at the same time justified and a sinner'. Paul goes on to say, 'I do not do the good I want, but the evil I do not want is what I do' (Romans 7.19). We know that deep-seated confusion – that we, who are 'dead to sin', continue to live lives that somehow always fall short of God's expectations.

The deeper narrative in this passage is that, by faith, we are bound up tightly by God in what was already done when Christ was raised from the dead. A future full resurrection life is promised to the faithful, and our daily lives in the here and now are lived in the light that such a promise shines upon us. 'We too might walk in newness of life' as that promise brings new possibility, bringing to our attention what needs to change and enabling us to live into that future.

*Reflection by* **Libby Lane**

**Easter Vigil**

*See page 127 for a list of
the Easter Vigil readings*

### Mark 16.1-8

*'... terror and amazement' (v.8)*

They missed it! The women who came to the tomb early on Sunday morning missed the resurrection. As far as we know, there were no witnesses to Jesus' resurrection – not human ones anyway. By the time the women arrived with spices, by the time the stone was rolled away, by the time the white-robed man took his place, it had already happened. Without an announcement of any kind, Jesus got on with what God alone can do, and for which he needed no help. In the dark of the night, he had quietly risen from the dead.

Crucifixion is public. It is loud, explicit and nauseating. But resurrection is not like that. It happens out of sight and unannounced. This is true of our lives. When the weight of life is brutal on our shoulders, those are the conditions that most resemble the first Easter. But personal resurrection may already have begun – life returning inside the shroud, inside the tomb.

Terror and amazement. Is that really a resurrection experience? Yes, actually! One day in eternity the resurrection will be complete. There will be alleluias, trumpets and triumph. But that isn't how the resurrection began. It began with three scared women who had nothing to say.

Today, as the choirs begin exulting and the worship bands burst into song, some people will find themselves wishing they could share their Church's jubilant certainty. There is a wonderful, godly precedent.

*Reflection by* **Peter Graystone**

¹**Acts 10.34-43** *or* Isaiah 25.6-9
Psalm 118.1-2, 14-24 [*or* 118.14-24]
1 Corinthians 15.1-11 *or* ¹Acts 10.34-43
John 20.1-18 *or* Mark 16.1-8

**Easter Day**

## Acts 10.34-43

### *'Then Peter began to speak to them' (v.34)*

The audience Peter is speaking to is a gathering of the family and friends of a Roman centurion, Cornelius, who is stationed in the town of Caesarea. The previous verses have been full of the detailed preparations for this visit, which has been spiritually inspired on both sides, given that it is unlawful for Peter to visit a gentile at home. We know that Peter is a powerful speaker; all that we see of him in the Gospels is that he is passionate, sometimes impetuous, but always totally committed. Earlier in Acts we heard that the crowd were 'cut to the heart' by how Peter spoke (Acts 2.37), and here his words seem just as influential.

Cornelius' household begin to accept the truth of his testimony and want to change their lives in response. Peter in turn declares that they should be baptized: included, admitted, welcomed right then and there. It's dramatic stuff, and begins a series of helter-skelter events in the streets, synagogues and houses of the towns visited by these first apostles. The way Peter tells the story of Jesus' life, death and resurrection and the effect it has had on him personally is something people can't resist; it becomes an irresistible invitation to live differently. Crowds of people from every layer of society want to hope again, want to start a new life. Now. At once.

The infectious energy of this meeting leaps off the page, and maybe convinces us that it's never too late to make new choices, take a different path. An inspiring reminder on Easter Day that it's never too late to be surprised by God.

*Reflection by* **Lucy Winkett**

¹*The reading from Acts must be used as either the first or the second reading.*

**Easter Day**

[1]Acts 10.34-43 *or* **Isaiah 25.6-9**
Psalm 118.1-2, 14-24 [*or* 118.14-24]
1 Corinthians 15.1-11 *or* [1]Acts 10.34-43
John 20.1-18 *or* Mark 16.1-8

### Isaiah 25.6-9

*'This is the Lord for whom we have waited' (v.9)*

Isaiah's vision of a day when God, in universal blessing (note the 'all'), will wipe away tears from all faces and take away his people's disgrace, presupposes situations when tears and humiliation are the only appropriate response.

The context of this generous promise was exile in Babylon, whose army razed Jerusalem to the ground in horrific acts of violence early in the sixth century BC. With these memories hanging heavily, amazingly God will wipe away all tears from people's faces. Imagine people weeping over their destroyed homes in cities like Aleppo, being bombarded as I write, being comforted by God himself, tenderly mopping away tears as a mother with her sobbing child. Against that background of suffering, God's promises sound at best far-fetched, if not simply unbelievable.

This devastation had put an end to wine-drinking (Isaiah 24.9), but now God provides well-matured wines strained clear for people used to diluting rough wine with water to make it drinkable. Now God's wine cellar has nothing but the best, mature, clear wines. If this vision was and still is hard to believe, we can recall the resurrection when God destroyed the power of death, enabling saints through the ages to live with hope beyond all reasonable hope. That leads to the joyous affirmation: 'This is the Lord for whom we have waited; let us be glad and rejoice in his salvation.' We may have to wait, but we wait in hope.

*Reflection by* **Rosalind Brown**

[1]*The reading from Acts must be used as either the first or the second reading.*

¹Acts 10.34-43 *or* Isaiah 25.6-9
Psalm 118.1-2, 14-24 [*or* 118.14-24]
**1 Corinthians 15.1-11** *or* ¹Acts 10.34-43
John 20.1-18 *or* Mark 16.1-8

**Easter Day**

## 1 Corinthians 15.1-11

*'... he appeared' (vv.5, 6, 8)*

Through the Easter season, Christians will explore the resurrection stories, one by one, rejoicing as each proclaims that Christ is risen. But, as if we cannot wait to unpack them one by one, these opening verses of 1 Corinthians 15 are given to us on the first day of Easter, with Paul pouring out a whole list of resurrection appearances – interestingly, most of them different from the ones the Gospels recount.

Equally interesting is that Paul apparently has no interest in empty-tomb stories. For him, what matters are resurrection appearances, people encountering the Risen Lord. His list of these encounters reaches a kind of climax with his 'Last of all, as to someone untimely born, he appeared also to me'. That appearance, the gracious confrontation on the Damascus Road that we call Paul's conversion, was long after the ascension and the giving of the Spirit at Pentecost, yet Paul experiences it as a resurrection appearance.

That encourages us to see our own moments of encounter with Jesus Christ as appearances of the Risen Lord. And, though we will value the story of the empty tomb and the appearances long ago to Mary Magdalene, Thomas and the others, we shall know that the evidence of the resurrection is that we too have met the Risen Lord. He is risen indeed. Alleluia!

*Reflection by* **Michael Perham**

¹*For a reflection on Acts 10.34-43, see page 135. The reading from Acts must be used as either the first or the second reading.*

**Easter Day**

Acts 10.34-43 *or* Isaiah 25.6-9
Psalm 118.1-2, 14-24 [*or* 118.14-24]
1 Corinthians 15.1-11 *or* Acts 10.34-43
**John 20.1-18** *or* ¹Mark 16.1-8

## John 20.1-18

### *'Do not hold on to me' (v.17)*

That women are among the first witnesses of Jesus' resurrection overturns assumptions about status – for women were not permitted to be witnesses in Jewish courts. Yet here, it is Mary Magdalene who sees the empty tomb first and who alone perceives the divine messengers. It is Mary who meets the risen Christ first and talks to him. And her name is the first one that he speaks, this Good Shepherd who calls by name his own sheep, who know his voice (John 10.3-4, 14).

Is this because Mary's loss and her longing are so acute – and so personal ('They have taken away my Lord, and I do not know where they have laid him')? Yet verse 17 warns us against drowning in devotion, however strong our emotions. 'Do not continue to cling to me', Jesus insists. Whatever the rest of this puzzling sentence means (and one scholar suggests it should simply read: 'it is true that I have not yet ascended to the Father but I am about to do so'), the next command is clear. Mary is to release her hold on the Lord who has so recently returned, to go and share his words with the other disciples.

As so often, to quote the poet C. Day Lewis, 'love is proved in the letting go'.

*Reflection by* **Jeff Astley**

¹*For a reflection on Mark 16.1-8, see page 134.*

¹Exodus 14.10-end;15.20, 21
**²Acts 4.32-35**
Psalm 133
1 John 1.1 – 2.2
John 20.19-end

**Second Sunday of Easter**

### Acts 4.32-35

*'... everything they owned was held in common' (v.32)*

The members of the early Church lived as one big family, sharing all they had. They took seriously the promise found in the book of Deuteronomy that there should be no poor among God's people – and they lived out that promise by asking everyone to give everything that they had to the common cause. In that way, the richer members subsidized the poorer members and no one was in any kind of need.

If only we lived with that same vision of generosity and common purpose today, there would be far less of a gap between rich and poor, between the obese and the starving, between those in security-protected, lavish homes and those who live on the streets.

In the Anglican Communion, wealthy dioceses often support poorer ones; likewise, richer parishes often subsidize poorer ones so that everyone has a parish priest, regardless of whether or not they can afford one. Thankfully, many take that charge seriously, but, sadly, many don't, and cling on to their 'reserves'. Somewhere along the line, we've lost the will to share what we have, unless that sharing doesn't cost us very much at all.

If we read on to verse 36, we meet Barnabas, who sells his field and gives the proceeds to the apostles. He models the kind of self-giving, abundant generosity that God shows towards us. Why do we find it so difficult to do the same?

*Reflection by* **Jan McFarlane**

¹ *For a reflection on Exodus 14.10-end;15.20, 21, see page 129.*
² *The reading from Acts must be used as either the first or the second reading.*

**Second Sunday of Easter**

Exodus 14.10-end;15.20, 21
[1]Acts 4.32-35
Psalm 133
**1 John 1.1 – 2.2**
John 20.19-end

### 1 John 1.1 – 2.2

*'... what we have heard, what we have seen with our eyes, what we have looked at and touched with our hands' (1.1)*

'Our eyes saw, our ears heard, our hands handled!' John unveils a mystery, not with philosophical abstraction or theological gobbledegook, but with these familiar human senses; with the world of touch, taste and sight, the daylight world of real people with real needs. Here is a theology of the Word, but always the Word made flesh. He guards against the disaster that later befell the Church – what Edwin Muir, the Orkney poet and mystic, in his poem 'The Incarnate One', called our 'abstract calamity', our attempts to disincarnate the Word, to retreat from the flesh and turn religion into an abstract language game. As Muir lamented: 'The word made flesh here is made word again.'

Not so with John: 'we declare to you what we have seen and heard'. Why? So that you can write a PhD about it? No, so that you may have fellowship with us and with God. Here is a truth that sets us free, free for relationship, free for love. And, even in this opening chapter, we see the themes of light, life and love all meeting, in the flesh – and all to one end, to make joy complete, to invite us, in the phrase of a deeply Johannine hymn, to revel in 'solid joys and lasting treasures' ('Glorious things of thee are spoken').

*Reflection by* **Malcolm Guite**

[1]*The reading from Acts must be used as either the first or the second reading.*

Exodus 14.10-end;15.20, 21
Acts 4.32-35
Psalm 133
1 John 1.1 – 2.2
**John 20.19-end**

### Second Sunday of Easter

### John 20.19-end

*'These are written so that you may come to believe ...' (v.31)*

We live in a sceptical age. Seeing is believing. The story of Thomas reaching out to touch Jesus appeals to us because we understand why he asked for proof.

But the experience of millions of Christians is that believing leads to seeing. When you live from day to day assuming that there is a good and loving God, changes take place. You are acutely aware of a purpose in life. You become a better person because you start living for the benefit of others. Things make sense that previously didn't.

Jesus made it clear to Thomas that proof is a privilege, not a right.

Suppose we could go back 2, 000 years and tell Thomas about a smartphone. He would be staggered. 'I won't believe that unless I can stretch out my hand and touch it,' he would say. So you would hold it out and he would put his finger on the screen. And there would be Google, YouTube and Wikipedia – he could look himself up!

Ridiculous, of course! But because this story has been preserved, Thomas can come forward 2, 000 years to us with this message: 'There is a Saviour. He is risen and he is alive. If that belief forms the basis of your life, you will discover a fuller, more secure, more meaningful way of being. And that will turn out to be more compelling than proof. Reach out your hand. I did.'

*Reflection by* **Peter Graystone**

**Third Sunday of Easter**

**Zephaniah 3.14-end**
[1]Acts 3.12-19
Psalm 4
1 John 3.1-7
Luke 24.36b-48

## Zephaniah 3.14-end

*'I will bring you home' (v.20)*

The book of Zephaniah ends with a paean of praise to the nation and city which, in the foregoing text, have been the butt of much righteous indignation.

A glorious future is now anticipated, as the Lord takes up residence again 'in your midst', protecting people from their enemies and taking away their reproach and shame to the extent that Jerusalem can now be acknowledged as the daughter of God.

While the actual text may be unfamiliar, the themes, phrases and even cadences of the language will strike a chord to many readers: 'he has turned away your enemies ... the Lord is in your midst' – 'he will renew you in his love – 'I will save the lame and gather the outcast'.

Especially resonant, perhaps, is the phrase in verse 20, thought by many commentators to be a later addition, which conveys a promise to those who have by now been exiled to the far country of Babylon: 'I will bring you home.'

For Christian readers at Eastertide, home is – as the cliché puts it – 'where the heart is', and thus wherever our risen Lord is. Following Jesus brings us home.

*Reflection by* **Jeff Astley**

[1]*The reading from Acts must be used as either the first or the second reading.*

Zephaniah 3.14-end
[1]**Acts 3.12-19**
Psalm 4
1 John 3.1-7
Luke 24.36b-48

## Third Sunday of Easter

### Acts 3.12-19

*'... you killed the Author of life, whom God raised from the dead. To this we are witnesses' (v.15)*

'We are witnesses,' says Peter. These three words sum up the whole of this book of the Bible. The Acts of the Apostles are the acts of those who witness to the death and resurrection of Christ and the continuing work of his Spirit in the life of the Church. Remember how in Chapter 1 of Acts the Eleven choose a replacement for Judas on the basis of that person being a witness with them to all that had happened from Jesus' baptism by John up to the present time (Acts 1.22). Through these witnesses, God's purposes will be made known and faith in Jesus Christ will spread from Jerusalem to Rome.

The Acts of the Apostles tells the astonishing story of how this happens: the Christian faith changing from a small Jewish sect to a global faith – and all in a few years and by the witness of an unlikely group of people. But the Holy Spirit is bearing witness through them.

Hence, the man who has been healed clings to Peter and John, amazed and confused by what has happened to him. The people are also astonished. And Peter bears witness. He says it is Jesus, the one they rejected and crucified, who has done this thing. It is by faith in his name that the man has received health. This Jesus is alive and working through his Church

*Reflection by* **Stephen Cottrell**

[1] *The reading from Acts must be used as either the first or the second reading.*

## Third Sunday of Easter

Zephaniah 3.14-end
[1]Acts 3.12-19
Psalm 4
**1 John 3.1-7**
Luke 24.36b-48

### 1 John 3.1-7

*'... what we will be has not yet been revealed' (v.2)*

Christian hope is not for this world only. It is for a state far beyond this world. It is not for some sort of disembodied immortality, but for an existence as the same persons we now are, embodied and in social relationships with others. Yet Paul says, in 1 Corinthians 15, that in such a life our bodies will be imperishable, glorious, powerful and spiritual, not physical, and as different from our present bodies as full-grown wheat is from the seed.

We shall be sharers in the divine nature, abiding in Christ, transfigured by the Spirit into an existence like his. Paul saw the risen Christ, and what he saw was a blinding light. When Jesus rose from death, his physical body was able to appear to his disciples for short periods, sometimes 'in another form' (Mark 16.12), but his true spiritual body is, as Paul says, far beyond all physical forms.

What is it like? We do not know. We only know that Jesus shares the divine nature, and that he lives in us. Because he lives in us, we are able to grow into his true likeness, and we shall be like him when we 'see him as he is'. Only then shall we live as truly fulfilled persons in God.

*Reflection by* **Keith Ward**

[1]*The reading from Acts must be used as either the first or the second reading.*

Zephaniah 3.14-end
Acts 3.12-19
Psalm 4
1 John 3.1-7
**Luke 24.36b-48**

## Third Sunday of Easter

### Luke 24.36b-48

*'Touch me ...' (v.39)*

Whatever he was, the risen Jesus was not a ghost. Luke describes Jesus eating 'broiled fish'. (My concordance said 'roast or grilled fish', which sounds so much more appetizing!) And Luke and John (1 John 1.1) use the same word for touch – *psēlaphaō* – which my concordance also translates as 'handle' or even 'grope'! There is something embarrassingly tangible about the resurrection. Why?

Because this is resurrection, not the liberation of the spirit from the body. Part of what the resurrection seems to suggest is that the conquering of death by God in Christ includes the redemption of the material order. This is not the same as its preservation. The risen Jesus has a very odd 'body' by our normal standards, but he has a body. Conquering death does not mean leaving embodied reality behind, rather the triumph over death is total. All is raised, albeit transformed.

I think this is good news. It is good news because much of the time, this world is beautiful. I do not want its beauty to perish. I do not want to lose 'me', and how can I conceive of 'me' except in a personal form? I do not want to lose those 'I have loved and lost a little while'. I want to meet them as persons.

None of this is, however, surprising. What else would we expect from a God whose love for us counts even the hairs on our head, as Luke so vividly taught us?

*Reflection by* **Alan Bartlett**

**Fourth Sunday of Easter**

[1]Genesis 7.1-5, 11-18; 8.6-18;
9.8-13
[2]**Acts 4.5-12**
Psalm 23
1 John 3.16-end
John 10.11-18

## Acts 4.5-12

*'By what power or by what name did you do this?' (v.7)*

What's in a name? Doesn't a rose by any other name still smell sweet? But the name of Jesus is different. His name carries power and authority. It opens doors. It is by faith in the name of Jesus that the crippled beggar at the beautiful gate is healed. And when the Jewish rulers ask Peter what authority he has to heal this man and in whose name he has done it – for the name corresponds directly to the authority to do it – he replies that is in the 'name of Jesus Christ of Nazareth' that this man stands before them in good health. Indeed, he goes on: 'there is no other name under heaven ... by which we must be saved'.

And so the Christian faith is not about 'what you know' but 'who you know'. To know and be known by Jesus is free entry to the banquet of heaven. In fact, the name Jesus means 'God rescues'. God has come in Jesus to gather us into his kingdom. This ministry of gathering and welcoming, of healing and saving, is continued by the Church. No ticket is required, the queue can be jumped, the lunch is free and the drinks are on the house. All you need do is mention his name.

*Reflection by* **Stephen Cottrell**

[1] *For a reflection on Genesis 7.1-5, 11-18; 8.6-18; 9.8-13, see page 128.*
[2] *The reading from Acts must be used as either the first or the second reading.*

Genesis 7.1-5, 11-18;8.6-18;
9.8-13
[1]Acts 4.5-12
Psalm 23
**1 John 3.16-end**
John 10.11-18

## Fourth Sunday of Easter

### 1 John 3.16-end

*'... let us love, not in word or speech, but in truth
and action' (v.18)*

The writer of 1 John has no time for believers who are all talk
and no action. His view is clear: if you refuse to help a brother
or sister in need, then God's love cannot be within you. The
Greek expresses this more colourfully, speaking of the one
who closes his heart (here, *splanchna*) to his brother. The
*splanchna* symbolizes the source of compassion and mercy
towards others: the seat of emotion. It helps explain why
God's love cannot abide within such a person: a heart that is
closed to a brother is a heart closed to Christ.

The initiative for any act we seek to do finds its source in the
action of God. It is in the tender (*splanchna*) mercy of our God
that the dawn from on high will break upon us (Luke 1.78),
and we only know love at all through the act of Christ laying
down his life for us. Self-giving is the purest form of 'love in
truth and action' and is the pattern set before us. Some of us
can give in practical ways, but even the most powerless person
in the most limited circumstances can help a brother or sister
by choosing to open rather than close their heart. Indeed,
bringing someone who is in your heart in prayer to the one
whose heart poured out its lifeblood on the cross may be the
most significant help that can be given.

*Reflection by* **Helen Orchard**

[1]*The reading from Acts must be used as either the first or the second reading.*

**Fourth Sunday of Easter**

Genesis 7.1-5, 11-18;
8.6-18; 9.8-13
Acts 4.5-12
Psalm 23
1 John 3.16-end
**John 10.11-18**

### John 10.11-18

*'I am the good shepherd' (v.11)*

What makes Jesus the 'good' shepherd? This passage makes the answer clear. He cares for his sheep in a way that a hired helper wouldn't understand. He knows, loves and protects his sheep and even lays down his life for them. Every Christian can pray the opening words of Psalm 23 with confidence: 'The Lord is my shepherd, I shall not want.'

Jesus also says here that his sheep know him. One of the things that people recognize as belonging to a shepherd is the shepherd's crook. Bishops carry one too as a sign of their pastoral vocation. Because of the curved end of the crook, it's usual to think that they are primarily used for reaching out and grabbing sheep around the neck, hauling them back in when being too independent or naughty. A Shropshire farmer once corrected this image for me. He said the crook was really for sticking deeply into the ground so that he could hold himself so still that the sheep eventually began to trust him.

This has many implications for bishops, and for all of us, as to what it is that establishes within us what is trustworthy and true. The rooted stillness of prayer and attention is where our compassion and responsibilities must all start. It is the same rootedness in the love of his Father that draws us to Christ. His voice, with its words of life, is a part of that divine magnetism of mystery that brings peace to the human soul.

*Reflection by* **Mark Oakley**

**Genesis 22.1-18**
[1]Acts 8.26-end
Psalm 22.25-end
I John 4.7-end
John 15.1-8

**Fifth Sunday of Easter**

### Genesis 22.1-18

*'On the mount of the Lord it shall be provided' (v.14)*

It is a dreadful story, Abraham setting out to sacrifice his beloved son. Inevitably, we ask whether this really was God testing Abraham. Was Abraham simply misunderstanding a God who would never make such an awful demand? The Christian tradition might have left it among the other obscure stories that are hidden in the Scriptures but not given much exposure.

Instead, the story is given prominence: it is read on Good Friday, the morning when Jesus hangs upon the cross, himself a sacrifice, an offering for the sin of the world. The Lectionary sets it for the Easter Vigil and again for today. This story could once again look like the work of an unacceptable God, demanding something dreadful of a beloved son. As such, we might want to turn away from it and, at the same time, be thankful that our understanding of God has moved on. The God in whom we believe doesn't need to punish the innocent in order to appease his anger.

But, as we gaze at the cross, we are looking not at one punished by a wrathful God, but at God himself. God did not require some other to demonstrate his love and compassion. In the mystery of the Trinity, this is God incarnate shouldering all this himself. The God of love ascends the cross and from it looks out in compassion on the world that he alone redeems.

*Reflection by* **Michael Perham**

[1]*The reading from Acts must be used as either the first or the second reading.*

## Fifth Sunday of Easter

Genesis 22.1-18
¹**Acts 8.26-end**
Psalm 22.25-end
1 John 4.7-end
John 15.1-8

### Acts 8.26-end

*'... the eunuch saw him no more, and went on his way rejoicing' (v.39)*

We begin with angels, always a good place to start, and end our reading with a disappearance – all very curious.

Philip was a 'seer': one who glimpsed angels, one who felt impelled to move on. Not for him the power of Jerusalem, but instead the restlessness of the long-distance traveller. He set out on the desert road and there, by chance, met an international diplomat, representing the royal court of Ethiopia. He was reading a passage from Isaiah, chapter 53, about the suffering servant, and was deeply puzzled about its meaning. Philip, invited to join him, explained that the passage referred to Jesus of Nazareth, and such were Philip's advocacy and teaching skills that the courtier asked to be baptized immediately.

And there, this gem of a story stops. Philip, like Elijah, disappears, and the Ethiopian has to make his own way home. We do not know what might have happened next. Did the diplomat take the Christian message back to Ethiopia? And what of Philip? Whom did he tell about his encounter? And what was the impact of the telling?

For many of us, it is also true that an apparently casual conversation with a stranger can cause our lives to change. Looking back on such events, what seemed casual takes on the appearance of an epiphany: a moment when the angel of God reveals to us the Most High ...

*Reflection by* **Christopher Herbert**

¹*The reading from Acts must be used as either the first or the second reading.*

Genesis 22.1-18
[1]Acts 8.26-end
Psalm 22.25-end
**1 John 4.7-end**
John 15.1-8

## Fifth Sunday of Easter

### 1 John 4.7-end

*'God is love, and those who abide in love abide in God,*
*and God abides in them' (v.16)*

If we had only this passage, we would have the heart of Christian faith. 'God is love' is a perception of God that is evoked by the life, death and resurrection of Jesus. It is not just that God is loving. 'God is love' means that the ultimate reality of God defines what love is, and unveils the inner character of being.

Divine love is not centred on itself, on contemplation of God's own divine beauty and perfection. It creates and enters a world of other persons, taking the risk of separation and rejection, so that others may have life. Love gives itself, so that we might share in it and be raised up to participate in the community of giving and receiving that God is creating, and that will live in God for ever.

John says that God 'sent his only Son into the world'. But it is of course God who enters the world of sin and self-centredness, who suffers pain and death in human form so that we might be freed from sin, and who unites us to eternal love in and through Christ. Divine love empties itself so that we might be filled with the undying life of God. Our calling is to live in that love, and to let it live in us.

*Reflection by* **Keith Ward**

[1]*The reading from Acts must be used as either the first or the second reading.*

**Fifth Sunday of Easter**

Genesis 22.1-18
Acts 8.26-end
Psalm 22.25-end
1 John 4.7-end
**John 15.1-8**

### John 15.1-8

*'Abide in me as I abide in you' (v.4)*

The Gospel of John seems to suggest that one of the key words or ideas to help us understand the ministry of Jesus and the subsequent blueprint for the Church is that of 'abiding'*. The word is linked to another English word, 'abode'. God abides with us. Christ bids us to abide in him, and he will abide in us. He bids us to make our home with him, as he has made his home with us. Christ tells us that there are many rooms in his father's house. There are many places of gathering and meeting there. And central to the notion of an abode is the concept of abiding.

To abide is to 'wait patiently with'. God has abided with us. He came to us in ordinary life, and he has sat with us, eaten with us, walked with us, and lived among us. That is why John ends his Gospel with Jesus doing ordinary things. Breaking bread, or eating breakfast on the seashore. God continues to dwell with us. He was with us at the beginning, and he is with us at the end. He will not leave us.

And he wants his Church to abide with the world – and especially to be with all those who have no one to be with them. The friendless, the forlorn, the forgotten – God wills us to abide with them, and with each other. Deep, abiding fellowship is God's will for creation, not just well-organized congregations.

*Reflection by* **Martyn Percy**

*cf. Ben Quash, *Abiding*, London: Bloomsbury, 2013

**Isaiah 55.1-11**
[1]Acts 10.44-end
Psalm 98
1 John 5.1-6
John 15.9-17

**Sixth Sunday of Easter**

## Isaiah 55.1-11

*'Incline your ear, and come to me;
listen, so that you may live' (v.3)*

How do we hope in time of crisis? When chapters 40 to 55 of Isaiah were written, the Jews were in exile in Babylon (beginning in 597 BC), having lost most of what they held dear. Chapter 55 is the powerful culminating section, a prophecy of hope for Israel's return from exile. It is practical – material and spiritual go together. Water, wine, milk and bread are images of full life given by God. It is also religious, social and political, with implications for all 'the peoples'.

To receive this new life, the one essential is to hear what God says: 'listen, so that you may live.' God's word brings unimaginable realities, above all forgiveness, joy and peace, and it is utterly reliable in bringing about God's purposes. At the heart of it lie the mystery and initiative of a God whose thoughts and ways far transcend ours.

Can we let our minds and plans be stretched by God's thoughts and ways? The picture is of God's word like rainwater, getting inside plants as they grow day by day. The listening you are doing now by reading Scripture is life-giving. Its promise is nothing less than joining all creation in an ecstasy of delight in the God of 'steadfast, sure love'.

*Reflection by* **David Ford**

[1]*The reading from Acts must be used as either the first or the second reading.*

## Sixth Sunday of Easter

Isaiah 55.1-11
¹**Acts 10.44-end**
Psalm 98
1 John 5.1-6
John 15.9-17

### Acts 10.44-end

*'While Peter was still speaking, the Holy Spirit fell upon all who heard the word' (v.44)*

I have long suspected that God is not as tidy as I am. God's ways seem at times to be quite careless of our well-crafted systems of belief and practice. Here in Caesarea, God decides to pour out the gift of the Holy Spirit on a group of 'Johnny-come-latelys' who haven't even been circumcised, let alone baptized. It's a scandal.

Peter had been doing his bit. He came to Caesarea under the compulsion of a dream and proceeded to do what any good apostle would do – he reminded them of the story of Jesus from arrival to departure. However, the Spirit interrupted, as he often does. 'While Peter was still speaking', the Holy Spirit 'fell' (not just 'alighted gently'), and all heaven broke loose. All Peter could do was to try to regularize what God was doing and to baptize the group forthwith.

There's always a danger that we Christians will try to make systems out of the reckless freedom of God, and that we'll try to make God manageable and the Church tidy. A rather more faithful strategy is to watch closely for what God is doing and to respond gratefully. We'll find ourselves in strange company and in edgy situations, but it makes the Christian life much more exciting.

*Reflection by* **John Pritchard**

¹*The reading from Acts must be used as either the first or the second reading.*

Isaiah 55.1-11
[1]Acts 10.44-end
Psalm 98
**1 John 5.1-6**
John 15.9-17

## Sixth Sunday of Easter

### 1 John 5.1-6

*'... the one who came by water and blood' (v.6)*

'If you cut me do I not bleed?' Shylock's appeal is also Christ's.

The Gnostics taught that the Christ came only 'by water', that at the moment of Jesus' baptism, the divine son, 'the Christ', came down for a three-year furlough, inviolate, immaculate, untouched and unsullied, disclosing gnosis, hidden wisdom, through Jesus' lips, then cutting back to heaven before that bloody business on Calvary.

You can meet Christianity like that today: ideal, bloodless, crystal clear. But, when the blood rushes to my cheeks in shame, or when it boils over in anger, when my pulse races with passion, and always when I am wounded, when the hidden life of my blood spills out from me, then I want a God who has heard the blood singing in his ears, a God who walks with me into the bloody mess of life, not away from it, a God who says of all the blood that's ever shed: 'This is my blood.'

'God is Love', says St John, and in his poem 'The Agony', the poet-priest George Herbert adds:

> *Love is that liquor sweet and most divine,*
> *Which my God feels as blood, but I as wine.*

### Reflection by **Malcolm Guite**

[1]*The reading from Acts must be used as either the first or the second reading.*

**Sixth Sunday of Easter**

Isaiah 55.1-11
Acts 10.44-end
Psalm 98
1 John 5.1-6
**John 15.9-17**

### John 15.9-17

*'I have called you friends' (v.15)*

Here is the deepest secret of a fruitful life: friendship that loves as Jesus has loved. The essence of us abiding in Jesus and him in us is daily, long-term friendship with him that overflows into loving others with the love we find in Jesus.

It is extraordinarily simple, endlessly fresh and deep. This is a communion of hearts and minds in which Jesus emphasizes that he shares with his friends his own understanding of what he is about. He does not demand the blind obedience of slaves. We are to stretch our minds in questioning, making as full sense as possible of who Jesus is and what he does. We learn more and more as we live in the intimacy of communication with him through prayer, study and conversation with other friends of his.

This friendship is utterly committed and radically free. The sign of commitment in love is willingness to lay down one's life for one's friends, as Jesus did. Our friends in Jesus include countless people who have had to do this literally, and even more who have lived it out in lives of love that is often hidden.

One sign of the freedom of this friendship is that 'the Father will give you whatever you ask him in my name'. Think of something to ask the Father that would please Jesus. Then ask in his name.

*Reflection by* **David Ford**

<sup>1</sup>**Acts 1.1-11** *or* Daniel 7.9-14
Psalm 47 *or* Psalm 93
Ephesians 1.15-end *or* <sup>1</sup>Acts 1.1-11
Luke 24.44-end

## Ascension Day

*Principal Feast*

## Acts 1.1-11

*'But you will receive power when the Holy Spirit
has come upon you' (v.8)*

St Luke, the doctor and writer, starts recording in this book
not the acts of the apostles but the act of the Holy Spirit. Luke
is passionate and enthusiastic about the presence and the role
of the Holy Spirit in the Church. He writes the account of the
ascension, but his focus is on the work of the Holy Spirit,
which is the continuity of the presence of Christ in the world.
Jesus is not with us in the body, but he is always with us
through the Holy Spirit. This is an account of hope and power.
The ascension is not a sad occasion when the world 'lost
Christ'. Even today, it is a time to celebrate the era of the work
of the Holy Spirit in us.

Through our baptism and the Eucharist, we go out into the
world as the disciples of Christ, the risen and the ascended
Lord, empowered just like the first disciples with the Holy
Spirit. Through that same power of that same Spirit, we
continue Christ's mission to be the light, the salt and the
leaven in the world. By living our faith well, people do not
see us – they see Christ in us!

This is how we shine and how we become true agents of the
Holy Spirit.

*Reflection by* **Nadim Nassar**

<sup>1</sup>*The reading from Acts must be used as either the first or the second reading.*

**Ascension Day**

*Principal Feast*

[1]Acts 1.1-11 or **Daniel 7.9-14**
Psalm 47 or Psalm 93
Ephesians 1.15-end or [1]Acts 1.1-11
Luke 24.44-end

### Daniel 7.9-14

*'... his kingship is one that shall never be destroyed' (v.14)*

Through stories and visions the book of Daniel explores a question that is no less difficult and troubling for us as for its original readers: who truly rules the universe? Our lives as people of faith depend on the answer.

The language of Daniel 7 is symbolic. It draws on the myths of other nations as well as the traditions of Israel. The 'beasts' represent the powers that have ruled over Judaea: Babylon, Persia and Greece. It is likely that the original readers of the book of Daniel were living under the rule of the Greek Antiochus IV, who was particularly arbitrary and brutal. Being a Jew and staying alive became a minefield of negotiation and danger.

All is not lost, however. The Ancient One is still on his heavenly throne, and in his courtroom justice is still done. Before him stands one in human form who is given delegated authority over the world. Who is it? Christian readers inevitably see here the figure of Christ, especially today when we celebrate the reign in God's kingdom of the one who called himself 'Son of Man'. This ancient text is, however, enigmatic. It tells us that all human kingdoms will ultimately fall before God's kingdom, and that God will share his rule with a representative of humanity. Even now we cannot know how and when the tyranny of evil will be overthrown, but Daniel encourages us to believe that day will come.

*Reflection by* **Gillian Cooper**

[1] *The reading from Acts must be used as either the first or the second reading.*

[1]Acts 1.1-11 *or* Daniel 7.9-14
Psalm 47 *or* Psalm 93
**Ephesians 1.15-end** *or* [1]Acts 1.1-11
Luke 24.44-end

### Ascension Day

*Principal Feast*

### Ephesians 1.15-end

*'... a spirit of wisdom and revelation' (v.17)*

'Get wisdom; get insight.' This exhortation from Proverbs 4.5 characterizes a book packed full of practical advice. The prayer in today's reading echoes the centrality of wisdom to well-being, but, rather than expounding it through a set of skills to be acquired and pitfalls to be avoided, it is sought as a gift from God.

Wisdom, revelation, knowledge and illumination: all forms of understanding are encompassed here, but Paul's prayer is not that the Ephesians should be more intellectually alert or shrewd in their dealings; rather that the eyes of the heart may be enlightened. It's a strange phrase but very evocative – with the eyes of the heart open, the hope to which God has called us, and the greatness of his power, can readily be seen.

The role of the heart in acquiring wisdom is well testified in Scripture, which claims: 'The fear of the Lord is the beginning of wisdom' (Proverbs 9.10). This is a helpful reminder for those who live in a culture saturated with information. Knowledge of the deep things cannot be verified by that contemporary font of all wisdom, Wikipedia; rather, it is forged in the crucible of Christian discipleship – the application of the mind coupled with the yielding of the heart to God.

*Reflection by* **Helen Orchard**

[1] *For a reflection on Acts 1.1-11, see page 157. The reading from Acts must be used as either the first or the second reading.*

**Ascension Day**

*Principal Feast*

Acts 1.1-11 *or* Daniel 7.9-14
Psalm 47 *or* Psalm 93
Ephesians 1.15-end *or* Acts 1.1-11
**Luke 24.44-end**

### Luke 24.44-end

*'... he ... was carried up into heaven' (v.51)*

Here we are, reading the end – for now – of Luke's story. Perhaps we feel relief: here's a happy ending, a quick tying-up of loose ends – the ascension, described in almost matter-of-fact terms, marking the end of Jesus' time on earth. It might almost be true to say that they all lived happily ever after. It's like a cosy jumper and a cup of cocoa at the end of a busy day ...

It isn't, though, is it? Luke tells of fear and doubt. The disciples were 'startled and terrified' (Luke 24.37). How did it feel to be there – to touch, to see and to hear Jesus once more? Did they feel foolish, as if they ought to have known what was going on all along? Is that Jesus' meaning? Or is he opening their minds to the fact that the ways of God are nearly always about things being bigger, better and more wonderful than we can ever think for ourselves?

Like the disciples, we have to meet Jesus with an open mind. Reading in this way can mean being profoundly disturbed – being open to his presence, accepting the consequences of suffering, resurrection, repentance, forgiveness.

It's such a lot to take in that retreat to the cosy jumper has quite an appeal. But the promise of Jesus holds so much more: a complete clothing, with power from on high. And so (as T. S. Eliot says in *Little Gidding*), the end is where we start from.

*Reflection by* **Jane Maycock**

**Ezekiel 36.24-28**
[1]Acts 1.15-17, 21-end
Psalm 1
1 John 5.9-13
John 17.6-19

## Seventh Sunday of Easter
### Sunday after Ascension Day

### Ezekiel 36.24-28

*'I will remove from your body the heart of stone' (v.26)*

This is a passage full of hope, but costly hope. God promises to gather the scattered people home, which is the thing that they long for above all else. But this will be entirely the action of God, to which the people themselves will contribute nothing, because they have nothing to offer. God will rescue his people because he is God, faithful and unchanging, not because the people have done anything to deserve God's action on their behalf. They must not begin to tell themselves that their exile was unfair or undeserved. Their hope comes only from the Lord.

God will have to perform radical surgery on the people before they can start their new lives. When they were left to their own devices, they fouled up everything they touched. If they are not to go on endlessly repeating that destructive cycle, they will have to go onto the operating table. As with any surgical procedure, first they will be disinfected (v.25), and then their hearts will undergo surgery, to replace their diseased organs with ones that will pump life-restoring blood around their bodies again.

Of course, Ezekiel did not know about open-heart surgery. He thought of the heart as the root of all thought, feeling and motivation, and it all needs to change. This is a fierce and painful metaphor, a symbol of the radical change that God must bring about in his people before they are fit to live again.

*Reflection by* **Jane Williams**

[1]*The reading from Acts must be used as either the first or the second reading.*

**Seventh Sunday of Easter**

**Sunday after Ascension Day**

Ezekiel 36.24-28
¹**Acts 1.15-17, 21-end**
Psalm 1
1 John 5.9-13
John 17.6-19

### Acts 1.15-17, 21-end

*'... and the lot fell on Matthias' (v.26)*

Who? When I was a theological college tutor and we kept the 'red letter days', Matthias would come around regularly and it became a sport among the staff to categorize our Matthias Day homilies. They covered a range from 'God can use anyone, even you' to 'even God's unknown servants have a worthy ministry'. To be honest, without dabbling into early Church legends, there was not much more to be said about Matthias.

But he had a job to do. He had the right qualifications. He met the 'person spec'. And we trust that he got on and did his job properly. It is just the case that not all ministry for Christ is glamorous. I serve in a 900-year-old church. I am just the latest in a long line of faithful (mostly) parish priests who have served Christ here. Not long after I am gone, I will be forgotten. And I have some nice jobs to do while I am here, and some tough ones. For the moment, the 'lot has fallen' on me here. That is just how it is in God's economy.

When I start getting stressed or pompous – and the two are not so far apart – it may be because in my own mind I have exaggerated my role. I am serving here, now, for a little while. I will then be gone. The Church will go on because it is God's.

*Reflection by* **Alan Bartlett**

¹*The reading from Acts must be used as either the first or the second reading.*

Ezekiel 36.24-28
[1]Acts 1.15-17, 21-end
Psalm 1
**1 John 5.9-13**
John 17.6-19

## Seventh Sunday of Easter
### Sunday after Ascension Day

### 1 John 5.9-13

*'And this is the testimony: God gave us eternal life,*
*and this life is in his Son' (v.11)*

In this letter, John presses one point firmly: because God is this God, we are free to love – we must be reconciled. In today's reading, the point is intensified. God's love cannot become abstract, nor can our piety remain self-contained. Both must be resolutely Christ-shaped, because only there – in him – do we find the perfect coincidence of all that John is saying. Jesus is the twofold identity of love: our brother, God, has died in our stead.

And suddenly we again sense the scandal of what's happening here. Amid our lives of love, the Spirit is God testifying to God from God, the delight of the Father and the Son. And this lively overflowing testimony is miraculously in our hearts, our lives pierced by the endless delight of the Father in his Son. Somehow we are between the Father and the Son, our lives reverberating with divine testimony, resonating with the liveliness of God, identified in Christ.

To confess Christ is therefore to become the testimony of the Father, the gift of the Spirit, their unending delight in Christ. Somehow, amid the blood, the sweat, the watery tears, we are the Father's testimony to the love of his Son, alive in the Spirit. Our minds can only boggle at the enormity of John's claims. Nonetheless, the task remains simple: love one another.

*Reflection by* **Lincoln Harvey**

[1]*The reading from Acts must be used as either the first or the second reading.*

**Seventh Sunday of Easter**

**Sunday after Ascension Day**

Ezekiel 36.24-28
Acts 1.15-17, 21-end
Psalm 1
1 John 5.9-13
**John 17.6-19**

### John 17.6-19

*'As you have sent me into the world ...' (v.18)*

The unknown author of the late-second-century Epistle to Diognetus took the view that Christians were ordinary folk going about their ordinary business. We don't have special food or modes of dress. We live where we are, and not as a separate tribal or ethnic group. But, Diognetus continued, Christians 'reside in their respective countries, but only as aliens ... they take part in everything as citizens and put up with everything as foreigners ... every foreign land is their home, and every home a foreign land'.

This echoes the words of Jesus. We belong here – and yet we do not. Our true home is yet to come, and our true kingdom has not arrived, but it is coming. So wherever we live, we pray 'thy kingdom come, thy will be done, on earth as it is in heaven'.

So, where do you belong? The answer from Jesus is that we are in the world, yet not of it. For some early Christians, this meant the world did not have to be taken too seriously. It was a temporary place of transit. But Jesus' words are rather more subtle – and certainly stronger. Just as he was sent into the world, so are we. And our calling and mission, like his, is one of deep abiding engagement and sanctification. We may not, ultimately, belong to the world. But we are to love, cherish and bless it without limit.

*Reflection by* **Martyn Percy**

[1]**Acts 2.1-21** *or* Ezekiel 37.1-14
Psalm 104.26-36, 37*b* [*or* 104.26-end]
Romans 8.22-27 *or* [1]**Acts 2.1-21**
John 15.26-27; 16.4*b*-15

## Day of Pentecost
## (Whit Sunday)

### Acts 2.1-21

*'All of them were filled with the Holy Spirit' (v.4)*

Today we reach the astonishing story of Pentecost. The Church is born from the wind and fire of the Spirit.

The wind represents God's power, but is also a reference to God's breath: God's still small voice that spoke to Elijah in his need (1 Kings 19.12, KJV), and the very breath that brought life to Adam and Eve in the first place (Genesis 2.7).

The fire of the Spirit that illuminates but does not consume reminds us of the burning bush out of which God spoke to Moses (Exodus 3), and the burning fiery furnace that could not overwhelm the faith of Shadrach, Meshach and Abednego when they were asked to worship a statue made from human hands (Daniel 3).

The remarkable ability of the disciples to speak in different languages reverses the confusion that was brought into the world at Babel, when human vanity and greed created warring faction from harmonious diversity (Genesis 11.1-9). Joel's prophecy that one day all God's people will receive God's spirit is dramatically fulfilled (Joel 2.28-29).

All these Old Testament stories and prophecies are consummated as the disciples – thought to be drunk with wine – pour onto the streets of Jerusalem telling of God's love in Christ, drunk on the intoxicating joy of the Spirit. A new age begins, where everyone who calls on the name of the Lord will be saved. This spirit is available to everyone.

*Reflection by* **Stephen Cottrell**

[1] *The reading from Acts must be used as either the first or second reading.*

**Day of Pentecost**
**(Whit Sunday)**

<sup>1</sup>Acts 2.1-21 *or* **Ezekiel 37.1-14**
Psalm 104.26-36, 37*b* [*or* 104.26-end]
Romans 8.22-27 *or* <sup>1</sup>Acts 2.1-21
John 15.26-27; 16.4*b*-15

### Ezekiel 37.1-14

*'I will put my spirit within you, and you shall live' (v.14)*

On this feast of Pentecost we encounter one of the strangest and most vivid passages in Scripture. The dry bones represent the people of Israel, exiled and cut off from life. Only the life-giving God has the power to alter their fate. The prophet is commanded to call the bones back, first to support real bodies with flesh and muscles, then to true life as the prophet calls to the four winds (wind also means spirit or breath) to enter them.

Though in its context the vision is about the revival of the nation of Israel, its vivid imagery inevitably turned it into a prophecy of the resurrection. In the creed we speak of the Holy Spirit as 'the Lord, the giver of life'. We can trust the Life-Giver to recreate us again and again, both in life and through death. The Spirit confers both our natural life and the eternal life God desires for us.

This new life is not an inherent property of human beings. We receive the Holy Spirit in baptism as pure gift. It is the way God shares his being with us and it encourages us to make gifts of ourselves. The life to come is also a shared life. It is not the possession of individuals so much as the inheritance of the whole community of those who have loved and trusted in Christ.

*Reflection by* **Angela Tilby**

<sup>1</sup>*The reading from Acts must be used as either the first or the second reading.*

¹Acts 2.1-21 *or* Ezekiel 37.1-14
Psalm 104.26-36, 37*b* [*or* 104.26-end]
**Romans 8.22-27** *or* ¹Acts 2.1-21
John 15.26-27; 16.4*b*-15

**Day of Pentecost**
**(Whit Sunday)**

### Romans 8.22-27

*'The Spirit helps us in our weakness' (v.26)*

In my nightmare I turn the corner on my way home and discover that my flat is on fire. I reach into my pocket and grab my water pistol. (Don't ask – it's a dream!) I squirt pathetic droplets into the flames. Then from behind me I hear the siren of a fire engine. A mighty torrent of water shoots over my shoulder, gathers up the dribble from my water pistol and thunders it with awesome force into the blaze.

That is what the Spirit of God is doing to my words and thoughts when I pray. It gives us confidence to pray about situations so complex that we can see no solution, so dread that we can see no hope. It doesn't matter if we know that our words are weak, full of doubt, confused or even selfish. Because of the part the Holy Spirit plays in our own spirituality, God 'hears' our prayers translated into his own good will for us and with inestimable power. So take heart, because it is impossible to do prayer incorrectly.

This same Spirit, through whom God is vividly present in our world, is our reason to hope. The Spirit is our reassurance that the joy of life in God's direct presence will be overwhelmingly superior to our time in this worrying world, just as the joy of holding a newborn baby follows the pain of labour. This Pentecost, wait expectantly.

*Reflection by* **Peter Graystone**

¹ *For a reflection on Acts 2.1-21, see page 165. The reading from Acts must be used as either the first or the second reading.*

**Day of Pentecost
(Whit Sunday)**

Acts 2.1-21 or Ezekiel 37.1-14
Psalm 104.26-36, 37b [or 104.26-end]
Romans 8.22-27 or Acts 2.1-21
John 15.26-27; 16.4b-15

### John 15.26-27; 16.4b-15

*'When the Spirit of truth comes, he will guide you into all
the truth' (v.13)*

There is a note of sadness in Jesus' words of farewell to the
disciples. The sadness is one of loss, the loss of belonging,
which the disciples will experience as the infant Church and
the Synagogue become estranged in the early years of the
Christian era.

Jesus' words here apply beyond his lifetime, and they echo
down the centuries to the present day. There has been terrible
intolerance between Church and Synagogue, and Jews and
Christians are impoverished because of it. But Jesus points
beyond his earthly lifetime to the coming of the Holy Spirit.
He still has many things to say to his disciples, 'but you cannot
bear them now'. The Spirit does not bring his own revelation
but continues and expands the teaching of Christ: 'he will take
what is mine and declare it to you'. The Spirit is a spirit of
prophecy: 'he will declare to you the things that are to come'.
The Christian Church has developed through time in ways that
would have astonished the early disciples. We can see
distortions through history, but also an unfolding of richness
and depth that is still going on. The life of the Trinity lived
out through the diverse Christian communities around the
world is evidence of the Spirit guiding into all truth. That
guidance continues into our time because, in the end, truth is
inexhaustible. There is always more of God to discover.

*Reflection by* **Angela Tilby**

**Isaiah 6.1-8**
Psalm 29
Romans 8.12-17
John 3.1-17

### Isaiah 6.1-8

*'Holy, holy, holy is the Lord of hosts' (v.3)*

This verse is repeated in the Book of Revelation and in our Eucharistic prayer – but what does it mean?

Holiness is to be set apart, and, as God is uniquely set apart in his uncreatedness and transcendence, holiness is a quality belonging to God. Joining in this holiness is God's gift to us, and our worship allows us to grow personally into God's holy nature.

Our calling to holiness is shown in our Eucharistic prayers. We sing 'Holy, holy, holy, Lord God of hosts' just before we ask God to enact change, thus making holy. Following this chant, we invoke the Holy Spirit over the bread and the wine, and over the people. We also repeat the transforming words of Jesus: 'this is my body ... this is my blood'. We call upon God's promise of transformational holiness.

The early African bishop Augustine reminds us that this is not primarily about transforming bread and wine, but about our own calling to change. We are to become holy by being the body of Christ. Augustine shows this in his reflection on receiving communion: 'What you hear ... is "The body of Christ", and you answer, "Amen". So be a member of the body of Christ, in order to make that Amen true.'

*Reflection by* **Paul Kennedy**

**Trinity Sunday**

Isaiah 6.1-8
Psalm 29
**Romans 8.12-17**
John 3.1-17

### Romans 8.12-17

*'Abba! Father!' (v.15)*

Why suddenly insert an Aramaic word in a letter to those who spoke no Aramaic? There must be only one explanation. The word 'Abba' must have become well known and much used in Christian circles. And, like the Hebrew 'Amen', it has stood the test of time, failing to be airbrushed out by the translators' pen.

'Abba' has its roots in the Hebrew word 'Ab', meaning 'father'. It developed into the Aramaic word as a term of affection and endearment, closest in our language to 'daddy'. It was the word Jesus used when he talked with God in the intimacy and agony of the Garden of Gethsemane that first Maundy Thursday. It was not the usual term used in religious circles when addressing God, and so it shows us something of that unique relationship Jesus enjoyed with his Father. The use of 'Abba' by those first Christians shows that they too were now a part of that special relationship. One of the family.

What does it mean to you to be an adopted son or an adopted daughter of God? It is only when we really stop to ponder and let the truth sink in that its significance hits us. Not a slave, but a son. Not a servant, but a daughter. And, in the same way that adopted children so often take on the mannerisms, speech patterns, behaviour and facial expressions of their adoptive parents, in the fullness of time our intimate relationship with our Father should cause others to see in us the likeness of God.

*Reflection by* **Jan McFarlane**

Isaiah 6.1-8
Psalm 29
Romans 8.12-17
**John 3.1-17**

### John 3.1-7

*'You must be born from above' (v.7)*

The Nicodemus who comes secretly to Jesus by night, and therefore out of the darkness towards the light (John 3.21), is probably well intentioned and sounds sympathetic, but he still doesn't quite get it. Readers of this Gospel frequently find themselves in a similar position, for John's retelling of Jesus' teaching is more allusive and elaborate than in the other ('Synoptic') Gospels. John's intention, however, is to show that the difference between those who do and those who don't get Jesus' message – in this case, unusually, over the reign of God – can be a profoundly spiritual difference. Despite what some contemporary Christians believe, it is those who take Jesus' teaching literally who often miss the point of it: that is, its spiritual depth.

In Nicodemus' case, the mistake is compounded by the fact that the same word can mean either 'anew' (and therefore 'again') or 'from above'. The first understanding leads to a literal and temporal cul-de-sac; only the second points to the deeper (higher) dimension and meaning of a birth that is from and of God. This is what it means to be born of the Spirit, without which we cannot enter, and cannot even see, God's kingdom when it comes.

Mysterious stuff, then, but not complicated or clever, reserved only for the learned. This passage is the equivalent of the Synoptics' teaching that we can only receive and enter the kingdom of God 'as a child' (Matthew 18.3; Luke 18.17).

*Reflection by* **Jeff Astley**

**Proper 4**

**Sunday between**
**29 May & 4 June inclusive**
*(if after Trinity Sunday)*

*Continuous:*
**1 Samuel 3.1-10 [11-20]**
Psalm 139.1-5, 12-18
2 Corinthians 4.5-12
Mark 2.23 – 3.6

### 1 Samuel 3.1-10 [11-20]

*'Here I am, for you called me' (vv.5, 6, 8)*

We catch a glimpse of Samuel's strange and lonely childhood with Eli, an ageing man, with failing sight, which could almost be his chosen defence mechanism: out of sight, out of mind. At night, the little boy sleeps in the temple, amid the smell and smoke of the burnt offerings, the flickering light of the lamp, and with the terrifying presence of the ark of God for company.

Yet, in the midst of all of these reminders, Samuel does not immediately understand his call. It's hard not to see this as Eli's failing: he failed to give his own sons any sense of the reality of God, and in the same way he has apparently not given Samuel any expectation of the presence of God in the sacred space where he lives, works and sleeps.

The first message God gives to Samuel is a brutal one, a hard test of whether Samuel is willing to be a truthful speaker of the word of God. Samuel is not to know that Eli has already heard this news, but we, the readers, know and wait to see what Samuel will do. Samuel chooses, and sets the pattern of faithful response that is to shape the rest of his days.

With awe, God's people, who have come to despise Shiloh under the ministry of Eli and his sons, come back, to hear and meet their God again, at last.

*Reflection by* **Jane Williams**

*Related:*
**Deuteronomy 5.12-15**
Psalm 81.1-10
2 Corinthians 4.5-12
Mark 2.23 – 3.6

## Deuteronomy 5.12-15

*'The seventh day is a sabbath to the Lord' (v.14)*

We are not yet half way through the year, but I'm already exhausted by this endless stream of weekdays stretching from Boxing Day to Christmas Eve. When I was young, I found Sunday afternoons, when nothing was open, boring. Now there is virtually no difference between a Sunday and any other day, and it feels more like drudgery than boredom.

The Ten Commandments were given to a people who looked back to an enslaved past. Their lives had been used as commodities to achieve wealth for others. They were given no care, no day off, no rest.

Now the Hebrews were free. But they were commanded never to forget what they had experienced. At some future date they would not be slaves, but employers. So long as they remembered what their past had involved, they would never replicate it. That was why a Sabbath was so important. It was a different kind of day, once in every seven. The people rested, the working animals rested, the land rested. It created space to reflect, to care for others, and to worship.

When I was young, I didn't realize that marking a Sabbath is about workers having conditions that ensure their wellbeing, about attention to animal welfare, and about fields and oceans being protected from those who would farm them into sterility. If I had, I might have realized that a Sabbath is not just about honouring God, but also about honouring human life.

*Reflection by* **Peter Graystone**

**Proper 4**

*Continuous:*
I Samuel 3.1-10 [11-20]
Psalm 139.1-5, 12-18
**2 Corinthians 4.5-12**
Mark 2.23 – 3.6

*Related:*
Deuteronomy 5.12-15
Psalm 81.1-10

## 2 Corinthians 4.5-12

*'... death is at work in us, but life in you' (v.12)*

In one of the greatest passages of Scripture, Paul mounts an eloquent self-defence. He starts the chapter by claiming to have renounced shameful behaviour, duplicity and false teaching in favour of open statement of the truth. However, he reaches beyond self-assertion by appealing to the conscience of his hearers 'in the sight of God' in verse 2.

This brings us to the verses in today's reading, which is the heart of the epistle. Paul's ministry is not his own, but the gift of God's mercy. What he focuses on is not himself but the glory of Christ, in whose face the light of creation shines again to re-create a dark world. What he preaches is not himself but the Jesus whose Lordship is made known in dying and coming to life. What sustains him is the knowledge of God, who keeps company with those at the end of their tether and promises to raise the dead.

This remarkable testimony illuminates the interchange of suffering and comfort in Christ. Radical openness to God's life-giving presence in experiences of brokenness brings discovery of treasure, not only to the apostle but also to those he serves – 'life in you'. In that faith, we can all look beyond the agonies of the present to the prospect of glory unlimited, unseen and eternal.

*Reflection by* **Christoher Jones**

| | | |
|---|---|---|
| *Continuous:* | *Related:* | **Proper 4** |
| I Samuel 3.1-10 [11-20] | Deuteronomy 5.12-15 | |
| Psalm 139.1-5, 12-18 | Psalm 81.1-10 | |

2 Corinthians 4.5-12
**Mark 2.23 – 3.6**

## Mark 2.23 – 3.6

*'Look, why are they doing what is not lawful on the sabbath?' (2.24)*

To what extent do we know this 'gentle Jesus, meek and mild …'? Not very well, according to Mark. For here in this rather breathless narrative, we meet Jesus the radical, Jesus the lawbreaker, Jesus the challenger and disturber of tradition. This is the Jesus who will not be an easy, passive member of your average congregation. He's a nuisance. And it is early days in so far as his ministry goes. Lord knows how it will end – though you can begin to see quite early on why so many would turn against him at the end.

In today's reading, Jesus first of all breaks a common and customary interpretation of the sabbath with almost casual determination. Just like Gandhi making salt from the sea and defying the British Empire salt tax in 1930, Jesus simply breaks the law to point out its absurdity. But it does not stop there. For next, he goes into the synagogue on the sabbath and breaks the law again by healing a man with a withered hand.

What do these gestures tell us about Jesus and the law? That Jesus is intent on redefining the relationship between humanity and the law. And that, in the new kingdom, the law must live under the love of God and with the compassion that God has for all humanity. A religious tradition that cannot feed and heal others, because of its compliance to an apparently divinely inspired code of ethics, has rather lost the plot.

*Reflection by* **Martyn Percy**

**Proper 5**

**Sunday between**
**5 & 11 June inclusive**
*(if after Trinity Sunday)*

*Continuous:*
I Samuel 8.4-11[12-15]
16-20 [11.14-end]
Psalm 138
2 Corinthians 4.13 – 5.1
Mark 3.20-end

### 1 Samuel 8.4-11[12-15] 16-20 [11.14-end]

*'Appoint for us ... a king to govern us, like other nations'*
*(v.5)*

Today's reading marks a turning point in the story of Israel. Samuel has been both priest and judge, but his sons are simply not cut from the same cloth, and the people seize the opportunity to demand a king, like other nations. The Lord assures Samuel that they're rejecting Yahweh, not him, and Samuel tries to warn them what this will mean in terms of royal oppression of all kinds. It's a sorry list, but the people are hell-bent on having their king, so the Lord says a king they shall have.

I once saw a notice in a shop in South Africa addressed to potential robbers. It stated simply: 'These premises are protected by God.' No arguing with that then! Israel had been protected by God, but the people somehow thought they would be better off being protected by a king. Mistake. If only we would understand that no human institution can offer us safety from harm, but God can offer us security in whatever life throws at us.

It was going to be a hard lesson for the Israelites to learn. And we're not doing much better in our own day. A bit more protection, we think; more missiles, more police, more gated communities. But that's not it.

Safety lies in faith, not in certainty; in God, not in kings.

*Reflection by* **John Pritchard**

*Related:*
**Genesis 3.8-15**
Psalm 130
2 Corinthians 4.13 – 5.1
Mark 3.20-end

**Proper 5**

## Genesis 3.8-15

*'Who told you that you were naked?' (v.11)*

This chilling question that God asks Adam pulls into sharp focus the reality of Adam's sin. The bubble has been burst, and Paradise is lost forever. There can never again be the state of innocence that characterized life for humanity before that fateful bite of the forbidden fruit.

Yet, with the first sin came the dawning of consciousness: we are naked and now we can see we are naked. Our eyes have been opened, and we know both good and evil.

In one sense, this is the most tragic moment in the relationship between God and people. What Adam and Eve did was to put their wishes and desires above what God had told them to do. It encapsulates all human rebellion and wilfulness. All other wickedness and evil come from this primal sin: disobedience born of wanting our own way.

In another sense, though, this is the moment when free will became activated. If our eyes had not been opened, would we have ever needed to choose between good and evil? Wouldn't we always have acted in accord with God's will?

The profound change in our consciousness described in the story of the forbidden fruit is the challenge of our whole spiritual journey. Every minute of every day, each of us now has to choose whom we will obey. Most of those choices are not really about good or evil; rather, they reveal who or what is my god.

*Reflection by* **Christina Rees**

| **Proper 5** | *Continuous:* | *Related:* |
|---|---|---|
| | I Samuel 8.4-11[12-15] | Genesis 3.8-15 |
| | 16-20 [11.14-end] | |
| | Psalm 138 | Psalm 130 |
| | **2 Corinthians 4.13 – 5.1** | |
| | Mark 3.20-end | |

## 2 Corinthians 4.13 – 5.1

*'So we do not lose heart' (v.16)*

The confident declaration that 'we do not lose heart' comes at the beginning and end of a unusually personal passage by St Paul in which he tells of the most harrowingly painful suffering for the faith. So the likelihood is he was writing to vulnerable communities of faith who were indeed on the edge of losing heart.

The great missionary theologian Lesslie Newbigin was once asked: 'What gives you hope for the world?' He immediately replied, 'that God raised Jesus Christ from the dead'. For Newbigin, like Paul, Christian resilience in the face of adversity and pain is not rooted in any human capacity for optimism or natural strength of character. It is based upon something God has done. By God's gift and choosing, we find ourselves part of a bigger story. So it is that tiny, vulnerable communities down through Church history witnessed with astonishing hope.

Like those moments under dark, wild-driven storm clouds when a break gives a brilliant glimpse of light beyond, we have glimpses. But more often this is a reality not yet visible to this world. Seeing is not believing. But for Paul it is a story so glorious he can describe his present sufferings as 'slight momentary afflictions' by comparison.

'Lift up your hearts' is the ancient liturgical call. Hold them in the story of what God has done in Christ – and hope.

*Reflection by* **David Runcorn**

| Continuous: | Related: | |
| --- | --- | --- |
| 1 Samuel 8.4-11[12-15] 16-20 [11.14-end] | Genesis 3.8-15 | **Proper 5** |
| Psalm 138 | Psalm 130 | |

2 Corinthians 4.13 – 5.1
**Mark 3.20-end**

### Mark 3.20-end

*'He has gone out of his mind' (v.21)*

We should not be surprised that the disruption Jesus' ministry caused – to the prevailing culture, society and faith of his day – prompts onlookers and commentators to surmise that this is the work of Satan. Jesus' critics are searching for an explanation of what is going on. The key to understanding their concerns lies in the telling comment that he (Jesus) 'has gone out of his mind'. And that is why the family of Jesus effectively try to serve a detention order on him: 'they went out to restrain him'.

But Jesus' ministry is not madness. Or evil. This is the arrival of the kingdom of God. And this entails letting out, freeing and liberating lots of issues, infirmities and people that have, hitherto, been locked up. But it is hugely traumatic and disruptive for wider society. People living with tormenting afflictions are suddenly, beautifully, wildly and wonderfully free. For the onlookers, this is unsettling, to say the least. Even today, when the mad start to say they are completely cured, we tend to proceed with caution. It was no different in Jesus' day. When the patients revert to being people again, society has suddenly to readjust. Sometimes it is easier to keep the delineations clear between sick and well, sane and insane. But Jesus, by healing so many afflicted people, radically reorders society. Some would prefer to restrain Jesus at this point, or say that he has gone out of his mind and has an unclean spirit. Jesus' response is simple: whoever does the will of God is my kindred.

*Reflection by* **Martyn Percy**

**Proper 6**

**Sunday between
12 & 18 June inclusive**
*(if after Trinity Sunday)*

*Continuous:*
1 Samuel 15.34 – 16.13
Psalm 20
2 Corinthians 5.6-10 [11-13]14-17
Mark 4.26-34

### 1 Samuel 15.34 – 16.13

*'... they look on the outward appearance, but the Lord
looks on the heart' (16.7)*

Today more than ever we find satisfaction in the appearance
of things. We are often deceived by what we see because we
have not scratched beyond the surface to discover the true
essence within. A good example is Christmas, when many
cover the true nature of the occasion – a celebration of God
becoming human – with a glitzy layer of consumerism and a
shiny secular façade; even the message is sanitized so that it
becomes unrecognizable and the Nativity becomes a
perfumed, tidy fairy tale.

Another example is when we divert our attention from being
a worshipping, serving Church and we worship and serve
buildings and all the rituals and paraphernalia that go with
them. The Church is the wall-less instrument that God uses to
transform people and serve humanity, and many of us have
lost this, distracted by the Church as an organization that
swallows everything else.

As it says in this passage, 'for the Lord does not see as mortals
see; they look on the outward appearance, but the Lord looks
on the heart'. This is also what Jesus said when he criticized
the religious leaders: 'Woe to you, scribes and Pharisees,
hypocrites! For you are like whitewashed tombs, which on the
outside look beautiful, but inside they are full of the bones
of the dead and of all kinds of filth' (Matthew 23.27). God is
calling us to look beyond the surface, to the heart of all
things.

*Reflection by* **Nadim Nassar**

*Related:*
**Ezekiel 17.22-end**
Psalm 92.1-4, 12-end [*or* 92.1-8]
2 Corinthians 5.6-10 [11-13]14-17
Mark 4.26-34

## Ezekiel 17.22-end

*'I bring low the high tree, I make high the low tree' (v.24)*

In 597 BC King Nebuchadnezzar II besieged Jerusalem, capital city of the Jewish people. Jehoiachin, a teenager who had only been king for 100 days, surrendered and was taken captive to Babylon. In his place Nebuchadnezzar appointed a puppet-king, Zedekiah. He survived for a decade by allying with Pharaoh Hophra of Egypt, but came to a sticky end when Nebuchadnezzar destroyed Jerusalem after a further siege.

In the first part of chapter 17, Ezekiel creates an elaborate allegory about this in which ferocious eagles damage a cedar tree. Then in these three verses he gives a radically different vision. This vision is God's plan.

In verses 22-24 the Lord himself takes a cutting. It's fragile, but God will tend it lovingly and it will become a great tree that offers wonderful protection. The cutting is the Messiah, the leader to whom the Jews would look for their salvation, and the imagery is echoed in Jesus' parable about God's Kingdom in Matthew 13.31-32.

Christians recognize that Messiah to be Jesus. These verses contain much that reminds us of the entirely unexpected nature of his ministry. It did not involve eagle-like ferocity, but sapling-like frailty. We have a God whose heart is set on raising up the weak and bringing down the tyrannical. I wonder whether Jesus' mother was thinking of these verses when she sang of the God who 'has scattered the proud in the thoughts of their hearts' (Luke 1.51).

*Reflection by* **Peter Graystone**

**Proper 6**

*Continuous:*
1 Samuel 15.34 – 16.13
Psalm 20

*Related:*
Ezekiel 17.22-end
Psalm 92.1-4, 12-end
[or 92.1-8]
**2 Corinthians 5.6-10 [11-13]14-17**
Mark 4.26-34

## 2 Corinthians 5.6-10 [11-13] 14-17

*'For the love of Christ urges us on' (v.14)*

What motivates us to serve? Sometimes it is friendship – we enjoy being with friends and those who share our common interests. We enjoy knitting so we form a knitting club and make garments for infant baptisms or donate them to disaster victims.

However, somehow extending loving acceptance is different – it's more personal – or, is it? Christ died to restore all humanity to right relationship with God. Understanding this should prompt us to form relationships with those who wouldn't otherwise enter our circle of friends.

We all know at least one person who is quick to point out the personal, shameful actions of another – often revealing their former sins or misdeeds. Little do we know that fear of rejection, ridicule for past deeds, or shame associated with former sin often prevents those who don't know Christ from entering our churches. We all share a common grace – a past buried in the death of Jesus and new life birthed in the love of Christ. Our relationship with him is the common thread that binds us together.

Today's reading challenges us to extend the grace we have received to others by becoming more inclusive in our relationships. When we reject those whom God brings through our doors, we also reject the diverse gifts he has given them needed to bless our communities.

*Reflection by* **Rosalyn Murphy**

*Continuous:*
I Samuel 15.34 – 16.13
Psalm 20

*Related:*
Ezekiel 17.22-end
Psalm 92.1-4, 12-end
[*or* 92.1-8]
2 Corinthians 5.6-10 [11-13]14-17
**Mark 4.26-34**

**Proper 6**

## Mark 4.26-34

*'It is like a mustard seed' (v.31)*

When Jesus reaches for metaphors that describe the kingdom of God, he often uses untidy images. 'I am the vine, you are the branches' comes to mind (John 15.5). No stately cedar tree of Lebanon here – Jesus chooses a gnarled, knotted plant that requires patient, careful husbandry. And one that is hardly pretty to look at either. Actually, it is bug ugly to look at – but taste the fruit of the vine, and don't judge on appearances.

In another short parable today, he compares the kingdom of heaven to a mustard seed – one of the smallest seeds that grows into 'the greatest of all shrubs, and puts forth large branches'. The image is ironic, and possibly even satirical. You might expect the kingdom of God to be compared to the tallest and strongest of trees. But Jesus likens the Church to something that sprouts up quite quickly from almost nothing, and then develops into an ungainly spindly shrub that barely holds up a bird's nest.

Churches, then, can take some comfort from the lips of Jesus. Like the mustard seed, a church can be an untidy sprawling shrub. Like a vine, it can be knotted and gnarled. Neither plant is much to look at. But Jesus was saying something quite profound about the nature of the Church: it will be rambling, extensive and just a tad jumbled. And that's the point. It often isn't easy to find your place in neat and tidy systems. And maybe you'll feel alienated and displaced for a while. But, in a messy and slightly disorderly Church, all may find a home.

*Reflection by* **Martyn Percy**

*Continuous:*

## Proper 7

**Sunday between
19 & 25 June inclusive**
*(if after Trinity Sunday)*

1 Samuel 17.[1*a*, 4-11, 19-23]32-49
Psalm 9.9-end *or*
1 Samuel 17.57 – 18.5, 10-16
Psalm 133
2 Corinthians 6.1-13
Mark 4.35-end

### 1 Samuel 17.[1*a*, 4-11, 19-23]32-49

*'Goliath, of Gath, whose height was six cubits and a span' (v.4)*

Most of us have experienced the feeling of being insignificant when we have compared ourselves to someone whom we judge to be wonderful or imposing or great, and we think, 'I can never be like that person', or 'I can never achieve that greatness'. Our hearts are filled with fear or awe, mixed with a feeling of weakness, perhaps even helplessness.

The people who witnessed Goliath's daily challenge were filled with fear and helplessness. David, however, rose to that challenge and resolved to stand up for what he believed in. This could have easily led to his death and the enslavement of his people. When David went to meet Goliath in battle, all present would have seen a heavily armoured giant, a hero of many battles, facing 'just a boy' with no military experience whatsoever; they saw only the appearance of the combatants and, based on their appearance alone, everyone would have felt sure that this could only result in David's death.

We do this too – we judge ourselves all too often in a shallow way, not appreciating the abilities that God has given us, including the power of our faith and the immense power of the Holy Spirit. When we face a big challenge in our lives, remember that we are not facing this challenge alone, and let's make sure that we know that God has equipped us for those times when we must carry our own cross.

*Reflection by* **Nadim Nassar**

*Continuous:*
1 Samuel 17.[1*a*, 4-11, 19-23]32-49
Psalm 9.9-end *or*
**1 Samuel 17.57 – 18.5, 10-16**
Psalm 133
2 Corinthians 6.1-13
Mark 4.35-end

**Proper 7**

## 1 Samuel 17.57 – 18.5, 10-16

*'Saul was afraid of David' (18.12)*

Saul and David are perfect examples of something that is crucial in our lives; the success of David, who was one of Saul's servants, filled Saul with jealousy, and he felt threatened by the young David's success. Many of us feel threatened when we see those around us thrive and apparently outshine us. The feeling of jealousy itself is a very human one; it is not wrong to feel some jealousy on occasions. The important thing is how we deal with these feelings. We have two choices: the first choice is to turn this jealousy into a motivational force so that we work to improve ourselves and to aspire and to celebrate the success of others. The other choice is to allow jealousy to fester in our hearts until it acquires a self-destructive power.

Turning jealousy into a force for good requires humility and a security in who we are – and that is much more achievable when we have faith. Why? Because we already believe that God loves us whatever we have achieved and that, out of this love, he has given us gifts – our responsibility is to make the most of these gifts and to make them fruitful. Our success in life should not be at the expense of others; rather, our success should benefit those around us, and the success of others should be a cause for celebration and gratitude.

*Reflection by* **Nadim Nassar**

**Proper 7**

*Related:*
**Job 38.1-11**
Psalm 107.1-3, 23-32 [*or* 107.23-32]
2 Corinthians 6.1-13
Mark 4.35-end

### Job 38.1-11

*'Who is this that darkens counsel by words
without knowledge?' (v.2)*

After 37 chapters of Job's protests and God's silence, finally, God speaks, and to indicate the profound nature of God's self-revelation, he speaks out of the whirlwind as one who commands the wind and the waves. Job has waited for this moment, but he has also feared it. Part-horrified by the idea of a God who would punish him unjustly, and part convinced that God has taken him by the collar and thrown him into despair, like other heroes of the Hebrew Bible, Job is ambivalent about meeting God face to face and senses that he will not come away unscathed.

Religious belief that does not expose itself to the awesome-ness of encounter with God is not faith at all but a last defence against God. This is perhaps part of the problem with Job's friends who have been 'comforting him' since chapter 2. Convincing themselves of their own orthodoxy, not once do they risk the kind of prayer in which their views might be challenged or reframed. So full of answers, how would they fare in the face of God's questions? Prepared to declare Job wrong, how would they cope with the demolition of their own world view and the pillars of sound reasoning, long-held tradition and divine inspiration on which they thought it was built?

And we – what defences do we use against God's awesome, wild and life-changing power?

*Reflection by* **Jane Leach**

*Continuous:*
1 Samuel 17.[1a, 4-11, 19-23]32-49
Psalm 9.9-end *or*
1 Samuel 17.57 – 18.5, 10-16
Psalm 133

*Related:*
Job 38.1-11
Psalm 107.1-3, 23-32
[*or* 107.23-32]

### Proper 7

[1]2 Corinthians 6.1-13
**Mark 4.35-end**

## Mark 4.35-end

*'Teacher, do you not care that we are perishing?' (v.38)*

One of my favourite Woody Allen lines is this: 'If you want to make God laugh, tell him your future plans.' The story of the stilling of the storm is hardly a barrel of laughs, but for anyone with faith, it ought at least to raise a wry smile. The disciples – not for the first time – find that their plans are about as stable as the sea that threatens to engulf them, and confronted by chaos, they quickly lose their faith. They even question the mindfulness and love of Jesus: '... do you not care that we are perishing?'

But all of this gives Jesus an opportunity to say two profound things in the face of apparent annihilation: 'Peace! Be still!' and 'Why are you afraid?' Sometimes we all find ourselves in the midst of what seem like great storms. We fear we will be engulfed. Even winds and waves are against us. Yet, we sometimes need to hear the words of Jesus that invite us out of fear and into peace. Sometimes what we need to do is reach out. Our salvation is nearer than we thought; it is within sight. Just not what we expected or thought.

The Scottish philosopher John Macmurray tells us that the maxim of illusory religion runs like this: 'Fear not; trust in God and he will see that none of the things you fear will happen to you'. But that of real religion is quite contrary: 'Fear not; the things you are afraid of are quite likely to happen to you – but they are nothing to be afraid of.' Peace be with you.

*Reflection by* **Martyn Percy**

[1] *For a reflection on 2 Corinthians 6.1-13, see page 91.*

## Proper 8

**Sunday between
26 June & 2 July inclusive**

*Continuous:*
**2 Samuel 1.1, 17-end**
Psalm 130
2 Corinthians 8.7-end
Mark 5.21-end

### 2 Samuel 1.1, 17-end

*'How the mighty have fallen and the weapons of war perished!' (v.27)*

A map helps us to understand this story. After springing a successful and violent attack on the Amalakites, David was camped nearly 100 miles south of Mount Gilboa, where Saul and Jonathan were killed fighting another enemy, the Philistines. It took three days for news of their deaths to reach him. Far from being thrilled at news that heralded the end of years as a fugitive from the unpredictable man whom he respected as king but whose vindictive violence he feared, David was devastated. Jonathan had been his closest friend and Saul had been his king, so there were very mixed emotions. His lament for both of them, not just for Jonathan, is an exquisite piece of biblical poetry.

David wanted the lament for the first king of Israel to be taught to his people of Judah, who had been fleeing from Saul as well as Saul's people of Israel further north. He wanted to remind them all of the good that Saul and Jonathan had done, not just the conflicts surrounding Saul's reign. David, previously anointed by Samuel as a future king, could easily have gloated at this news and pushed things too fast. Instead he allowed grief time to surface and ensured that, as people continued to sing the song, the good Saul had done was recorded for posterity.

Song is powerful: what do you sing of the moments of joy and lament in your life?

*Reflection by* **Rosalind Brown**

*Related:*
Wisdom of Solomon 1.13-15; 2.23, 24
*Canticle*: ¹**Lamentations 3.22-33** *or* Psalm 30
2 Corinthians 8.7-end
Mark 5.21-end

**Proper 8**

## Lamentations 3.22-33

*'... therefore I will hope in him' (v.24)*

The first line of today's reading is a popular worship chorus – an expression of confidence in the endless goodness of God, whose 'mercies never come to an end' (. But we do well to remember the original setting of these verses. They come in the midst of some of the most anguished poetry and lamenting in the Bible. The book of Lamentations is probably set in the suffering and devastation that followed the destruction of Jerusalem. It is rarely read in Christian worship, where the whole Biblical tradition of lament, protest and questioning is largely missing too. But it is a book for today's world, as some know well. A Sudanese priest, speaking of the sufferings of his Church insisted fiercely, 'lament is what keeps the church in the Sudan alive'.

Lament is a very particular theological response to God out of pain. It is a sign of faith, not the absence of it. In many of the Psalms, lament is closely linked to deliverance and praise. The same connection is found in the spirituals of past slave communities: 'Nobody knows the trouble I've seen – glory hallelujah!'

The challenge of this passage is not whether we hope and trust in God's goodness or not. It is where in life we insist on planting that hope. 'Therefore' – even here, where, by any visible measure, all signs of God seem to be absent.

*Reflection by* **David Runcorn**

¹*Lamentations 3.22-33 may be read as the first reading in place of Wisdom 1.13-15; 2.23, 24*

**Proper 8**

*Continuous:*
2 Samuel 1.1, 17-end
Psalm 130

*Related:*
Wisdom of Solomon
1.13-15; 2.23, 24
*Canticle:* Lamentations
3.22-33 *or* Psalm 30
**2 Corinthians 8.7-end**
Mark 5.21-end

## 2 Corinthians 8.7-end

*'Your present abundance and their need' (v.14)*

The decades after the resurrection of Jesus, during which the Christian Church expanded, coincided with a devastating famine in which the people of Jerusalem suffered particularly badly. Churches found themselves dealing for the first time with this question: As Christians are we responsible for people in need whom we don't know in places we will never visit?

The answer was an unambiguous 'Yes'. Church leaders launched a scheme whereby Christians in flourishing towns could give money that was transported in a trustworthy manner to towns where there was poverty. It is so much part of Christian practice today that we forget there was a first time. But these events were taking place as the first books of the New Testament were being written. Paul's letters were, in part, fundraising appeals.

The Christians in Macedonia got it right. They themselves were relatively poor. But when they heard what was happening in Jerusalem, they knew they had to help. In fact, they gave more than the relatively wealthy Christians in Corinth, which is why Paul wrote the reprimand disguised as an exhortation that we read today. The Church in Macedonia became a model for every succeeding generation of Christians because they wanted to be like their Lord – wholeheartedly generous to a needy world.

Why should Christians today give money to help suffering people rise out of poverty? Because it makes them like Jesus.

*Reflection by* **Peter Graystone**

*Continuous:*
2 Samuel 1.1, 17-end
Psalm 130

*Related:*
Wisdom of Solomon
1.13-15; 2.23, 24
*Canticle:* Lamentations 3.22-33
or Psalm 30
2 Corinthians 8.7-end
**Mark 5.21-end**

### Mark 5.21-end

*'Daughter, your faith has made you well' (v.34)*

The accounts of the haemorrhaging woman are always paired with the raising of Jairus' daughter. Jesus goes out of his way to affirm the faith of the older woman, yet apart from healing her, he also seems to challenge the social and religious forces that have rendered this woman 'contagious'; he calls her 'daughter' in all three Gospels, all of which stress the woman's faith. The significance of Jesus' action should not be underestimated, since her continuous menstruation renders her permanently 'unclean'. Her poverty – she 'had spent all that she had' – is a direct result of her affliction.

There is a double issue of impurity here: touching a corpse, and a continually menstruating woman. The girl is twelve, and her untimely death clearly prevents her from entering womanhood. Jesus declares her 'not dead, but sleeping', and his touch, resulting again in his defilement, raises her.

Mark gives prominence to the narrative by the sharing of the number twelve: the girl is twelve, the woman has been ill for twelve years. This coincidence suggests that there is a narrative relation of some kind between the woman and the girl. An older woman is cured of a menstrual disorder of twelve years' standing and is sent back into society; a girl who has not yet reached puberty is about to be reborn and take her place in society. Jesus, by absorbing and absolving their taint through the simple power of healing touch, enables this.

*Reflection by* **Martyn Percy**

**Proper 9**

**Sunday between
3 & 9 July inclusive**

*Continuous:*
**2 Samuel 5.1-5, 9-10**
Psalm 48
2 Corinthians 12.2-10
Mark 6.1-13

### 2 Samuel 5.1-5, 9-10

*'David became greater ... for the Lord of Hosts was
with him' (v.10)*

'There was a long war between the house of Saul and the house of David ...' (2 Samuel 3.1), but finally Saul's followers in the northern tribes of Israel recognized David as their king, as had the southern tribe of Judah seven years earlier. A covenant was agreed in God's sight and there was peace at last. To maintain this uneasy truce, David needed a neutral capital and, in a cunning and bold move using the water courses, he captured the independent, seemingly impregnable, city of Jerusalem, which had belonged to the Jebusites.

David's kingship was hard won through the years of conflict with Saul; during this time he refused to usurp the throne but continued to trust God, despite the continuing tension there between believing what God had promised years earlier through Samuel and his experience of living with the opposition to that fulfilment. Like John the Baptist, to whom Jesus said, when John was languishing in prison centuries later and tempted to doubt his calling, 'Blessed is anyone who takes no offence at me' (Matthew 11.6), David's was a testing, even gruelling, blessing. Over the years, through both success and hardship, he was being formed into the king who could unite his people and lead them in the ways of God.

How do we view our times of testing and unfulfilled dreams? And how do we steady ourselves when our dreams come true?

*Reflection by* **Rosalind Brown**

*Related:*
**Ezekiel 2.1-5**
Psalm 123
2 Corinthians 12.2-10
Mark 6.1-13

**Proper 9**

## Ezekiel 2.1-5

*'A spirit entered into me' (v.2)*

I was on a bus, sitting behind two mature ladies whose conversation I couldn't help overhearing. One said, 'Our grandson will be christened on Sunday.'

The other said, 'I forgot you go to church. Why are you a Christian?'

'Oh, you can't possibly ask me that,' said the first. 'You'd have to ask the vicar.' I was willing her to say something positive and was delighted when she added, 'I do find the services peaceful'.

'Ah, peace,' replied her friend. 'You should come to my pilates class. It's the most peaceful point in my week.' To my dismay the conversation ended with the Christian lady writing the date of the exercise class in her diary, not the other one being invited to the baptism.

Six centuries before Jesus, Ezekiel was charged with talking about God to his generation. He was warned that they had aggressively turned against the Lord and there was every chance they would ignore him. This is not dissimilar to the world in which we find ourselves today.

The problem is made more daunting by the fact that, like the lady on the bus, we have become so accustomed to keeping our faith private that it can be too embarrassing even to attempt to explain our beliefs to those who do not share them. I sense God saying, 'Stand on your feet. Get some spirit inside you!' After all, he's said it before.

*Reflection by* **Peter Graystone**

**Proper 9**

Continuous:
2 Samuel 5.1-5, 9-10
Psalm 48

*Related:*
Ezekiel 2.1-5
Psalm 123

**2 Corinthians 12.2-10**
Mark 6.1-13

## 2 Corinthians 12.2-10

*'My grace is sufficient for you, for power is made perfect in weakness' (v.9)*

Why wear an instrument of torture, a cross, around your neck? The cross speaks of a power that overcomes torture and death – of a power that, by God's good will towards all humankind, by grace, makes the cross empty. Christ crucified and risen is the true power of God. Christ was crucified in weakness and seemed to be defeated by the power of oppression and death. But God's power raised him from death and makes that death-defying power alive in us. And so we can boast of 'weakness' as Paul does, so that the grace, which overcomes the world, can work through and with our weaknesses to overcome the insults, the hardships, the persecutions and calamities, for the sake of Christ.

We are like earthen vessels, made of common clay with its cracks and grit, but have placed within us the immeasurable riches of Christ, so that even if the pottery vessel is chipped or breaks, the treasure holds its worth. This is the beautiful truth about ourselves.

This does not mean wallowing in weakness or becoming lethargic because we ourselves are weak but, rather, letting the beauty, light and power of the treasure course through us in prayer and sacrament, to make us strong, to rise up and walk in God's ways of justice and righteousness.

*Reflection by* **David Moxon**

*Continuous:*
2 Samuel 5.1-5, 9-10
Psalm 48

*Related:*
Ezekiel 2.1-5
Psalm 123

**Proper 9**

2 Corinthians 12.2-10
**Mark 6.1-13**

### Mark 6.1-13

*'Prophets are not without honour, except in their home town' (v.4)*

It is hard not to feel some sympathy for the complainants in today's Gospel reading. Jesus is someone they know. They have eaten with him, played ball with him, and watched him grow up. Now, almost suddenly, so it seems, he's different. He's preaching, healing, drawing large crowds, and everyone is interested in his background. What were his parents like? Tell us about his schooling? Has he always been special? How did he become a celebrity healer-preacher?

The friends and family of Jesus are a bit piqued, to say the least. But this causes Jesus not to acknowledge his humble origins, and affirm his nearest and dearest. Rather, he steps up a gear in proclaiming the kingdom of God project. He calls the Twelve, and clearly states that they are to come on this new mission without too many ties. The next few years will require utter dedication and few distractions.

Yet these exchanges in Mark 6 also serve to remind us of the deep importance of the Nazareth years. Simply put, Jesus has been with us. He has lived and eaten among us. He has slept in beds and on boats. He has, truly, richly and deeply, been Emmanuel – God with us. God knows what it is like to be human. In Jesus, we have heaven in ordinary, so that we too might, in the end, be ordinary in heaven. He became like us so we might become like him.

*Reflection by* **Martyn Percy**

**Proper 10**

**Sunday between
10 & 16 July inclusive**

*Continuous:*
**2 Samuel 6.1-5, 12b-19**
Psalm 24
Ephesians 1.3-14
Mark 6.14-29

### 2 Samuel 6.1-5, 12b-19

*'David brought up the ark of God … with rejoicing' (v.12)*

The frequent repetition of 'ark of God' and 'David' focuses us on the heart of this story. After consolidating his earthly power, King David's priority was to establish worship of God at the heart of his nation's life. The atmosphere was festive, even like a carnival, and the only sour note, when David's wife despised him for his actions, reinforces the exuberance of the revelling. The king's celebration of God's presence among his people was perhaps heightened by the fear recorded in the omitted verses when God's holiness was revealed very dramatically.

Michal, Saul's daughter, would have had her own conflicted memories of the past and was challenged by David's public display of emotion. But there is a leap from not being engaged in something to despising those who are and, tragically, Michal missed the import of the event when the kingdom's life was being refocused on God. There was as yet no central place of worship, only a few scattered shrines, and this bringing of the ark to Jerusalem was the beginning of establishing that city as the locus for the nation's worship and pilgrimage.

It is worth noting that the celebrations included distribution of food to people who were away from their homes, a reminder that worship cannot be separated from care for people's needs, something the later prophets such as Amos would have to remind God's people very sharply.

*Reflection by* **Rosalind Brown**

*Related:*
**Amos 7.7-15**
Psalm 85.8-end
Ephesians 1.3-14
Mark 6.14-29

## Amos 7.7-15

*'See, I am setting a plumb-line in the midst of my people Israel' (v.8)*

The famous picture of the plumb-line in verses 7-8 of Amos 7 has been speculated about for centuries. It's one of only two occasions where it appears in the Bible (the other being Isaiah 34.11). Nowadays, we have spirit levels to make sure our DIY projects are in line, while surveyors use laser measurements to check dimensions. What all these devices do is to measure against something else. In the case of this vision of God, the Lord is the builder, measuring Israel to see whether she meets with approval. Even though God shows mercy, we are also accountable to him.

This is not about 'measuring up' to standards, but balancing what we do against God and God alone. This is hard in a world where relativism holds sway – the notion that all points of view are equally valid, and that all truth is relative only to the individual. In such a world we just measure ourselves against ourselves, and define our morality against ourselves. For God, having a line – a plumb-line or any other measuring line – means that there is a clear marker, one that we do not write ourselves, but that God has written.

Today, think of this line not as a long plumb-line, but as the line around the heart of God – God who continually shows mercy. When we cause God grief, it is not just that our line does not measure up to God, but that it breaks the heart of God, who is still seeking to align his heart to ours.

*Reflection by* **Tim Sledge**

**Proper 10**

*Continuous:*
2 Samuel 6.1-5, 12b-19
Psalm 24

*Related:*
Amos 7.7-15
Psalm 85.8-end

**Ephesians 1.3-14**
Mark 6.14-29

## Ephesians 1.3-14

*'Blessed ... in Christ with every spiritual blessing' (v.3)*

Paul's letter to the Ephesians begins with a 'blessing', or act of praise expressed to God. This was, and is, a very common Jewish expression of prayer, whether at home over the bread or in the more formal setting of the synagogue. It is a response to what God has done in creation and redemption (for example, 'Blessed be the Lord, the God of Israel, who with his hand has fulfilled what he promised with his mouth to my father David' in 1 Kings 8.15; see also Psalm 103.1-5; Psalm 104.1-4). It is therefore a response to who God is and (in hope) to what God will do.

For Christian writers, like the author of Ephesians and 1 Peter (1.3-5), this Jewish prayer has become centred on Christ. God is no longer just 'O Lord our God, King of the Universe', but 'the God and Father of our Lord Jesus Christ'. And the blessings for which God is blessed are those that Christians have received through the words and works of Jesus: 'adoption as his children', redemption, forgiveness, grace, knowledge of 'the mystery of his will'. And – supremely – 'an inheritance', which is pledged by his mark, the 'seal' of his Spirit.

Everyone sees God from somewhere. For the Jews, God is seen mainly from the vantage point provided by the shape of their history; Christians, however, claim that the best views are to be had when they stand within the pattern of their Christ.

*Reflection by* **Jeff Astley**

*Continuous:*
2 Samuel 6.1-5, 12b-19
Psalm 24

*Related:*
Amos 7.7-15
Psalm 85.8-end

Ephesians 1.3-14
**Mark 6.14-29**

## Mark 6.14-29

*'...when Herod heard of it, he said,
"John, whom I beheaded, has been raised"' (v.16)*

The haunting image of a young woman carrying a human head on a platter and giving it to her mother is only one of many contrasts in the story. These include the contrasts between worldly power (Herod Antipas) and religious poverty (John the Baptist); between the immoral life of the king and the righteous, ascetic life of the prophet; and between the luxury of the palace and the barrenness of the prison cell.

Within the story of John the Baptist's execution, there are some links with Jesus' own death: both Jesus and John were subject to despotic injustice; both were tried by men who found them deeply perplexing. Herod knew in his heart of hearts that John the Baptist was 'a righteous and holy man'. Pontius Pilate said of Jesus at the trial: 'I find no case against him' (John 18.38).

The contrasts inside the story and the links with Jesus' life 'outside' the story give the episode its power and fascination. When the overarching hubris, vanity and amorality of Herod are confronted by an ascetic, self-forgetful and righteous prophet, the stage is set for a tragic confrontation. When the Herods of today murder the John the Baptists of today, is it not the duty of Christians to protest – and to work for a world where, instead of brutality, the watchwords become repentance and reconciliation?

*Reflection by* **Christopher Herbert**

**Proper 11**

**Sunday between
17 & 23 July inclusive**

*Continuous:*
**2 Samuel 7.1-14a**
Psalm 89.20-37
Ephesians 2.11-end
Mark 6.30-34, 53-end

### 2 Samuel 7.1-14a

*'The Lord will make you a house' (v.11)*

At last, David had peace from his enemies and – ever the man of action who had already built his own house – he turned to the idea of building a permanent house for the ark of God, which he had brought to Jerusalem with such rejoicing. It was perhaps not entirely coincidental that he thereby consolidated his own power by providing this temple for national worship. His good intention was initially endorsed by Nathan. But sometimes it is easier to start a project than wait for God to lead, and God had much greater ideas than David could imagine. While David thought of building physical houses for himself and God, God intended to build David a dynastic house beginning with Solomon (who would build a physical house for God), leading ultimately to the birth of the Son of God to a member of that dynastic house, Mary.

So God intervened to deflect David from his good idea in order to open the way for God's greater one. Centuries later, in a similar way, Peter proposed building dwellings to contain the experience of the transfiguration (Mark 9.5-7). But God will not be domesticated by us, however sincere our intentions. As Solomon later prayed at the dedication of his temple, even the highest heaven cannot contain God. The wonder is that this uncontainable God had begun to work in David's life and continues to do so in our lives.

*Reflection by* **Rosalind Brown**

**Jeremiah 23.1-6**
Psalm 23
Ephesians 2.11-end
Mark 6.30-34, 53-end

**Proper 11**

## Jeremiah 23.1-6

*'The days are surely coming, says the Lord' (v.5)*

Jeremiah takes us to the traumatic period after the Babylonians first conquered Judah in 597 BC. Over the next 15 years the remaining people were deported into exile or abandoned to eke out survival in Jerusalem's ruins. The theological challenges were as great as the physical survival challenges: the temple was destroyed, the supposedly eternal Davidic dynasty terminated, the land given by God to the people occupied by foreign enemies. Had God neglected and failed them, or been powerless to help?

'No!' said the prophet. It was all much more complex than that. Jeremiah claimed the Lord's action in this ending of the people's occupation of the land given to them (Jeremiah 21.5-7; 23.3, 8). The people's sin and the failure of their leaders had precipitated this disaster. The kings of Judah had scattered God's people, God's sheep. However, God was also involved, and the element of divine punishment driving them into exile reminds us never to lose sight of God's holiness and his call to his people to be holy.

God's involvement meant that this fate was not permanent, as it would be if only the leaders of nations were responsible. God alone could promise salvation. God was, and is, as determined to bless as to judge. God had salvific plans in mind and would do vastly greater things. The good news is that God is always doing something new.

*Reflection by* **Rosalind Brown**

**Proper 11**

*Continuous:*
2 Samuel 7.1-14a
Psalm 89.20-37

*Related:*
Jeremiah 23.1-6
Psalm 23

**Ephesians 2.11-end**
Mark 6.30-34, 53-end

## Ephesians 2.11-end

*'In him the whole structure is joined together' (v.21)*

Today's reading concludes with a number of construction metaphors. Christ is the master builder. He demolishes an old dividing wall – here between Jew and Gentile, circumcised and uncircumcised – and in its place he builds one temple. Himself he lays as the cornerstone; the prophets and apostles form the foundation, and from the cornerstone the whole building is constructed.

Human beings like to build walls – it makes us feel safe. In modern times, we have rejoiced to see some torn down, but we are just as adept at constructing them. It was little more than a decade between the tearing down of the Berlin Wall in 1989 and the commencement of the Israeli separation barrier in 2002. Even within the Church, it seems to be our natural inclination to construct barriers against those from different Church traditions and with opposing views on biblical or moral principles. Ephesians reminds us that the dividing walls that we establish to help us feel safe and secure against 'the others' are futile. There are no walls within the body of Christ; indeed, we need no walls, for our security is found in him, who loves and values all equally. Let us ask Jesus to show us those walls we need to begin dismantling – and start today.

*Reflection by* **Helen Orchard**

*Continuous:*
2 Samuel 7.1-14*a*
Psalm 89.20-37

*Related:*
Jeremiah 23.1-6
Psalm 23

Ephesians 2.11-end
**Mark 6.30-34, 53-end**

## Mark 6.30-34, 53-end

*'Come away to a deserted place all by yourselves' (v.31)*

Christian discipleship and ministry can be prone to high levels of guilt and exhaustion. It is to do with our expectations. Are we doing enough for God? The task is endless. The challenges are huge. And what is ever enough for God? So for some of us at least, a story of Jesus trying to arrange a few days off for his disciples because they are tired may come as a merciful reversal of our assumptions about what God expects of us.

Now, in my experience, no matter how far ahead a quiet day or retreat is planned in the diary, it is rarely convenient when it arrives. There are always compelling reasons for feeling we just can't take the time out. And in this story too 'the crowds' are pressing even as they arrive.

Do you need to hear Jesus say to you – 'come away for a while by yourself?' Notice the invitation is not to be with him in the first instance; it is to be with ourselves. What are you like at giving yourself space and solitude? It needs planning, but without it we can end up living at some distance from ourselves. As British psychotherapist and essayist Adam Phillips put it: 'Our lives take the form of an absence'. Jesus knows we need the spaces where we stop, we rest and we catch up with ourselves.

*Reflection by* **David Runcorn**

**Proper 12**

**Sunday between
24 & 30 July inclusive**

*Continuous:*
**2 Samuel 11.1-15**
Psalm 14
Ephesians 3.14-end
John 6.1-21

### 2 Samuel 11.1-15

*'But David remained at Jerusalem' (v.1)*

Things are very wrong from the start: kings should be with their troops in battle but David was lounging around on the roof of his palace. And so, 'it happened…' How much wrong happens because of a smaller wrong, a shirking of duty or a little relaxing of standards? The consequences turned this hitherto exemplary king, a man after God's heart, into a murderer.

This masterpiece of Hebrew storytelling leaves so much tantalizingly unsaid: for example, since most purification baths were covered, why was Bathsheba bathing naked in the open air? Did Uriah guess what was going on? Bathsheba's husband and father were members of David's personal bodyguard, so known to him, which makes his betrayal even worse. Uriah's utter loyalty to his king – and his rectitude when twice encouraged by his king to enjoy time with Bathsheba (to wash or uncover one's feet was a euphemism for sexual intercourse) while his colleagues ('my Lord Joab and the servants of my Lord') were sleeping on the battlefield – is expressed bitingly: Uriah refrained from commenting where his Lord the king was sleeping.

As a result, David dug himself deeper into a hole and had the temerity to send Uriah back with his own death warrant, relying on his trustworthiness not to open it. The Bible does not shirk from confronting us with unpleasant truths.

*Reflection by* **Rosalind Brown**

*Related:*
**2 Kings 4.42-end**
Psalm 145.10-19
Ephesians 3.14-end
John 6.1-21

**Proper 12**

### 2 Kings 4.42-end

*'A man came … bringing food from the first fruits' (v.42)*

This short vignette is too easily overshadowed by Jesus' feeding miracles. A map and some reading earlier in chapter 4 help us to understand what was going on and the distances Elisha travelled. Having been summoned to heal the child of a wealthy couple who had offered him hospitality in the past, Elisha then walked about 60 miles as the crow flies to Gilgal, where he found fellow prophets suffering from famine. He sent his servant to gather herbs but, unfortunately, the servant harvested something that gave them food poisoning. Elisha remedied the situation and they ate, but food remained scarce and faith was no doubt tested.

Then a stranger arrived. He too had travelled some distance, crossing from the foothills of the coastal plain over hills to the valley of the River Jordan. This was no simple journey and the man made it to fulfil the law by offering the first fruits of his harvest to the man of God. This faithful worshipper of God went to considerable inconvenience to fulfil his religious duty.

Elisha ordered that the food be shared, but his servant, ever the realist, complained it was not enough. However, as with Jesus' feeding miracles, there was enough and some left over. There is always abundance with God. But it depended upon the faithfulness of an unknown man who made a miracle possible, probably without realizing how urgently his gift was needed. There's a lesson in that.

*Reflection by* **Rosalind Brown**

**Proper 12**

*Continuous:*
2 Samuel 11.1-15
Psalm 14

*Related:*
2 Kings 4.42-end
Psalm 145.10-19
**Ephesians 3.14-end**
John 6.1-21

## Ephesians 3.14-end

*'I pray that you may have the power to comprehend' (v.18)*

Prayer, I suppose, is one of those activities that Christians engage in, but seldom pause to consider what it is they are doing. The habitual, impromptu and mysterious nature of prayer is part of its fascination. Here we have the language of faith, of desire, of hope, of healing – and even occasionally of justification and indignation.

Several years ago I was an honorary chaplain to a professional Rugby Club. I performed all the usual duties. Perhaps inevitably, in all the fracas and fury of a game, the name of God would often be invoked by the supporters. And after a crucial-but-missed-kick, my neighbour might turn to me and say, 'I don't think your boss is helping us much today.' The retort: 'Sorry. But I work in sales and marketing, not production.'

But prayer is not about success. Or even about winning. It is about attuning our hearts and minds to God, no matter what life throws at us. Today, across the world, there will be tragedy and triumph, joy and pain, birth and bereavement. Prayer won't change these realities. But it changes how we face them. There is only one place to begin with prayer, then. That in the midst of whatever we face, we will know the height, depth and breadth of God's love that surpasses all knowledge, and is made known in the fullness of Christ. If we know that, we won't know everything, but we will know enough.

*Reflection by* **Martyn Percy**

**Proper 12**

## John 6.1-21

*'Jesus ... withdrew again to the mountain by himself' (v.15)*

Jesus is persistently misunderstood by the crowds who flock to him. Today's passage opens with a large crowd following him 'because they saw the signs that he was doing for the sick'. He satisfies their physical hunger through a feeding miracle, and the pressure intensifies as they then hail him as a prophet and desire to make him king. This leaves Jesus little option but to withdraw to protect his true identity, because that identity can never be confined within human categories of power and authority, nor be twisted to serve a merely human self-interest.

But this withdrawal may signify more than simply a desire to disabuse the crowd of their wrong thinking. The graphic accounts of Jesus' time in the wilderness in Matthew (4.1-11) and Luke (4.1-12) make it vividly clear that the temptation to take the way of worldly power and acclaim was real. Earlier, Jesus made clear his total dependence on his Father and his inability to act rightly independently of that relationship (John 5.19). So this withdrawal enables Jesus to resist again the lure of earthly power and to strengthen his prayerful dependence on his Father (see Luke 5.16; Matthew 14.23).

When our actions bring praise and admiration, it can be difficult to resist the flattering ego-boost such praise generates. At such times an inner 'withdrawal' may help to remind us where the source of our abilities truly lies.

*Reflection by* **Barbara Mosse**

**Proper 13**

**Sunday between
31 July & 6 August inclusive**

*Continuous:*
2 Samuel 11.26 – 12.13*a*
Psalm 51.1-13
Ephesians 4.1-16
John 6.24-35

## 2 Samuel 11.26 – 12.13*a*

*'Why have you despised the word of the Lord?' (12.9)*

David's cunning plan worked: Uriah was killed and Bathsheba moved into the king's house (another reference to 'house', a theme running through all these stories of David). So far, so good.

But the Lord was angered and once more sent Nathan to speak to David about his actions. To be fair to David, when his actions were recast in story form and he fell straight into the trap set for him, he recognized his sin as being against God as well as Uriah and the other victims of his conniving. If we read on, we see that, in consequence, the baby died. This seems cruel, but God wanted to build a house for David and David's sinful action could not to be its foundation.

Bathsheba would later feature in the genealogy of the house of David (Matthew 1.6) through her son Solomon, but even there she is named as 'the wife of Uriah'. Just as God never forgot this episode, so neither do the biblical genealogists. Our sins cannot be written out of the story, but the good news is that there is redemption. God remained faithful to David and to Bathsheba, and she did become part of David's house, physical and dynastic. Furthermore, the wronged, foreign (Hittite) Uriah, the faithful bodyguard who was more righteous in this than David, also has his place in David's house.

*Reflection by* **Rosalind Brown**

*Related:*
**Exodus 16.2-4, 9-15**
Psalm 78.23-29
Ephesians 4.1-16
John 6.24-35

### Exodus 16.2-4, 9-15

*'Draw near to the Lord,*
*for he has heard your complaining' (v.9)*

After the jubilation of the crossing of the Red Sea, things have deteriorated quickly for Moses and the people. The water at Marah is bitter, until God sweetens it for them with a piece of wood (Exodus 15.25). The oasis of Elim gives way to the desert of Sin, and there they are hungry – so much so that they long to be back in Egypt.

God promises them 'bread from heaven'. It's a gift. Will they know the giver? God makes his presence known in a cloud of glory. It's a promise. Will they see? Even with life-giving bread in their hands they ask: 'What is it?'

'In the evening you shall know … and in the morning you shall see …', say Moses and Aaron in verses 6 and 7. Life is often tough, it's sometimes very bitter; it may be that your life is so at the moment. Whatever is going on, however much like the wilderness it seems, there are always signs of God's presence to be discovered. In the most difficult times and the hardest places, God is there; surprisingly seeking to refresh us, to feed us, to sweeten the bitterness and to remind us he hasn't left us. The question is, do we know it, do we see it?

Take time, in the evening and in the morning, to pause and to know that God is present and to see what God is doing.

*Reflection by* **John Kiddle**

**Proper 13**

*Continuous:*
2 Samuel 11.26 – 12.13a
Psalm 51.1-13

*Related:*
Exodus 16.2-4, 9-15
Psalm 78.23-29

**Ephesians 4.1-16**
John 6.24-35

### Ephesians 4.1-16

*'... maintain the unity of the Spirit in the bond of peace'*
*(v.3)*

When Christians get together, the unity they experience at those moments isn't something they create or decide among themselves. It is a gift – something given to them by God, when they begin to order their lives around one Lord, one faith and one baptism, growing through the exercise of the gifts of the Spirit in the Church, into 'the measure of the full stature of Christ'. That is why they are told in this passage to 'maintain' rather than 'create' the 'unity of the Spirit through the bond of peace' (v.3).

Yet it is a gift that is easily broken, damaged or lost. Proud, aggressive and impatient behaviour will find any excuse to break unity and cause division. So, these Christians are told to cultivate humility, gentleness, patience and forbearance – not the most exciting and dynamic set of qualities imaginable, but necessary if unity is to be maintained. True, Christian unity is not held at any cost. Yet, so often at the heart of disunity among Christians lies a lack of humility about our grasp of truth, pride that seeks power and control, a lack of sympathy and understanding of what makes others different.

Before unity is broken, we might at least ask ourselves whether we have really taken these factors seriously.

*Reflection by* **Graham Tomlin**

*Continuous:*
2 Samuel 11.26 – 12.13a
Psalm 51.1-13

*Related:*
Exodus 16.2-4, 9-15
Psalm 78.23-29

**Proper 13**

Ephesians 4.1-16
**John 6.24-35**

## John 6.24-35

*'I am the bread of life' (v.35)*

In the words of biblical scholar John Marsh, Jesus 'is the gift he brings'. 'The bread of life' is the bread that is the source of life, and also the 'living bread'. It nourishes us, fills us, satisfies us, enlivens us. The symbolism chimes with the Church's eucharistic practice, in which the body of Christ is ingested and becomes part of us, part of our life.

In the period between the Old and New Testaments, 'the manna in the wilderness' was interpreted as God's wisdom, which was itself the word of life and the fulfilment of the law. In taking to himself the divine word of revelation, 'I am', Jesus presents himself as this work of God's self-disclosure.

The bread is what God does: a gift that feeds the hungry; one that requires nothing of them but their acceptance that it is food and that it will indeed fill them. All we have to do – the only 'spiritual labour which makes it possible' to earn this food (as Anglican Franciscan scholar Barnabas Lindars put it) – is to accept and trust Jesus. John and Paul are at one in this.

To have this bread is to have life, life that is never going to be lost. The bread that 'comes down from heaven and gives life to the world' will not be lost, nor will any whom the Son has been given. Why? Because this filling up and making full, this fulfilment, is what God intends – and will ensure.

*Reflection by* **Jeff Astley**

## Proper 14

**Sunday between
7 & 13 August inclusive**

*Continuous:*
**2 Samuel 18.5-9, 15, 31-33**
Psalm 130
Ephesians 4.25 – 5.2
John 6.35, 41-51

### 2 Samuel 18.5-9, 15, 31-33

*'O my son Absalom, my son, my son Absalom!' (v.33)*

One consequence of David's adultery with Bathsheba was that his house would always experience violence (2 Samuel 12.10), and it did not take long to emerge. It began with his son Ammon raping his half-sister Tamar, thus setting in motion bitter revenge that led to Tamar's brother, Absalom, rebelling against his father and claiming the throne. David fled but regrouped his weary followers east of the River Jordan. The army insisted that, for his own safety, David should not fight when they went to battle against Absalom's soldiers in a forest some 40–50 miles away. The battle was widespread with a bloody outcome. Among the dead was the rebellious but beloved Absalom.

Guessing that David's grief would overshadow any joy at the victory, Joab sent a foreign mercenary (Cush was today's Ethiopia) as messenger. Apparently ignorant of the likely impact of his news, this man must have been open-mouthed at David's reaction of deep grief and inconsolable weeping which went on until a, no doubt panicked, message reached Joab and he came to remind the king of his royal duties (2 Samuel 19.1-8).

Absalom's death exposed all the ambiguity and unresolved issues for David in his complex relationship with Absalom. We cannot help but be moved by David's conflicted emotions and his heartache as the consequences played out. There is always room for compassion in the face of family breakdown.

*Reflection by* **Rosalind Brown**

*Related:*
**I Kings 19.4-8**
Psalm 34.1-8
Ephesians 4.25 – 5.2
John 6.35, 41-51

**Proper 14**

## 1 Kings 19.4-8

*'It is enough; now, O Lord, take away my life' (v.4)*

'What is God like?' This is faith's most fundamental question. It is one to which we return repeatedly, continually re-shaping our response as we catch further glimpses of the God who comes near to us and yet remains beyond our imagining. Each fresh revelation of his complexity deepens rather than clarifies the mystery of God.

Elijah has been contending alongside an elemental, rain-withholding, fire-breathing God who commands and directs his faithful lieutenant and battles against the powers of darkness. Yet in his exhaustion and brokenness, Elijah encounters not this relentlessness of God, but the tenderness of God who, like a mother, wisely ignores the petulant request of his over-wrought child and, instead, tucks him up in bed, cooks him his favourite dinner, wakens him to feed him and soothes him back to sleep again. And when, finally, God speaks with Elijah, it will not be with the irresistible command of a sergeant major but as 'a sound of sheer silence' (1 Kings 19.12) – in the silent dialogue of the soul with its Creator, where understanding is felt as much as it is articulated.

Elijah wants to die because he envisages only an implacable God with whom he can no longer keep pace. Instead Elijah encounters a deeply compassionate God who enables him to go on living. Settling for what we have already seen of God can obscure rather than reveal him. Instead, we are to continue to seek him and, when we think we have seen him, to go on looking.

*Reflection by* **Mary Gregory**

| **Proper 14** | *Continuous:*<br>2 Samuel 18.5-9, 15, 31-33<br>Psalm 130 | *Related:*<br>1 Kings 19.4-8<br>Psalm 34.1-8 |
| | **Ephesians 4.25 – 5.2** | |
| | John 6.35, 41-51 | |

## Ephesians 4.25 – 5.2

*'... be kind to one another, tender-hearted, forgiving one another, as God in Christ has forgiven you' (v.32)*

In the radical letter to the Ephesians, the Christian community is depicted as a foretaste of the coming age, when all things will be brought together under Christ (Ephesians 1.10). It is to be a place where a new way of life can be learned – one that anticipates the coming kingdom of God. This is a community unmarked by the common human traits of dishonesty, anger and greed. Instead, it is a place where we learn to 'clothe [our]selves with the new self' (Ephesians 4.24) – to put on a new way of life.

Christian behaviour, therefore, isn't simply a list of things you don't do. In this community, people don't just stop lying; they learn to speak the truth to each other, even if that is hard sometimes. They don't bottle up anger, but learn to deal with it quickly, rather than letting it fester and eat away at their spiritual and emotional health. Those with a tendency to grasp for themselves learn not only to stop thieving, but positively to start working so they have something to give away. They learn not just to hold back on hurtful words, but to find affirming things to say to build up other people.

Positive action, not just negative abstinence – how might that work out in your life this week?

*Reflection by* **Graham Tomlin**

*Continuous:*
2 Samuel 18.5-9, 15, 31-33
Psalm 130

*Related:*
1 Kings 19.4-8
Psalm 34.1-8

Ephesians 4.25 – 5.2
**John 6.35, 41-51**

### John 6.35, 41-51

*'Is not this Jesus, the son of Joseph …?' (v.42)*

To be known by our association to others – 'so you're Wendy's sister/George's wife/Peter's colleague/Anita's friend …' – can be both a blessing and a curse. Even with regard to the best of relationships, to be defined by our connection to others can feel belittling. We feel this not only when it means we are dismissed, but also if it seems as if it's the reason we are honoured.

Jesus was being discounted because of his family ties. Although we are told that he honoured Mary and Joseph, we also know that his identity, though shaped by them, was not determined by them. It was his identity as the son of his heavenly Father that provided his security: 'the one who is from God; he has seen the Father'.

Letting go of our labels may be a relief or it may be a threat. However we feel about our personal relationships, we too are offered a new identity in Christ as joint heirs of the kingdom and recipients of the promise of eternal life. Our identity in Christ is a gift from God, and frees us to become who God desires us to be, not what others expect us to be.

Our new identity offers security but is a challenge as well as a comfort. The bread of life, broken for us, is given for the life of the whole world. Like those first disciples, we too are required to share what we have been given.

*Reflection by* **Libby Lane**

**Proper 15**

**Sunday between
14 & 20 August inclusive**

*Continuous:*
I Kings 2.10-12; 3.3-14
Psalm 111
Ephesians 5.15-20
John 6.51-58

### 1 Kings 2.10-12; 3.3-14

*'Solomon loved the Lord ...; only, he sacrificed and offered incense at the high places.' (3.3)*

When God invites Solomon to ask him for what he wanted, he is setting the young man quite a challenge. The temptation for him must surely have been to take full advantage of the offer, in order to assure for himself riches and popularity. But Solomon's response indicates a depth of wisdom beyond his years, and God's response demonstrates the truth of some of the later teaching of Jesus about seeking God's kingdom first of all (Matthew 6.33).

Solomon's powers of discernment are soon, famously, to face an even sterner test as he is approached by two prostitutes, both claiming to be the mother of the same baby (1 Kings 3.16-28). Demonstrating God's gift of 'an understanding mind' and with acute psychological insight, Solomon quickly distinguishes the attitude and response of the true mother from that of the fraud.

Even at this early stage, however, one or two disquieting hints indicate that all is not quite as it should have been. Solomon's marriage to the daughter of Pharoah king of Egypt must, given the history of the two nations, have put the integrity of the kingdom at risk. And this was coupled with delays in the completion of the temple, forcing Solomon and his people to sacrifice 'at the high places', with all their negative associations of pagan worship (cf. Leviticus 26.30; Numbers 33.52). This lack of single-heartedness was ultimately to cost Solomon dear.

*Reflection by* **Barbara Mosse**

*Related:*
**Proverbs 9.1-6**
Psalm 34.9-14
Ephesians 5.15-20
John 6.51-58

## Proverbs 9.1-6

*'Lay aside immaturity, and live' (v.6)*

Some years ago, the Eagles had a big hit with a song called 'Hotel California'. It tells the story of a 'dark desert highway' where a driver found an alluring hotel to stop for the night. He found himself in a place of drinking and easy women where 'some dance to remember, some dance to forget'. The mood suddenly turns sinister and he hears distant voices calling, 'we are all just prisoners here of our own device'. And then the desperate last verse where the nightman says 'you can check out any time you like, but you can never leave'.

It sounds like a cover version of an earlier song in Proverbs 9, where a choice is set before the reader, between the House of Wisdom (vv.1-6) and the Hotel California (vv.13-18). Wisdom invites us in to 'lay aside immaturity, and live, and walk in the way of insight'. Clearly a good choice. But, if you skip ahead to the end of Proverbs 9, the woman outside the Hotel California invites us in because 'stolen water is sweet, and bread eaten in secret is pleasant'. And then in a terrible echo of the song, 'they do not know that the dead are there, that her guests are in the depths of Sheol'.

To a greater or lesser degree, this is the choice we face every day. Are we going to choose the way of life and hope, or the way of fear and folly? Very many of our decisions will turn us one way or the other – not dramatically but inexorably. Most of what we do today is charged with significance. Live well!

*Reflection by* **John Pritchard**

**Proper 15**

*Continuous:*
I Kings 2.10-12; 3.3-14
Psalm 111

*Related:*
Proverbs 9.1-6
Psalm 34.9-14

**Ephesians 5.15-20**
John 6.51-58

### Ephesians 5.15-20

*'... making the most of the time' (v.16)*

Time. Our relationship with it is one of the great stressors of our age. There is never enough of it. Our obsession with finding faster ways of doing things makes no difference. 'Time management' is one of the most frequent searches on the internet. But 'making the most of the time' suggests something different. There is certainly a call to live wisely and responsibly here, but rather than a call to improve our organizational skills we are being invited to live in time's fullness. This is not about the quantity of time managed so much as the quality of time lived.

If we are to make the most of the challenges and opportunities of life, we will a need a trusting relationship with time. Without it, our best intended activities will tend to be anxious, driven, reactive and increasingly lacking in depth.

What might it mean to live as if there really is time enough?

Time is God's gift. So the first response might be to develop a habit of gratitude in relation to it. God allows time to be time. Time gives life its priority and direction. There is gift in the constraints time places upon our activities. Without time, nothing would have any more significance than anything else. Time is not working against us or denying us our truest vocation.

Therefore thank God for time.

*Reflection by* **David Runcorn**

*Continuous:*
1 Kings 2.10-12; 3.3-14
Psalm 111

*Related:*
Proverbs 9.1-6
Psalm 34.9-14

**Proper 15**

Ephesians 5.15-20
**John 6.51-58**

### John 6.51-58

*'… my flesh is true food' (v.55)*

Nourishment is about calories and hydration, balance of proteins and carbohydrates, minerals and vitamins – necessary for our physical and mental wellbeing. But, for those of us blessed with plenty and choice, being well fed is not only about sustenance but is also one of life's pleasures. It is about taste and texture, aroma and visual stimulus. It is sensual as well as practical, often about experience as well as function.

'Taste and see that the Lord is good' the psalmist encourages us (Psalm 34.8). That sounds as though being nourished by God gives pleasure as well as sustenance.

Jesus says that he is our true food. The word made flesh, broken for us, is the source of real food that nourishes, sustains and delights us. What are the ways that we can 'feed' on him? If Jesus is our true food, perhaps there are other things that falsely claim to feed us. So, what else might we be relying on for that which Jesus best supplies?

It is not, necessarily, that other things that feed our sense of wellbeing are not good in themselves. But how do we avoid inappropriately relying on them instead of Jesus? Or allowing them to detract from Jesus rather than glorify him? How, instead, might we recognize and acknowledge Christ in life's pleasures, and in the people and things that give us support and help us to flourish?

*Reflection by* **Libby Lane**

**Proper 16**

**Sunday between
21 & 27 August inclusive**

*Continuous:*
1 Kings 8.[1, 6, 10-11] 22-30, 41-43
Psalm 84
Ephesians 6.10-20
John 6.56-69

## 1 Kings 8.[1, 6, 10-11] 22-30, 41-43

*'... this house that I have built' (v.43)*

The work on the temple is finally complete, and Solomon assembles all the elders and leaders of the tribes of Israel to witness the triumphant dedication. Central to the ceremony is the bringing up of the Ark of the Covenant, symbol of both God's presence with his people and a reminder of his covenant with them, to its final resting place in the inner sanctuary of the temple. But we step aside from the narrative of Solomon's life and reign for a moment in order to reflect on a significant crossroads in the faith and belief of the Israelites.

The text at this point is laden with images resonant of Israel's religious past. Once the Ark had been installed and the priests re-emerged from the holy place, 'a cloud filled the house of the Lord ... for the glory of the Lord filled the house of the Lord'. The image conflates two symbols redolent of the exodus, where the glory of the Lord appeared in the cloud that accompanied the Israelites on their daytime wanderings through the desert (Exodus 16.10). But alongside these images of the immediate presence of God, a more mysterious reality is emerging: one that sees God as dwelling in deep darkness (8.12). The temple has indeed been built as a fitting dwelling place for the Lord, but its dedication is accompanied by a growing awareness that 'even heaven and the highest heaven' cannot contain him.

*Reflection by* **Barbara Mosse**

*Related:*
**Joshua 24.1-2a, 14-18**
Psalm 34.15-end
Ephesians 6.10-20
John 6.56-69

### Joshua 24.1-2a, 14-18

*'... as for me and my household, we will serve the Lord'*
*(v.15)*

The 24 chapters of the book of Joshua tell of the Israelites' invasion and conquest of Canaan and the division of the land under the leadership of Joshua. In this final chapter, Joshua's parting shot is to throw out a challenge to his people who already were beginning to forget what God had done for them. They were starting to lose their cutting edge, and were flirting with idols and foreign gods. Joshua must have felt something close to despair when he saw how easily their faith in God would slip and slide away.

So, in verses 3–13 he reminds them how far they have come. Beginning with Abraham, he recounts the story of God's people and reminds them of just how much God has done for them. And then he throws out the challenge. 'Choose this day whom you will serve'. Who is it going to be – the foreign gods or the one true God? Make a decision.

How often do we challenge each other and ourselves about where our allegiance lies? What's it to be on Sunday – shopping and football practice – or worshipping God? What's it to be – a narrow focus on money and ambition, or a lifestyle that places God at its centre?

To follow Christ is a conscious decision – and one that we're challenged to renew from time to time, so that we can say with hand on heart, 'As for me – I will serve the Lord'.

*Reflection by* **Jan McFarlane**

**Proper 16**

*Continuous:*
1 Kings 8.[1, 6, 10-11]
22-30, 41-43
Psalm 84

*Related:*
Joshua 24.1-2a, 14-18
Psalm 34.15-end

**Ephesians 6.10-20**
John 6.56-69

### Ephesians 6.10-20

*'... take up the whole armour of God ... stand firm' (v.13)*

'Spiritual warfare' is a forceful image for some of our experiences of the Christian life, which often feels like a trial of strength with forces that work both against our human good and contrary to God's healing power.

For some, including the writer of this letter, these spiritual forces are real entities – divinely created agents to whom God gave limited power to exercise on behalf of his providential rule. But they have 'got above themselves', and perverted that authority to their own ends.

For others, including many readers today, this is figurative language that labels the 'false gods' that we chose to value above the one, true God. Putting our faith and vesting our hope in what is less than God is what gives these penultimate centres of value an alien power over us – one that we cannot bend by our own strength or break by our own efforts.

At any rate, this passage is certainly full of potent metaphors of determination and protection: 'standing', 'putting on' and 'taking'; 'armour', 'belt', 'breastplate' and 'shoes'; 'shield', 'helmet' and 'sword'. Kitted out in the figurative protection of this divine body armour – which represents the toughness of truth, righteousness, peace, faith and God's word – neither real nor symbolic evil forces will be able to shift us.

As long as we stand our ground.

*Reflection by* **Jeff Astley**

**Proper 16**

### John 6.56-69

*'You have the words of eternal life' (v.68)*

The author of the Father Brown stories, G. K. Chesterton, wrote: 'The Christian ideal has not been tried and found wanting. It has been found difficult; and left untried.' Jesus' listeners found much of what he said difficult, it seems. Jesus' words were not simply dismissed by those who were opposed to him. Those who were closest to him also struggled with what he was saying. There is a lot that we might find difficult about Jesus' teaching today too. Perhaps we find it too complex: what does he mean? Maybe we consider it too troublesome: what does he expect? For some it may seem too offensive: who does he think he is? It is demanding, difficult. Is it therefore too much?

'The Christian ideal', as Chesterton puts it, does stretch us in every way. Following Jesus makes demands on the ways we think, the ways we act, the ways we feel. However, it offers a great deal more than it demands. Jesus, Simon Peter recognized, has the words of eternal life. Indeed, the writer of the Gospel of John would have us realize, Jesus is the Word of Life.

Perhaps it's only possible to follow the demands that we hear through the words of Jesus if we hear them as those in a relationship with the one who speaks them. Perhaps this teaching is too difficult unless, through Jesus' love for us and in us, his words become 'spirit and life'.

*Reflection by* **Libby Lane**

## Proper 17

**Sunday between 28 August &
3 September inclusive**

*Continuous:*
**Song of Solomon 2.8-13**
Psalm 45.1-2, 6-9 [or 45.1-7]
James 1.17-end
Mark 7.1-8, 14, 15, 21-23

### Song of Solomon 2.8-13

*'Arise, my love, my fair one, and come away' (v.13)*

In the first century, Rabbi Akiva famously said of the Song of Songs: 'The entire age is not so worthy as the day on which the Song of Songs was given to Israel. For all the scriptures are holy, but the Song of Songs is the holiest of all.'

According to Genesis 3, humankind is created for intimate relationship. It is not good for anyone to be alone. We are created for relationship with one another, as man and woman become one flesh in marriage. We are created for intimate relationship with God in fellowship and in prayer. 'What is the chief end of man?' says the old catechism (meaning humanity). 'The chief end of man is to know God and enjoy him forever.' Knowing is, of course, the biblical word for intimacy.

The Song of Songs celebrates the passion and love that is possible between two people, which is itself a mirror and likeness of God's love for creation and for humankind as the pinnacle of creation. And so we place ourselves within this lover's song. In the words of the ancient poem, we praise the life and vitality we see in the risen Christ. And we hear the words of invitation as God's personal words of love to us this day: '… the winter is past … Arise, my love, my fair one, and come away'.

*Reflection by* **Steven Croft**

*Related:*
**Deuteronomy 4.1-2, 6-9**
Psalm 15
James 1.17-end
Mark 7.1-8, 14, 15, 21-23

**Proper 17**

## Deuteronomy 4.1-2, 6-9

*'... give heed to the statutes and ordinances' (v.1)*

The Hebrew verb for 'observance' (v.1) denotes having charge over, tending, and keeping watch like a sentinel. Such vigilance is required in responding to God's commands. There is a common misconception about the Old Testament religion – that it was all about works or observance of the law. We forget that these people did not become God's people by observing the laws but they were given these laws because they were God's people already.

But why laws? First, the laws of the Lord are the source of life. The purpose of obedience is 'that you may live'. Holding fast to the Lord is life. The nearness of God and the righteous laws are closely related. The righteous laws being kept by God's people are a manifestation of the presence of God.

The laws of the Lord are also seen as the rules that would govern the people of God. These statutes are 'just' or 'righteous'. They facilitate right relationships all around. They underline the communal and corporate dimension of faith. Our trust in God determines how we relate to each other and our concern for the weak, the poor and the stranger.

The laws of the Lord also have a missional dimension. When people observe the laws, their reputation for wisdom, intimacy with God and righteousness will grow (v.6). It will help them achieve their missionary role of bringing blessing to other peoples.

*Reflection by* **John Perumbalath**

**Proper 17**

*Continuous:*
Song of Solomon 2.8-13
Psalm 45.1-2, 6-9
[or 45.1-7]

*Related:*
Deuteronomy 4.1-2, 6-9
Psalm 15

**James 1.17-end**
Mark 7.1-8, 14, 15, 21-23

### James 1.17-end

*'... look into the perfect law, the law of liberty' (v.25)*

How do you live in the real world? What is the real world anyway? Is the bottom line, in reality, 'do to others before they do to you?' – a first-strike policy? Therefore, should Christians get real and leave humility and meekness behind, following the path of pre-emptive aggression by which we might create real security and defence? Certainly, some paths of the commercial and political world would tell Christians to 'Get real' in this way.

But James is uncompromisingly clear in his claim that the real world comes from the Father of lights, who purposed to give us birth by the word of truth. Reality is made up of deep listening, wise speaking, great patience, compassionate action and honest self-reflection. The real world involves caring for the marginalized and distressed without being contaminated by 'the world'. The world in this case is the way things are arranged by Caesar, whose commercial and militarist world view dehumanized and commodified thousands of human beings.

So, James says, 'Don't forget who you are': do not look at yourself as in a mirror, but look to the law of freedom in God and look to walking in humility and acting with justice. These are the real wheels that turn the world in the end, not the lords and governors.

*Reflection by* **David Moxon**

*Continuous:*     *Related:*

Song of Solomon 2.8-13    Deuteronomy 4.1-2, 6-9

Psalm 45.1-2, 6-9     Psalm 15

[*or* 45.1-7]

James 1.17-end

**Mark 7.1-8, 14, 15, 21-23**

### Mark 7.1-8, 14, 15, 21-23

*'This people honours me with their lips,*
*but their hearts are far from me' (v.6)*

'You hypocrite!' – the accusation we all dread, but have probably faced at some time or another. It is an easy insult for atheists to throw at Christians: we have a high calling in the pattern of Christ, but continually fail to live up to it and actually practise what we preach.

In today's passage, it is Jesus who accuses the overtly religious of his day, the Pharisees, of hypocrisy – not for failing to observe their traditions, but for overdoing it to a ridiculous degree and thereby missing the point. Their strict practices are derided by Jesus as external human traditions standing in opposition to the commandments of God, which instead make demands on the heart.

The fact of the matter is, however, that we all extend, distort and subvert the commandments of God to some degree because, despite being so straightforward, they are so very challenging to honour. They are no less than the whole-hearted love of God with heart, mind, soul and strength – and the genuine and sacrificial love of the most difficult neighbour. Far easier to busy yourself with ritual washing than grapple with what that means each day.

*Reflection by* **Helen Orchard**

**Proper 18**

**Sunday between**
**4 & 10 September inclusive**

*Continuous:*
**Proverbs 22.1-2, 8, 9, 22, 23**
Psalm 125
James 2.1-10[11-13] 14-17
Mark 7.24-end

### Proverbs 22.1-2, 8, 9, 22, 23

*'The rich and the poor have this in common:*
*the Lord is the maker of them all' (v.2)*

'The rich man in his castle, the poor man at his gate, God made them high and lowly, and ordered their estate.' These words comprise the long-omitted third verse of that perennial children's hymn, 'All things bright and beautiful'. They were written in the 19th century, a time when it was believed that the state of life into which a person was born was fixed, part of the divine order of things. A complacent reading of verse 2 of today's passage could be open to the same interpretation: the way people are and the position they hold in society is the way God created them and intended them to be.

It is possible, however, to read this verse as a critique of the human tendency to classify and fix people's status, rather than as an endorsement of it. In later verses (vv.7-8), weight is given to the view that society's injustices are human in origin, not divine. Jesus also continued to challenge society's judgements on the powerless. So the rich are condemned for their lack of charity towards the poor (Luke 16.19-31), and a child is held up as a model for those wishing to enter God's kingdom (Matthew 18.3). Jesus himself counted tax collectors and sinners among his companions (Mark 2.13-17), and he refused to condemn an adulterous woman, offering her the chance of a new beginning (John 8.1-8).

How do we think about, and behave towards, the 'poor' in our midst?

*Reflection by* **Christopher Herbert**

**Proper 18**

### Isaiah 35.4-7a

*'For waters shall break forth in the wilderness,
and streams in the desert' (v.6)*

In today's reading, the prophet Isaiah paints a picture of a twofold life-giving transformation – a people brought to life and a land restored to beauty and fertility.

Weak hands, feeble knees and fearful hearts are strengthened. The blind find sight, the deaf hear; legs and tongues are loosed in joy. These are the people of God, not superheroes, but simply and wonderfully those whose lives have been touched and changed by the beauty of God – ordinary children, women and men who daily know what it is to be extraordinarily strengthened, healed and set free by God's joyful transforming presence.

There is a further transformation in Isaiah's vision – the transformation of the desert. God brings life and strength to his people, and he brings water to the desert. As God's restored people walk the way, life is brought to the land through which they pass.

The people of God are not simply those who know God's transforming power in their own lives; they are those who, through their love and prayers, their life and generous courageous action, bring transformation and healing to the communities and the world in which they live and the deserts they walk through. Celebrate the transformation that God has brought to your life by living a transformed and transforming life. Walk the way gently, generously and gratefully.

*Reflection by* **John Kiddle**

**Proper 18**

## James 2.1-10[11-13] 14-17

*'You do well if you really fulfil the royal law ...' (v.8)*

The French Revolution's cry of 'Liberty, Equality, Fraternity' seems unexpectedly to find a precursor here in the Letter of James. God in Christ, according to James, has called Christians to 'the law of liberty'. And what is this law of liberty? It is to show no favouritism; to avoid making distinctions on the grounds of wealth or social status; to put such distinctions away forever. Equality is its watchword: equality of regard. And what is to be the fruit of this equality of regard? Love and mercy. These create the special bond of Christian fellowship whose French Revolutionary equivalent was fraternity.

Where the French Revolutionary would surely baulk, however, is in the claim that this 'law of liberty' is also a 'royal' law. What has royalty to do with such ideals? Why talk of kingship in the same breath as saying we must make no social distinctions?

Yet here is the secret: this is the true royalty that puts a revolutionary end to all the most unjust or self-serving pretensions of earthly rule. It is not the royalty that the Judges in ancient Israel knew was a dangerous burden for the people to take upon themselves: a royalty so easily corrupted. It is the royalty that alone guarantees the mercy, the love, the freedom from favouritism that allows humans to flourish together, while even the most high-minded revolutionaries fall back into being victims of their own 'evil thoughts'. It is the royalty of the crucified.

*Reflection by* **Ben Quash**

Continuous:
Proverbs 22.1-2, 8, 9, 22, 23
Psalm 125

*Related:*
Isaiah 35.4-7*a*
Psalm 146

James 2.1-10[11-13] 14-17
**Mark 7.24-end**

### Mark 7.24-end

*'Sir, even the dogs under the table eat the children's crumbs'*
*(v.28)*

A feisty, foreign woman argues with Jesus. We applaud her persistence, wit and guts, but we can also see the inner struggle of Jesus as he explores the expansion of his vocation to include the gentiles.

Jesus naturally feels drawn to minister among the 'chosen people' of God – but, instead of welcoming him, the Jewish religious leaders are suspicious, confrontational. In this encounter, we can almost hear Jesus wrestling with the paradox: he longs to bring to the 'children' the good news of God's grace, but his actual experience repeatedly tells him that those who grasp his divine uniqueness, who are open to his loving message, are often not the Jews but the 'others', those deemed 'outsiders' because of their gender, race, traditions or illness, or those whose work evokes public censure.

While Jesus' words to the woman might seem harsh to us initially, in this interaction she helps us to see the pivotal moment when part of old Simeon's prophecy (Luke 2.29-32) takes flesh. Jesus becomes for the desperate woman 'a light for revelation to the gentiles ...' as he shares with her something of his divinity, pronounces longed-for healing for her child, and consciously embraces both gentile and Jew.

How have you seen the call of God on your life change and expand in unexpected ways?

*Reflection by* **Sue Pickering**

## Proper 19

**Sunday between
11 & 17 September inclusive**

**Proverbs 1.20-33**
Psalm 19 [*or* 19.1-6] *or Canticle:*
Wisdom of Solomon 7.26 – 8.1
James 3.1-12
Mark 8.27-end

### Proverbs 1.20-33

*'How long will scoffers delight in their scoffing ...?' (v.22)*

Remember the worldwide banking crisis of 2007? At the time there was an outcry of anger about the leadership of the banks. One might have expected some radically serious changes to follow. There have been some, yet, according to the European Banking Authority, 160 of the UK's most senior bank executives enjoyed a huge increase in their 2014 average fixed pay, which more than doubled to 1.51 million euros ...

It looks as though the banking leaders have 'scoffed' at the public, treating us with insolence (as other translations of verse 22 put it). Insolence is a word more often used in the classroom ('Take that look off your face'), than it is in the boardroom. But it's a word with wide applicability and deserves to break out beyond the classroom's walls. It implies an attitude towards others that is dismissive. Scoffers, says Proverbs, with a sharp eye on human behaviour, delight in their scoffing. More than that, it continues, 'fools hate knowledge'.

And what follows for those who scoff and are foolish? There is, says Proverbs, a kind of universal moral retribution awaiting them ... 'the complacency of fools destroys them'. That, I gently suggest, is a statement of fact. And for us? How are we to deal with our own incipient desire to scoff? By learning humility – that is, by recognizing that integrity can only be achieved when we kneel before God and with as much honesty as we can muster, see ourselves as God sees us ... and seek his forgiveness and mercy.

*Reflection by* **Christopher Herbert**

*Related:*
**Isaiah 50.4-9***a*
Psalm 116.1-8
James 3.1-12
Mark 8.27-end

## Isaiah 50.4-9*a*

*'It is the Lord God who helps me' (v.9)*

Isaiah knew both the power of the tongue of a good teacher who chooses words to sustain weary listeners and his own calling to teach. With this knowledge he first took his place as a disciple and placed himself in the position of a listener woken every day by God. It was not just Isaiah who was wakened: specifically God wakened his ear so he could listen as one who is taught. That image suggests we can have sleepy ears that are unable to listen and prevent us from learning.

Because of his opened ear, Isaiah was not rebellious but could set his face like flint in the face of opposition. This deliberateness, even stubbornness, reflects Isaiah's experience that God's calling not only made him a disciple but also threw him on God's mercy and protection in the face of adversaries out to shame him. Even if he faced accusation in court, he could assert that God helped him, asking rhetorically 'who will declare me guilty?'

Yet, as Jesus knew, this does not result in instant deliverance because God's ways are not like our ways. Hence the paradox that there can be insult and spitting as well as not being put to shame: one day accusation will simply wear out and, in the ultimate indignity, a tiny moth will eat up the accusers. To comprehend that requires open, non-rebellious listening to the God who wakes us each morning.

*Reflection by* **Rosalind Brown**

**Proper 19**

*Continuous:*
Proverbs 1.20-33
Psalm 19 [*or* 19.1-6]
*or Canticle:* Wisdom of
Solomon 7.26 – 8.1
**James 3.1-12**
Mark 8.27-end

*Related:*
Isaiah 50.4-9*a*
Psalm 116.1-8

### James 3.1-12

*'Does a spring pour forth from the same opening both fresh and brackish water?' (v.11)*

If Jesus had only a few seconds to speak of the kingdom that was coming through and around him, many scholars think he would say something like 'It is not what goes into a person that defines them, but what comes out of them ... for out of the heart comes good and evil.' Jesus is recorded as saying this kind of thing in all three Synoptic Gospels, and it seems to be at the heart of his message.

James, his disciple, in this passage is picking up this central point by commending us to guard our heart, have a care for what comes out of us, to use our mouths to elevate, not desecrate, to build up, not to tear down. There is no point in having a reformation of structures and a revolution in politics if what comes out of the mouths of people continues to be prejudicial, or cruel or malicious. We are called to an internal reformation, a revolution of the heart that brings forth a new way of thinking or speaking.

We are called to be transformed by the renewal of our minds, as Paul said. Then, the renewal of structures becomes viable. It can go something like this: love, then justice, then peace, although they are all totally interdependent in a holistic gospel. Jesus brings in a new creation through our hearts and minds.

*Reflection by* **David Moxon**

*Continuous:*
Proverbs 1.20-33
Psalm 19 [or 19.1-6]
*or Canticle:* Wisdom of
Solomon 7.26 – 8.1
     James 3.1-12
     **Mark 8.27-end**

*Related:*
Isaiah 50.4-9*a*
Psalm 116.1-8

**Proper 19**

### Mark 8.27-end

*'... he rebuked Peter and said, 'Get behind me, Satan!' (v.33)*

Poor Peter: one minute he's top of the class, and the next he's being ticked off.

Jesus has been growing in popularity as he travels about teaching, healing and feeding thousands, and now Peter is convinced: Jesus is the Messiah. But then something unexpected happens. Instead of capitalizing on his popularity, Jesus starts talking about suffering, rejection and death. This doesn't square with Peter's expectations. The Messiah was going to be a powerful leader who would defeat the Romans and establish a prosperous Israel. At least, that's the plan he signed up for.

But Peter has to learn that the road of revolutionary triumph is not the route they will be taking. Instead, it's a path involving denial of self and the giving up of life to gain life. Peter's whole understanding of why he was following Jesus has been swept away. It's not going to be glorious; it's going to be grim. Why does he stay? Because, even though he doesn't understand or like the sound of the new plan, it is God's plan and he trusts in Jesus, the one who will bring it to completion. Peter will come to know that, as the famous nineteenth-century preacher C. H. Spurgeon said: 'There are no crown-wearers in heaven who were not cross-bearers here below.'

*Reflection by* **Helen Orchard**

**Proper 20**

**Sunday between
18 & 24 September inclusive**

*Continuous:*
**Proverbs 31.10-end**
Psalm 1
James 3.13 – 4.3, 7-8*a*
Mark 9.30-37

### Proverbs 31.10-end

*'… more precious than jewels' (v.10)*

Over the years there have been many different reactions to this passage. Some have laughed at the impossibility of any woman fulfilling this 'superwoman' image: managing the household, buying land, providing food 'while it is still night', while at the same time planting a vineyard 'with the fruit of her hands'. Some branches of feminism have rejected it outright, seeing it as either offensively patriarchal, or simply an impossible ideal.

But are both these reactions missing the point? These verses form a hymn to wisdom where the illustration on this occasion happens to be 'a woman who fears the Lord'. For a proper sense of balance we should also read Psalm 112, where 'the man who fears the Lord' (ESV) acts as a counterpart. In the psalm, the man who fears the Lord is praised for a corresponding faithfulness and set of accomplishments. Both the psalm and our passage from Proverbs are acrostics (where each line begins with successive letters of the Hebrew alphabet), and both focus on the wise and energetic activity of the person described.

The aim here seems to be neither to devalue women, nor to demand that they fulfil an unattainable ideal. Rather it seems to point to the values of wisdom and discernment that enable a person – man or woman – to live rightly, justly, and to the full measure of their God-given ability. These values are as vital today as they ever were.

*Reflection by* **Christopher Herbert**

**Proper 20**

### Jeremiah 11.18-20

*'I was like a gentle lamb led to the slaughter' (v.19)*

Jesus is a prophet yet much more than a prophet. He stands in the long line of God's messengers who came not simply to deliver words but to bear witness in their lives to God's great love for his people.

The prophets' witness was often costly and involved pain, rejection, suffering and sometimes death. This is true of Jeremiah more than anyone. His ministry was in the generation leading up to the destruction of Jerusalem, and his word was one of judgement. His prophecy is punctuated by cries of lament and many tears for the suffering he endured.

This passage is one such lament. Jeremiah protests his innocence. The image of the gentle lamb led to the slaughter will be echoed in Isaiah 53.7 and again in all the language that describes Jesus as the Lamb of God. Jesus, too, is innocent of all charges against him and the victim of schemes and false accusation leading to his trial and his death.

Yet there is also a key difference between Jeremiah and Jesus. The prophet cries out, as we would do, for judgement and vengeance on his persecutors. The one who is more than a prophet is the one who prays even from the cross: 'Father, forgive them; for they know not what they do' (Luke 23.34).

*Reflection by* **Steven Croft**

**Proper 20**

*Continuous:*
Proverbs 31.10-end
Psalm 1

*Related:*
Wisdom of Solomon
1.16 – 2.1, 12-22 *or*
Jeremiah 11.18-20
Psalm 54
**James 3.13 – 4.3, 7-8*a***
Mark 9.30-37

### James 3.13 – 4.3, 7-8*a*

*'Draw near to God, and he will draw near to you' (4.8)*

Every Christian wears an invisible sign around their necks, which reads 'work in progress' or 'be patient with me, God has not finished with me yet', or 'you should have seen what I was like before'. James reminds us that conversion is an ongoing evolution as we are transformed spiritually. This is not a super-religious, pious activity, but a day-by-day growing in integrity, faithfulness and hope. We are always growing out of the ways of the world and always growing into the ways of God. There is some ambiguity in this that every Christian learns to understand and work with. We have been saved, we are being saved, we shall be saved.

Each little victory over the ways of the world such as gluttony, aggression or hardness of heart is a possibility of growth in God. By contrast, James' description of envy, leading to murder, is the most dramatic of all the New Testament, challenging us to be so careful with the state of our emotions. We are called to see ourselves as learners in 'the way' by paying deep attention to the state of our heart and by shaping what we feel and think with consistent, attentive prayer, so that we are guided by the light within us rather than the shadows around us.

*Reflection by* **David Moxon**

| Continuous: | Related: |
| --- | --- |
| Proverbs 31.10-end | Wisdom of Solomon |
| Psalm 1 | 1.16 – 2.1, 12-22 *or* |
| | Jeremiah 11.18-20 |
| | Psalm 54 |

James 3.13 – 4.3, 7-8*a*
**Mark 9.30-37**

**Proper 20**

### Mark 9.30-37

*'Whoever welcomes one such child in my name*
*welcomes ... the one who sent me' (v.37)*

The other day, a church member asked me what I was going to do about the behaviour of two young children who had recently started coming to church. This incident put me in mind of this verse, where Jesus, having declared that true greatness is a matter of humble service, goes on to give as an example of humble service the way in which we welcome young children. Children had little by way of rights or status in the Greco-Roman world, and so Jesus says that how we welcome young children is actually a measure of how we welcome God the Father.

The status of children in society may have risen hugely since Jesus' day, but are we any better at welcoming children in our churches? When I was a diocesan missioner, I was invited to speak to many different Parochial Church Councils about how to help their churches grow. I used to ask them, 'What do you really, really want?' Time and again their replies boiled down to this: 'What we really, really want is to see more children and young people coming to the kind of services that we (the PCC members) like.' How realistic is that?

And yet Jesus said the welcome we give to a child is the welcome we give to God the Father.

*Reflection by* **Mark Ireland**

*Continuous:*
**Esther 7.1-6, 9, 10; 9.20-22**
Psalm 124
James 5.13-end
Mark 9.38-end

### Esther 7.1-6, 9, 10; 9.20-22

*'... as they were drinking wine' (7.2)*

One of the striking motifs of the book of Esther is the repeated description of lavish banquets. Three are called by the king, the second in honour of Queen Esther (Esther 2.18); one is called by the deposed queen Vashti; two are called by Esther; and the book closes with joyful Jewish banquets foreshadowing the great festival of Purim.

Today's reading shows Esther using the social apparatus of the banquet to triumphant political effect. With an impeccable sense of timing, our heroine holds her nerve until the second day of her second banquet before disclosing her true identity as an imperilled Jewess.

By this stage Ahasuerus, the Persian king, is both curious and merry with wine. Seizing the moment to gain his ear, Esther speaks out boldly to reveal the genocidal plan that will not simply threaten her own life but, more tellingly as far as the king is concerned, bring shame and dishonour to his royal court.

It is this combination of shrewdness and audacity that plays so effectively into the purpose of a guiding providence. If we can speak of a theology in the book of Esther, then the working of the unnamed God of the Jews is decisively enacted through the astuteness and courage of his endangered people. Even with horrific consequences at stake, Esther appreciates that there is 'a time to keep silence, and a time to speak' (Ecclesiastes 3.7).

*Reflection by* **Margaret Whipp**

*Related:*
**Numbers 11.4-6, 10-16, 24-29**
Psalm 19.7-end
James 5.13-end
Mark 9.38-end

**Proper 21**

### Numbers 11.4-6, 10-16, 24-29

*'Would that all the Lord's people were prophets ...!' (v.29)*

So, here we have a congregation numbed by nostalgia, crying out for the good old days when things were better done, and a put-upon pastor, wearied by the back-biting crying, to God: 'It's all too much for me!' Sound familiar?

Now, as then, our God hears and addresses both these complaints; now, as then, he challenges the fantasies and meets the true needs. Moses must learn to delegate, and the people must learn to find the real goodness that God gives in the here and now, not the fantasy food of memory. Ah, but delegation is no easy thing. You may share a burden, but you put people's backs up too. Joshua had basked in the glory of being Moses' one and only number two, and was jealous of the likes of Eldad and Medad, who prophesied just where they were in the camp. But Moses looks forward with us to Pentecost and says: 'Would that all the Lord's people were prophets, and that the Lord would put his spirit on them!'

Even today, most congregations have an over-zealous Joshua, who needs to take a step back, and some shy 'Eldads' and 'Medads', who need encouraging. If we can let the past be past, and meet God in the here and now, there will indeed be meat and manna for the journey.

*Reflection by* **Malcolm Guite**

241

**Proper 21**

*Continuous:*
Esther 7.1-6, 9, 10;
9.20-22
Psalm 124

*Related:*
Numbers 11.4-6, 10-16,
24-29
Psalm 19.7-end

**James 5.13-end**
Mark 9.38-end

### James 5.13-end

*'The prayer of the righteous is powerful and effective' (v.16)*

This passage presents us with a conundrum. It suggests that prayer is answered (especially, in this case, prayer for the sick) in a real and healing way: 'The prayer of faith will save the sick, and the Lord will raise them up'. But the writer makes the prelude to this claim a series of injunctions to learn from those who are especially patient – those who are models of how to wait. Be like a farmer, the writer says; be like a prophet; be like Job (James 5.7-12).

This is to capture two aspects of the experience of prayer, both of which are well and widely attested to in the Christian Church. There are very many Christians who will testify with joy to the fact that they have known their prayers to be answered and felt the effectiveness of God's grace powerfully in their lives. But there are others who have dwelt in a dark night of the soul, questioning where God is and what God's will might be.

I am not sure that the Letter of James wants to resolve the apparent tension between these two aspects of prayer; equally, it does not want to deny either type of experience. Christians are to pray with a patience that sets no ultimatums. And yet ... they are to pray in the real expectation of an answer. The waiting that strains forward needs accompaniment by a straining forward that knows how to wait.

*Reflection by* **Ben Quash**

### Proper 21

### Mark 9.38-end

*'Whoever is not against us is for us' (v.40)*

You can hear Jesus gearing up for what is to come. It's no good shilly-shallying around anymore. The disciples are missing the point; they just don't get it. And unless they do, they are worse than useless – 'a stumbling block' to others – and no fate is bad enough for them. They need to know that their discipleship is for real. It's not about who belongs to the in-group, and who doesn't; it's much bigger than that. Jesus exaggerates for effect, to stress just how crucial it is that these disciples of his are there, for him, as he faces life and death. His call burns like fire; it purifies like salt.

Think of the times when a commitment is required, a decision has to be made. The run-up is hard: your mind goes back and forwards, weighing over different options, arguments with others rehearsed in your mind, unsure what to do for the best. Then, suddenly, sometimes out of the blue, the way forward becomes clear. You know where you are going. The doubts and uncertainties fall away.

Jesus uses the image of an ordinary cup of water, given to you to drink. You are thirsty, and the water is fresh and cold. You feel the shock as it reaches your stomach and begins to revive you. That's what the clarity is like, when an ordinary decision is made, commitment taken. How much greater the clarity when we respond and say 'yes' to the name of Jesus Christ!

*Reflection by* **Frances Ward**

**Proper 22**
**Sunday between**
**2 & 8 October inclusive**

*Continuous:*
Job 1.1; 2.1-10
Psalm 26
Hebrews 1.1-4; 2.5-12
Mark 10.2-16

### Job 1.1; 2.1-10

*'Shall we receive the good at the hand of God,*
*and not receive the bad?' (v.10)*

The book of Job starts with an almost fairy-tale 'once upon a time' introduction, and the story is set in 'the land of Uz', somewhere to the east. We are dealing here not with history, nor the salvation-saga of Israel, but with universal human experiences and dilemmas, reflected on through story telling.

The story teller depicts for us the Lord presiding over heavenly beings ('sons of God', in the original) who act as courtiers in heaven and divine agents on earth. Among them is Satan 'the accuser' (Revelation 12.10), whose role seems to be to sniff out hypocrisy and disaffection among human beings and to draw it to the Lord's attention.

And so we meet him today, casting aspersions on the sincerity of Job's outstanding piety. Already Job has lost his whole wealth, and heard of the deaths of all his children at a single stroke, and yet remained devout and resigned. But Satan is suspicious. Can resignation and piety persist in the face of extreme physical pain?

How admirable is resignation, anyway? In the voice of Job's wife, the question is posed whether human nobility might not rather reside in defiance and death. What do *you* think about that?

*Reflection by* **Maggie Guite**

*Related:*
**Genesis 2.18-24**
Psalm 8
Hebrews 1.1-4; 2.5-12
Mark 10.2-16

**Proper 22**

### Genesis 2.18-24

*'... whatever the man called each living creature,
that was its name' (v.19)*

Gratuity is under threat in our world. We are trained in more and more aspects of our lives to justify our expenditure – of effort, of time, of money – in ways that are quantifiable and goal-oriented – that are, in other words, narrowly utilitarian.

In this passage, Adam is invited into God's delighted work of naming the creatures. He is a participant in the generous dynamic of blessing that is at Creation's very source. He finds himself surrounded by a world of trees, planted by the Lord God, and these God-given trees are first described as pleasant to the sight, and only second as good for food (Genesis 2.9).

Perhaps there is a hint here of what our world has lost. The pleasure of the eyes may not be a bare necessity of life, but when our only priority is with how we can make things *work* to serve our needs, we make lives that are hard to live and impossible to enjoy. The gratuitous 'excess' in things is not just some trivial 'icing on the cake' compared with the mechanics of production and consumption; it is a witness to why it is worth producing and consuming at all. We can live in a way that corresponds to this 'excess' in things by enjoying and not just using them.

Adam and Eve changed their relationship to that 'gratuitous' tree that was not for their use when they began to suspect it might do something for them.

*Reflection by* **Ben Quash**

**Proper 22**

### Hebrews 1.1-4; 2.5-12

*'... crowned with glory' (2.9)*

We hear in the Eucharistic prayer that we sing together 'with angels and archangels, and all the company of heaven'. But isn't this fanciful and an unreachable reality?

This passage encourages us to imagine it in such a way that we give it some space in our heads and hearts: perhaps we give it some contemplative attention, so that in the end we're inspired to live differently, knowing that this beauty exists perhaps just out of earshot.

In Chronicles, we read that David appointed Asaph and other musicians, including trumpeters, to 'make one sound ... in praising and thanking the Lord' (2 Chronicles 5.13, KJV). In worship, we sing to express not only our earthly unity, but also our unity with the angels and with the whole of creation. Angels are not rulers of creation, but they are the invisible bonds of creation. Worship binds heaven and earth together, and we worship in time and eternity each time we pray. The 'glory' that the writer speaks of is a translation of the Hebrew word that also means to shine. Music makes glory visible (and audible) in the temple and the worship of God. Joining with the angels is our purpose on earth.

As philosophers have seen a link between beauty and justice, so we are to understand that the glory of God that we experience in worship gives us energy and inspiration to live the life Jesus lived, even though we know we are bound to die. We are, like he was for a while, just a little lower than the angels.

*Reflection by* **Lucy Winkett**

*Continuous:*
Job 1.1; 2.1-10
Psalm 26

*Related:*
Genesis 2.18-24
Psalm 8
Hebrews 1.1-4; 2.5-12
**Mark 10.2-16**

**Proper 22**

## Mark 10.2-16

*'Because of your hardness of heart ...' (v.5)*

These words of Jesus shocked the first disciples. And perhaps that is the first thing we must allow them to do to us – just shock us.

Invited to join a debate about divorce, Jesus completely ignores the long-running rabbinic discussions about 'strict' or 'liberal' approaches that we now know to be the hidden background to this discussion. He insists on returning to God's first intention, re-centring the debate around the original gift and vocation to marriage in Creation. But it is still hard to hear.

And isn't the gospel about God's mercy upon humanity in its brokenness and failures? But it may be that the debate had become so absorbed with defining the provisions for what is broken that it had lost touch with the original gift and call – and therefore with God's judgement or mercy upon our frailty within it. There is no other starting place. Our hope is found here.

For wherever we, in the rawness of our broken dreams, failed intentions or wilful misdoings, come to Jesus for his mercy, we are not turned away against some pitiless measure of religious perfection. There is another shock in store here. He welcomes us – takes us up in his arms and blesses us into the hope of healing and new beginnings.

*Reflection by* **David Runcorn**

**Proper 23**

**Sunday between
9 & 15 October inclusive**

*Continuous:*
Job 23.1-9, 16-end
Psalm 22.1-15
Hebrews 4.12-end
Mark 10.17-31

### Job 23.1-9, 16-end

*'O that I knew where I might find him,
that I might come even to his dwelling!
I would lay my case before him' (vv.3-4a)*

The book of Job presents us with a God-fearing and righteous man who finds his whole life in ruins: his cattle, sheep and camels have been stolen and his servants have been killed; his sons' and daughters' lives have been lost to a tornado and Job himself has been afflicted with terrible sores. Beyond these disasters, however, Job's torment is compounded by the way in which his only remaining friends are convinced that he must have done something to deserve his misfortune.

Job's laments and protests occupy much of the book. He cannot accept that he deserves this fate and he cannot believe that God is unjust. So he wrestles with his friends and with God, choosing to believe that he would be acquitted if only God would meet with him.

In this passage, Job complains at the paradox that though he searches for God, he cannot find him in order to put his case to him. At the same time he feels God's hand heavy upon him and wishes he could hide from the pressure of God's seemingly terrible impact upon his life.

When disaster strikes in our own lives it can be easy either to blame ourselves or to blame God. Job offers a third path, which is to live with the questions themselves and keep on asking until, perhaps, in Rainer Maria Rilke's words, 'we might live into the answers'.

*Reflection by* **Jane Leach**

*Related:*
**Amos 5.6-7, 10-15**
Psalm 90.12-end
Hebrews 4.12-end
Mark 10.17-31

### Proper 23

## Amos 5.6-7, 10-15

*'Hate evil and love good, and establish justice in the gate' (v.15)*

Reading Amos is like walking on burning coals. His words were written to shake a complacent world and to proclaim God's judgement. Here he speaks of the coming judgement in the form of a lament – a song that puts into words the grief and pain of the community. There are many laments in the book of Psalms, so this is a familiar kind of song. But Amos has not composed his lament for something that has happened but for something that is going to happen. It is a song for the future tragedy being played out before the prophet's eyes.

All of the sins of the Israelites are described in striking images: turning justice to wormwood and bringing righteousness to the ground; trampling the poor; pushing aside the needy. The two great virtues of justice and righteousness are lifted up. The violence underneath the pictures is condemned. Christians cannot read the words of Amos without reflecting on the injustice in our own society and across the world.

Yet, there is a glimmer of hope here and a clear indication that it is not yet too late for Israel. Three times the appeal rings out in this chapter: seek me and live; seek the Lord and live; seek good and not evil that you might live. There is space yet for turning and renewal, and that is the purpose of the prophet's preaching. The renewal of justice and righteousness will begin with a renewal of personal faith in the Lord.

*Reflection by* **Steven Croft**

**Proper 23**

*Continuous:*
Job 23.1-9, 16-end
Psalm 22.1-15

*Related:*
Amos 5.6-7, 10-15
Psalm 90.12-end
**Hebrews 4.12-end**
Mark 10.17-31

### Hebrews 4.12-end

*'Since, then, we have a great high priest who has passed through the heavens' (v.14)*

In today's passage, the writer to the Hebrews makes a bold assertion: Christ is the great high priest whose inner sanctuary is heaven itself. Jesus is like any priest in that his personal sufferings are part of his offering to God. He prays for himself and for others, he deals gently with those who are struggling because he is aware of his own weakness. He has been through the same trials and temptations as we have, and yet, unlike us, he has not fallen short. All this should give us the ultimate confidence to trust him as we approach God with our particular needs.

Yet we misunderstand our great high priest if we assume his obedience was effortless. Even as the Son of God, he needed the discipline of prayer. 'In the days of his flesh, Jesus offered up prayers and supplications, with loud cries and tears' (Hebrews 5.7). He was not spared the dilemmas and ambiguities that test us every day. His human life, like ours, was a pilgrimage towards God's perfection.

The fourth-century theologian Gregory of Nazianzus insisted on the reality of Christ's humanity with the statement, 'That which he has not assumed he has not healed'. Our salvation depends not only on Christ's divine Sonship, but on the authenticity of his human struggle.

*Reflection by* **Angela Tilby**

Continuous:
Job 23.1-9, 16-end
Psalm 22.1-15

Related:
Amos 5.6-7, 10-15
Psalm 90.12-end
Hebrews 4.12-end
**Mark 10.17-31**

**Proper 23**

### Mark 10.17-31

*'Jesus, looking at him, loved him ...' (v.21)*

You can't help feeling rather sorry for this rich young man.
And it seems that Jesus did too. Again, from Mark's Gospel we
receive a clear and unequivocal message about what it takes,
and what it means, to follow Jesus. Jesus has been teaching
about eternal life, the age to come, when God will bring in his
kingdom. Who enters that kingdom was the big question for
those who lived around Jesus, as they began to realize that
he held the key. So, it is not enough to fulfil the
commandments – the rich young man had done so since he
was young. Entry into the kingdom means total response, so
that nothing is more important. That's treasure in heaven.

The conversation evidently left Peter uncomfortable. 'How
much is enough?' He wants to know. Jesus' response has a
sting in the tail that challenges even further. Yes, Peter, you
have left everything – and in due course you'll receive
everything back a hundredfold. But don't forget the
persecutions thrown in for good measure: Peter, who will
hang upside down on a cross to die. It's hardly an attractive
option, the way Mark presents discipleship. This good news is
strange indeed.

I wonder what happened to the rich young man. Did life just
continue as before? Or did that gaze of love enter his soul?
Perhaps, in an age to come, he was St Francis.

*Reflection by* **Frances Ward**

**Proper 24**

**Sunday between
16 & 22 October inclusive**

*Continuous:*
**Job 38.1-7[34-end]**
Psalm 104.1-10, 26, 35c [or 104.1-10]
Hebrews 5.1-10
Mark 10.35-45

### Job 38.1-7[34-41]

*'Then the Lord answered Job out of the whirlwind' (v.1)*

After 37 chapters of Job's protests and God's silence, finally God speaks, and to indicate the profound nature of God's self-revelation, he speaks out of the whirlwind as one who commands the wind and the waves. Job has waited for this moment, but he has also feared it. Part-horrified by the idea of a God who would punish him unjustly, and part convinced that God has taken him by the collar and thrown him into despair, like other heroes of the Hebrew Bible, Job is ambivalent about meeting God face to face and senses that he will not come away unscathed.

Religious belief that does not expose itself to the awesome-ness of encounter with God is not faith at all but a last defence against God. This is perhaps part of the problem with Job's friends who have been 'comforting him' since chapter 2. Convincing themselves of their own orthodoxy, not once do they risk the kind of prayer in which their views might be challenged or reframed. So full of answers, how would they fare in the face of God's questions? Prepared to declare Job wrong, how would they cope with the demolition of their own world view and the pillars of sound reasoning, long-held tradition and divine inspiration on which they thought it was built?

And we – what defences do we use against God's awesome, wild and life-changing power?

*Reflection by* **Jane Leach**

**Proper 24**

### Hebrews 5.1-10

*'... he learned obedience through what he suffered' (v.8)*

Two features of Israelite priesthood are mentioned in our passage: every priest was *called* and every priest must *sympathize*. Those two features are worked through, first in relation to the ancient Hebrew priesthood and then in relation to Christ. The Hebrew priest had to 'deal gently' with the wayward, remembering that he himself is a sinner. The Greek here actually goes beyond externalities ('deal gently') to the priest's inner life: he is to 'feel for' the people. As for the second point, as we have seen, the priest is also called, since 'one does not presume to take this honour' – even if that calling comes through family and birth.

What was said last about the ancient Hebrew priesthood is said first about Christ. He was called, or 'appointed' by God. Then, just like the priesthood of old, he is also full of sympathy. In his case, that follows not from being a sinner among sinners, but from having suffered every human woe as one of us. In a reference that reveals the author to be familiar with gospel stories, he invokes the agony in the Garden of Gethsemane. Jesus, who was perfect as God, became also the perfect human being. He was 'made perfect', not in the sense of having previously been lacking, but in the sense of having offered his life perfectly to God, right to the end. In this way, his divinely perfect humanity becomes what will perfect our errant humanity: 'having been made perfect, he became the source of eternal salvation for all who obey him'.

*Reflection by* **Andrew Davison**

[1] *For a reflection on Isaiah 53.4-12, see page 124.*

**Proper 24**

*Continuous:*
Job 38.1-7[34-end]
Psalm 104.1-10, 26, 35c
[*or* 104.1-10]

*Related:*
Isaiah 53.4-end
Psalm 91.9-end

Hebrews 5.1-10
**Mark 10.35-45**

### Mark 10.35-45

*'... whoever wishes to be great among you must be your servant' (v.43)*

Whether or not the audacious appeal from James and John is consistent with their nickname, 'sons of thunder' (Mark 3.17), it reveals the universal, human dynamic of wanting to be first, 'a cut above' everyone else.

Jesus responds to their request for places of honour by questioning their understanding. Their eyes still shuttered by ego-driven needs, the wider wonder of the nature of the kingdom of God eludes them. Nor can they grasp the cost of discipleship when, without hesitation, they answer 'yes' to Jesus' question: 'Can you drink ...?' They are oblivious to the solemnity of his reply – they *will* 'drink his cup' and experience the same 'baptism', but not in the way they expect. Their request naturally angers their fellow disciples and draws a clear reminder from Jesus that he came *to serve* and that that is what he expects of his disciples – then and now.

The miracle is that, in the early days of Christianity, both James and John lived and died *in the service* of others. Their attitude of 'me first' was transformed by the Holy Spirit into 'others first', expressed in James' martyrdom and in John's foundation of a vibrant community and, authenticated by recent scholarship, the gift of the Gospel that bears his name.

Are we living a 'me first' or an 'others first' life?

*Reflection by* **Sue Pickering**

**Job 42.1-6, 10-end**
Psalm 34.1-8, 19-end [*or* 34.1-8]
Hebrews 7.23-end
Mark 10.46-end

**Proper 25**

**Sunday between**
**23 & 29 October inclusive**

### Job 42.1-6, 10-end

*'... therefore I despise myself,*
*and repent in dust and ashes' (v.6)*

Job listens to what God has to say. He is not intimidated by God into retracting his questions. He is not crushed by God into acknowledging a guilt he does not feel. He is treated as a person of dignity who will be heard and will be trusted to discern wisdom when he hears it, for God is no bully. God is simply good – and, faced with God's goodness and wisdom and strength in the face of chaos, Job's heart begins to sing.

Translating verse 6 creates all sorts of problems. Does Job end despising himself? What does he retract? Of what does he repent? Although scholars disagree, the Latin American liberation theologian Gustavo Gutiérrez suggests that the Hebrew is best translated as Job turning away from his attitude of 'dust and ashes' – Job puts away mourning and lamenting, and begins, in spite of all his troubles, to dance. No longer putting himself at the centre of things, he can praise God for God's goodness; he can pray for those who have wronged him and know the joy of being one who forgives.

And, although the story ends with the restoration of Job's fortunes – his wealth and standing, and even his descendants – this is no reward to reinforce the doctrine of retribution. Rather, God's free grace simply overflows as a sign of the life he wills and labours to bring to birth for all.

*Reflection by* **Jane Leach**

**Proper 25**

*Continuous:*
Job 42.1-6, 10-end
Psalm 34.1-8, 19-end
[*or* 34.1-8]

*Related:*
¹Jeremiah 31.7-9
Psalm 126

**Hebrews 7.23-end**
Mark 10.46-end

### Hebrews 7.23-end

*'... a high priest, holy, blameless, undefiled, separated from sinners, and exalted above the heavens' (v.26)*

The argument in Hebrews for the supreme effectiveness of Christ's priesthood continues as the comparison between the old and the new is developed further. The old Levitical priesthood was inevitably imperfect. Its imperfection actually pointed towards 'another priest' (Hebrews 7.11, 13, 15), who would be different and better, whose new powers would not be compromised by his having been part of an 'imperfect' priestly family.

The coming of Christ as high priest transforms the law requiring priests to be descended from Levi, because the life he brings is simply indestructible; its validity is proved by its total efficacy. In addition, Christ's priesthood is not ended by death, nor is it weakened by his need to offer sacrifice for his own sins before performing the sacrifices for his people. Christ as high priest simply cannot let us down. He is eternally ready to save us; 'he always lives to make intercession' for us.

The profound invitation of this chapter is to offer our prayer consciously through Christ, to see him in our mind's eye as one who stands before the Father on our behalf, taking with him into God's presence all our needs and fears and failures. He is our guarantee of God's good intent towards us, the ultimate fulfilment of God's promise to visit and redeem his people.

*Reflection by* **Angela Tilby**

¹ *For a reflection on Jeremiah 31.7-9, see page 55.*

*Continuous:*
Job 42.1-6, 10-end
Psalm 34.1-8, 19-end
[*or* 34.1-8]

*Related:*
Jeremiah 31.7-9
Psalm 126

Hebrews 7.23-end
**Mark 10.46-end**

### Mark 10.46-end

*'... he cried out even more loudly, 'Son of David, have mercy on me!' (v.48)*

This is one of the stories that forms the basis of the ancient 'Jesus Prayer', a rhythmic prayer taught and practised within the Eastern Orthodox tradition: 'Lord Jesus Christ, Son of God, have mercy on me a sinner.' The plea for mercy can sound, to Western ears, rather grovelling and negative. But here, on the lips of this blind man, it is a bold cry of hopeful longing for healing and transformation.

It is clear from this and other stories in the Gospels that Jesus loves a faith that takes him on. He teaches us to ask, knock and seek. There is an important place for bold initiative in Christian faith that balances a tendency to stress careful submission.

Bartimaeus models for us this less-encouraged way of approaching Jesus. It is a long way from lowered voices, polished phrases and the bowed heads of Sunday intercession: 'Lord in your mercy, hear our prayer.' This is faith shouted aloud by the public roadside, crying out for what he cannot see but hears is near, enduring the hostility of those around and refusing to be quiet until Jesus stops and pays attention. And Jesus does just that. And the man's prayer is answered.

*Reflection by* **David Runcorn**

[1]Isaiah 55.1-11
Psalm 19.7-end
2 Timothy 3.14 – 4.5
John 5.36b-end

## 2 Timothy 3.14 – 4.5

*'All scripture is inspired by God and is useful for teaching,*
*for reproof, for correction, and for training in righteousness'*
*(v.16)*

In verse 16 of this chapter we find one of the few occasions where Scripture takes a step back and says something about itself as Scripture. The rest of the chapter in which this verse sits helps us to understand what is being said. The overall setting is one of distress, temptation and persecution. Against that background, the role of Scripture becomes all the more clear. It provides stability, right judgement, and a plumb line in uncertain times.

Our passage also sets its statement about Scripture within the context of Timothy's wider human experiences. In particular, it sets Scripture within the story of the various examples who have helped him to faith and theological understanding: both Paul ('you have observed my teaching, my conduct' and so on) and Timothy's family ('continue in what you have learned ... knowing from whom you learned it, and how from childhood you have known the sacred writings').

2 Timothy 3.16 sets out an important statement about the authority and usefulness of the Bible. In the rest of the passage, we learn why this 'teaching ... reproof ... correction, and ... training in righteousness' is important, and why the family of the Church is the natural and best place to receive the truths of the Scriptures with full understanding.

*Reflection by* **Andrew Davison**

[1] *For a reflection on Isaiah 55.1-11, see page 153.*

Isaiah 55.1-11
Psalm 19.7-end
2 Timothy 3.14 – 4.5
**John 5.36b-end**

### John 5.36b-end

*'... seek the glory that comes from the one who alone is God' (v.44)*

Who is in the dock here? Jesus calls his witnesses for the defence: himself (but this, regrettably, is inadmissible in the law), John the Baptist (who is described as the lamp lit from the light), Jesus' own works and the Father. An impressive line-up.

But the author knows that it is Jesus' enemies who are really on trial. They have ignored all the evidence, even the testimony of God. They have pored over the Scriptures but entirely missed the point of them, neither hearing God's voice through them nor allowing God's word to live within themselves.

The problem here is the problem of the source of glory. Seeking and accepting it 'from human beings', 'from one another', has blinded them to the true light that can only come from God – from the one whose glory transcends everything that the world has to offer.

Perhaps it does all begin, as it must end, with love. Unless we want God, unless we have love for God, we will never want the Son or acclaim his works as the works of a loving father. Love comes first, before worship and before belief. If we want a God we can 'believe' in – a God whom we can love and praise – we must first believe in love. For 'whatever your heart clings to and confides in, that is really your God' (Martin Luther). And we can only worship the true God.

*Reflection by* **Jeff Astley**

Wisdom 3.1-9 *or* [1]Isaiah 25.6-9
Psalm 24.1-6
**Revelation 21.1-6a**
John 11.32-44

## Revelation 21.1-6a

*'See, the home of God is among mortals' (v.3)*

The message of the last chapters of Revelation (20–22) is that God chooses to make his home with redeemed humanity. This beautiful vision of the new Jerusalem 'coming down out of heaven from God' illustrates God's desire for all human beings to find their true home with one another – in other words, to be saints, living icons of God's presence. This can only come about as an act of new creation. 'See, I am making all things new'. Yet the author cannot conclude the vision without declaring judgement against those who reject that call to holiness and homeliness with God and one another. Those who have betrayed God's trust cannot endure the heavenly city. So, according to the agonized logic of Revelation, even the heavenly city is incomplete without its opposite, the lake of fire, described in the verses following today's reading. This is the ultimate deterrent and safeguard. There must always be a place where destructive behaviour can be contained by destruction.

This warning note may be disturbing. But the finality of judgement is qualified by the inviting words of the one sitting on the throne: 'To the thirsty I will give water as a gift from the spring of the water of life'. The thirst for life always meets a response from God. The emergence of the city of God may be a certainty, but the chance for life is never withheld from those who desire it. While there is life, there is, indeed, hope.

*Reflection by* **Angela Tilby**

[1] *For a reflection on Isaiah 25.6-9, see page 136.*

Wisdom 3.1-9 *or* Isaiah 25.6-9
Psalm 24.1-6
Revelation 21.1-6*a*
**John 11.32-44**

**All Saints' Day**

**1 November** *Principal Feast*

### John 11.32-44

*'Jesus began to weep' (v.35)*

The characters of Mary and Martha come to the fore in this passage. Martha, the frank-speaking one, has already gone out to meet Jesus to tell him that, if he had been with them, her brother wouldn't have died. Mary, though equally puzzled, reluctantly comes out and, weeping, kneels at his feet.

Together these women reveal the parts of bereavement that we will know something about – the questions and anger and frustration – and then the helplessness and submission to what has happened. When Jesus sees Mary crying, John says he did something. The English translation says that Jesus wept. John does not quite say this though. He says that Jesus shuddered with anguish; the Greek word implies a sort of snorting with fury, with flared nostrils, displaying an anger in his sadness. Perhaps it was an anger at the powers of sickness, death and human pain. If so, it reminds us in a Gospel that might sometimes appear to lead us another way, that Christ was fully human.

The seventeenth-century bishop Jeremy Taylor sometimes spoke of the 'gift of tears', an important challenge to the embarrassment we can often feel at our own or others'. Likewise, the poet John Donne prays that God will 'pour new seas into mine eyes' so that his world might be either drowned or washed. Jesus cried and, in doing so, blesses our tears and confusions and hurt. It may be part of the Christian vocation to help people cry better.

*Reflection by* **Mark Oakley**

## Fourth Sunday before Advent

**Sunday between 30 October &
5 November inclusive** *(For use if the
Feast of All Saints is celebrated on 1 November)*

Deuteronomy 6.1-9
Psalm 119.1-8
Hebrews 9.11-14
Mark 12.28-34

### Deuteronomy 6.1-9

*'The Lord is our God, the Lord alone. You shall love...' (v.4)*

The Great Commandment in verse 4 is the pivot around which everything else in Deuteronomy revolves. This is also known as the Shema, meaning 'hear' or 'listen', which became the creed that Jews recited every day. Everything else – obedience to God's law, not testing God, passing on our faith to the next generation, and avoiding the pitfalls of prosperity – comes out of our love for God.

The commandment starts with a statement. The phrase 'Lord alone' – literally 'YHWH one' in Hebrew – is ambiguous. We are not sure whether it suggests oneness in God's being or it means that in the midst of other gods Israelites should worship this God alone. Our language of God is always ambiguous and inadequate.

We have difficulty finding a language to understand the God of the Old Testament stories. More often we think about a warrior and violent God, but a passage like this underlines the lovingness of God and God as worthy of love. It also paints people's commitment to God in a fresh light. Loving God is not performance of some external duties but a matter of heart searching and looking inward too.

The Great Commandment tells us not to fall into the trap of legalism and the pursuit of works as the way of salvation. Awesome demands of the law are certainly present but assertions of love and grace are too. God's positive action is love always and it begs our love as response.

*Reflection by* **John Perumbalath**

Deuteronomy 6.1-9
Psalm 119.1-8
**Hebrews 9.11-14**
Mark 12.28-34

**Fourth Sunday before Advent**

## Hebrews 9.11-14

*'[Christ] entered once for all into the Holy Place' (v.12)*

Are there still holy places? In this section of the letter to the Hebrews, the writer contrasts the elaborate arrangements made for creating a holy place in which sacrifices for sin could be made under the old covenant – with 'cherubim of glory overshadowing the mercy-seat' (Hebrews 9.5) – with the new covenant under which Jesus 'entered once for all into the Holy Place' to make the sacrifice that can never be repeated. It's as if Christ himself has become the Holy Place. And he is with us, and he is everywhere.

So are there still holy places? Many of us have an instinct that some places have a tangible feeling of holiness. A medieval church building can feel prayed in. The open moor can seem full of the Creator's presence. And on the holy islands around our shores (including, of course, the Holy Island of Lindisfarne), we can sense the 'thin' quality of the setting and the presence of the saints. So can these places be holy? I think they can – but perhaps what's going on is that their particular holiness is a gift to show us that all places are holy, and that the Christ can be found in every place. So wherever you are today, may you sense the holiness of each place you are in, and the presence of Jesus the Christ, the Holy Place.

*Reflection by* **Ian Adams**

**Fourth Sunday before Advent**

Deuteronomy 6.1-9
Psalm 119.1-8
Hebrews 9.11-14
**Mark 12.28-34**

### Mark 12.28-34

*'There is no other commandment greater than these' (v.31)*

Nowadays, in our secular society, many people reverse the order of the two great commandments on which Jesus and this young lawyer are both agreed. A good relationship with other people is recognized as the overriding public imperative for everyone, but a good relationship with God is often written off as an optional extra, the private choice of a religious minority of no importance to anybody else.

But the wisdom of ancient Israel knows that how you understand the second commandment is defined by whether or not you acknowledge the priority of the first. Whom I recognize as my neighbours and what I think is involved in loving them depends on what I believe about what ultimately makes the world tick the way it does. If it is a Darwinian world ruled by the survival of the fittest, there will not be many neighbours and not much love. But if it is the world created, claimed and redeemed by the triune God of the gospel, then his love as shown in Christ will be the model that challenges and inspires all my relationships with other people.

As John put it, 'We love because he first loved us' (1 John 4.19).

*Reflection by* **Tom Smail**

**Jonah 3.1-5, 10**
Psalm 62.5-end
Hebrews 9.24-end
Mark 1.14-20

### Third Sunday before Advent
**Sunday between
6 & 12 November inclusive**

### Jonah 3.1-5, 10

*'The word of the Lord came to Jonah a second time' (v.1)*

Jonah, when first called to go to Nineveh, had gone in exactly the opposite direction but now had a second chance to get his map reading right. God repeated the instruction and Jonah finally headed to this imposing city, surrounded by nearly 8 miles of ramparts with 15 gates, which was situated on trade routes near Mosul in modern Iraq. Its population was at least 120, 000 and its magnificent architecture expressed Assyria's power and wealth.

This pagan capital city of Israel's oppressor was to experience God's judgement. Yet God first sent Jonah to call it to repent. When Jonah reluctantly obeyed, the miraculous happened, and even the king of Nineveh put on sackcloth and sat in ashes, decreeing that everyone, human or animal (!), should fast and pray. No preacher could ask for a better response! God in turn responded, changing his mind about the city's fate.

Both Jonah and Nineveh had second chances from God and the chapter ends on a high note. But, read on, and we realize that Jonah had a big problem with God's mercy. As we approach Advent, with its call to prepare for the coming of the Lord, Jonah's message about repentance is as pertinent today and challenges us: when we pray for forgiveness ourselves, are we ready for God to show mercy to our opponents?

*Reflection by* **Rosalind Brown**

**Third Sunday before Advent**

Jonah 3.1-5, 10
Psalm 62.5-end
**Hebrews 9.24-end**
Mark 1.14-20

### Hebrews 9.24-end

*'... he has appeared once for all ... to remove sin
by the sacrifice of himself' (v. 26)*

There are several images that the New Testament presents to us that attempt to convey the meaning and the depth of Christ's death. Some of those images (such as 'ransom' or 'sacrifice') are imaginative metaphors that seek to communicate a range of complex truths. Our scriptures don't give us one single notion of atonement to subscribe to, but rather several that are simultaneously competitive and complementary.

The ones offered in today's scripture are essentially contractual. Even though images of blood and purity flow through the reading, the central issue is value. What is our value to God, and what is the value of Christ's sacrifice for us? The English phrase 'paid on the nail' relates to the bronze pillars, also called nails, that have large flat tops – the size of large plates. These nails can still be seen outside the Corn Exchange in Bristol and the Stock Exchanges in Limerick and Liverpool. From late medieval times, business deals were often sealed by money being exchanged on these large flat-headed nails. The songwriter and worship leader, Graham Kendrick's folk song from 1974 ('How Much Do You Think You Are Worth?') takes this idea up, and says that our lives have been valued, and 'a price had been paid on the nail' for each of us. The great beauty of the Christian story is that we can't get to heaven and abide with God in our own strength. The good news is that it is God who reaches down, touches us, bleeds and dies for us, enabling the door of heaven to be opened to all. Christ's death is a one-off, single payment for entry.

*Reflection by* **Martyn Percy**

Jonah 3.1-5, 10
Psalm 62.5-end
Hebrews 9.24-end
**Mark 1.14-20**

## Third Sunday before Advent

### Mark 1.14-20

*... and his brother John' (v.19)*

Right from the start of his ministry, Jesus begins to subvert and play with our assumptions about those to whom we are related; those to whom we have obligations; those to whom we belong. The poor and the socially repugnant are celebrated as near to God. Jews are asked to accept that Samaritans are their neighbours. Gentiles, tax-collectors and women are shown special treatment by Jesus. Perhaps most dramatically of all, the natural family is redefined. All who love God and do his will are Jesus' mother and brothers and sisters.

Traditional Jewish interpretation of Scripture (and a long Christian tradition too) makes the distinction between plain-sense readings and deep-sense readings of the text. Perhaps Jesus wants us to think about 'deep-sense family' (spiritual family) and not suppose that the only meaning of family is the 'plain-sense' (natural) one.

However, Jewish interpreters will also insist that deep-sense readings do not undo or replace plain-sense ones; they extend and deepen them, and are based on them. It is very striking that the Jesus who preached a radical reconsideration of what the meaning of 'family' might be also called two pairs of 'natural' brothers as some of his first disciples: Simon and Andrew, James and John. Even this moment of radical decision, dramatic in its reconfigurations of relationship, is not in every way a break. Family bonds are both sundered and preserved – our kith and kin given back in a new light.

*Reflection by* **Ben Quash**

## Second Sunday before Advent

**Sunday between
13 & 19 November inclusive**

**Daniel 12.1-3**
Psalm 16
Hebrews 10.11-14
[15-18]19-25
Mark 13.1-8

### Daniel 12.1-3

*'... those who lead many to righteousness,
like the stars for ever and ever' (v.3)*

Angels are the neon lights on God's messages and God's purposes. When he has something to which he specially wants to draw our attention, they appear to highlight it, as they did in the fields at Bethlehem and the empty tomb of Easter.

Their function is never to speak of or for themselves, but to be the faithful heralds of the message that God has entrusted to them – and we honour them best when we pay heed to the gospel they are sent to convey.

In their heavenly calling, we can see the prototype of our earthly mission. Our function also is so to live and speak that we floodlight the gospel in a way that enables others to heed and receive it.

This passage points to another, even more mysterious, angelic ministry. The Archangel Michael is appointed the heavenly patron and protector of Israel, and Jesus hints that God has allocated such an angelic guardian to each of us (Matthew 18.10). Just as we are helped and protected in ways we can see by good friends on earth, so our interests will be looked after in ways beyond our knowing in the hidden realms of heaven.

*Reflection by* **Tom Smail**

Daniel 12.1-3
Psalm 16
**Hebrews 10.11-14**
**[15-18]19-25**
Mark 13.1-8

## Hebrews 10.11-14[15-18]19-25

*'... he sat down at the right hand of God' (v.12)*

What Christ achieved for us is final and complete, and this is emphasized by his seated posture. He is no longer standing like a temple priest to offer sacrifice every morning and evening. We live in the time between the victory and the end, waiting and praying that all that remains opposed to him is won over or defeated (compare Hebrews 10.13 with 1.13: 'Sit at my right hand until I make your enemies a footstool for your feet').

So what should our attitude be in this waiting time? The writer suggests, rather optimistically perhaps, that those who are cleansed once for all will cease to have any consciousness of sin and even that we should no longer be in need of forgiveness. His perspective is that of one who is living in 'the last days'. But for us, this raises different issues. How are we to live in response to the finality of Christ's sacrifice?

The quotation from Psalm 40 earlier in this chapter (vv.5-6) suggests an answer: 'Burnt-offering and sin-offering you have not required ... I delight to do your will, O my God' (Psalm 40.6, 8). We are not to live in anxiety about whether or not we are acceptable to God. This anxiety might tempt us to try to appease God or bargain with him. But God takes no pleasure in such strategies. Instead, our prayer should be, 'I have come to do your will, O God'. Offering ourselves afresh in God's service is the response to all that Christ has done for us.

*Reflection by* **Angela Tilby**

**Second Sunday before Advent**

Daniel 12.1-3
Psalm 16
Hebrews 10.11-14
[15-18]19-25
**Mark 13.1-8**

### Mark 13.1-8

*'Not one stone will be left here upon another;*
*all will be thrown down' (v.2)*

A former dean of Salisbury used to stand every morning at his deanery door, look over to the magnificent pile facing him and say: 'O great Cathedral, the day will come when the Lord has no more use for you.'

Great buildings and the ancient traditions they incorporate can reach a point where they impede or resist the very purposes they were set up to serve, and then, like the Jerusalem temple, they become idolatrous sources of temptation that must be removed.

Universally, whenever and wherever Christ comes, the more powerful his presence, the more tumultuous is the resistance to it. The true Messiah will be challenged by false prophets, there will be outbreaks of murderous strife on an international scale; even the forces of nature will, in earthquake and famine, be stirred into a rebellion that frustrates the life-giving will of their Creator.

The Church, where in word and sacrament Christ is most explicitly present, will feel the full brunt of persecuting opposition and internal division, and will be driven to pray for that quality of endurance that will bring it to its goal of salvation in the fully unveiled majesty of its crucified and risen Lord.

*Reflection by* **Tom Smail**

¹Daniel 7.9-10, 13, 14
Psalm 93
**Revelation 1.4b-8**
John 18.33-37

**Christk the King**

**The Sunday next before Advent**
**Sunday between**
**20 & 26 November inclusive**

### Revelation 1.4b-8

*'I am the Alpha and the Omega' (v.8)*

As we celebrate the festival of Christ the King, it's good to be made to examine the scale of our vision of God. I have a horrible suspicion that for some of us God is a worthwhile accessory, a family-sized, flat-packed, easy-assembly deity, one that doesn't interfere too much with our plans or ask too many questions of our lifestyle.

John will have none of that. The God whose greetings he sends to the seven churches is the One 'who is and who was and who is to come', whose seven spirits are before his throne, whose Christ is 'the firstborn of the dead and the ruler of the kings of the earth'. Indeed he is the Alpha and the Omega who encompasses the entirety of history, past, present and future.

What difference would it make to our worship on Sunday if we took with us a vision of the sheer scale, the terrifying beauty, the heart-stopping vastness of that uncontainable Mystery we have the temerity to name 'God' (as if we knew)? The writer Annie Dillard says that when we come to worship: 'We should all be wearing crash helmets. Sidesmen should issue life-preservers and signal flares; they should lash us to our pews ...'

And yet, astonishingly, this God loves us and sets us free and has made us to be a kingdom, priests to serve him. Aren't these powerful images the ones that should be the foundation of our faith and the inspiration of our days?

*Reflection by* **John Pritchard**

¹*For a reflection on Daniel 7.9-10, 13, 14, see page 158.*

**Christt the King**

**The Sunday next before Advent**

Daniel 7.9-10, 13, 14
Psalm 93
Revelation 1.4b-8
John 18.33-37

### John 18.33-37

*'Are you the King of the Jews?' (v.33)*

In this scene, an intense human and spiritual drama plays out behind locked doors. Outside, nationalist feeling is running high. Pilate, alert to potential disturbance during the Passover, must maintain relations with the temple authorities while upholding Roman law and his own position.

The Jews want Pilate to put Jesus to death. An irony that swirls around John's telling of this scene is that the Jews are tacitly acknowledging the kingship of Caesar in order to be rid of their true king, Jesus.

Our sense of the private interchange between Jesus and Pilate depends on tone of voice as they parry questions with questions. Jesus's reply to Pilate's first question takes up the subject and introduces doubt into Pilate's mind – 'on your own' challenges Pilate to move beyond expediency and reveal what he personally thinks. Jesus reframes the encounter, establishing that kingship has a meaning beyond the politics of the Roman world. Jesus is able to draw Pilate to the heart of the matter.

As we ask Pilate's question of Jesus ourselves, 'Are you the King of the Jews?', we face the same challenge he did. He is a king who calls us to face the truth. Do we accept or reject his kingship? All future decisions will be made in the light of that choice.

*Reflection by* **Libby Lane**

Genesis 28.11-18 *or*
Revelation 21.9-14
Psalm 122
1 Peter 2.1-10
John 10.22-29

### Dedication Festival

*If date not known, observe on the First Sunday in October or Last Sunday after Trinity.*

### Genesis 28.11-18

*'The Lord is in this place – and I did not know it! (v.16)*

People go travelling for all manner of reasons. Sometimes – like Jacob, who has scurrilously tricked his brother, who now wants revenge – we are running away. Sometimes we have a destination in mind. Sometimes we are just on a voyage of discovery. Whatever our journey is – even the daily commute – when we are on the move, there can be a sense of us being 'neither here nor there', and so the usual rules do not apply. We are in a liminal state, on the threshold (the meaning of the Latin word *limen*) between two worlds, even if only between home and work.

Often God catches us as we are in transition between one settled place and another. In this unrooted space, outside comfort zones, we may be more open to being surprised by him. Taken beyond our habituated certainties, we, like Jacob, may glimpse new understandings of God, and his call on our lives.

On Dedication Sunday, we generally reflect on churches as solid, settled places, where people may come with an expectation of finding God present. Surely that is the case, especially when we visit churches not our own.

Yet the true church is the community of its people, far more than the building. And the settled people of God of every congregation need to be open to the possibility of being 'on the move' so they too may encounter God in new and unexpected, but life-enhancing, ways.

*Reflection by* **Sarah Rowland Jones**

**Dedication Festival**

Genesis 28.11-18 *or*
**Revelation 21.9-14**
Psalm 122
1 Peter 2.1-10
John 10.22-29

## Revelation 21.9-14

*'Come, I will show you the bride' (v.9)*

What is the significance of John's presentation of the New Jerusalem, the bride of the Lamb, the perfected Church, as an immense, transparent, jewel-like, golden cube?

The key to the logic-defying symbolism of this passage is to contrast it with its sister image, the whore Babylon (compare verse 9 with Revelation 17.1). The whore gives allegiance to whichever suitor seems most advantageous (17.2). The whore is encrusted with gold, jewels and pearls in a gaudy display to enhance her capacity for unfaithfulness (17.4). The whore reels in her drunkenness (17.6) and with the instability of the beast upon which she rides (17.7). The whore is chaos.

The bride, by contrast, is utterly pure. Her purity is such that even the solid elements of which she is made – gold, pearl and jewels – are 'clear as crystal'. This bride has nothing to hide; she is one, single, pure and consistent entity from top to bottom, side to side and back to front.

This vision of purity reflects Revelation's primary concern, which is to alert the churches to the dangers of compromising the singularity of their allegiance to Christ. It is challenging to our own churches that from this singular allegiance is fashioned a dwelling-place of beauty and order, capable of sheltering a vast population in stability and peace.

*Reflection by* **Alan Garrow**

Genesis 28.11-18 or
Revelation 21.9-14
Psalm 122
**1 Peter 2.1-10**
John 10.22-29

## Dedication Festival

### 1 Peter 2.1-10

*'... like living stones, let yourselves be built into a
spiritual house' (v.5)*

Stones that live and houses that are made of spirit seem to belong to the world of cartoons, not of scripture. But Peter is using metaphors and images, piled one on top of the other, to persuade his diverse readers that they are now truly part of God's people, not also-rans outside God's covenant. They are 'a chosen race, a royal priesthood, a holy nation, God's own people'. He lays it on with a trowel. And they are now part of God's temple because of the cornerstone of the building, Jesus, over whom many are stumbling but over whom they themselves are rejoicing, as they come 'out of darkness into his marvellous light'. The argument is closely packed but deeply liberating.

As we gather on a Sunday morning with the usual suspects in a luke-warm church for a somewhat predictable service, we may not feel that we are much of a chosen race or a royal priesthood. Something more mundane may come to mind. But beneath the surface something much more important is going on. Christians have been dipped in God and are being re-formed by the Spirit. There's no hurry about this process; God deals in eternities not weekends. So we meet as freshly minted Christians on the royal road to freedom. And on this festival day of Dedication, we give thanks for Peter, freshly minted after the resurrection, whose passion inspires us still.

That motley band of worshippers you meet on Sundays might turn out to be rather special. Pray for them today.

*Reflection by* **John Pritchard**

**Dedication Festival**

Genesis 28.11-18 or
Revelation 21.9-14
Psalm 122
1 Peter 2.1-10
**John 10.22-29**

### John 10.22-29

*'How long will you keep us in suspense? If you are the Messiah, tell us plainly' (v.24)*

John's Gospel is thick with irony, and this passage is no exception. Isn't it obvious that Jesus is the Messiah, we might say to ourselves? The point is made persistently: many people failed to recognize Jesus, and even when it must have been impossible not to see it, this failure intensified. This, in turn, led to persecution and death, suggested in the verses following today's reading by the threat of stoning on the grounds of apparent blasphemy (John 10.31-34).

John leads us deeper into the mystery of Jesus' divine identity by increasing the risk, a sure indication that the path of following Jesus is not easy. Risk here doesn't only mean threat of death, though that is certainly possible (and worryingly probable in some places); risk also implies that we might lose heart because following Jesus becomes too hard. Risk also invites us to participate in God's mission because God and Jesus 'are one' (John 10.30).

The dynamic incarnational wisdom at the heart of this Gospel remains the mystery that unfolds as the narrative winds its way towards the cross and resurrection. Thus it is through engagement in God's mission that we come to know and understand more fully who Jesus is – and so often it is far from plain sailing! Jesus' opponents struggle to admit Jesus' identity, or even comprehend it. It is only through involvement that we can begin to recognize the fullness of life that is offered to us.

*Reflection by* **Helen-Ann Hartley**

**Joel 2.21-27**
Psalm 126
1 Timothy 2.1-7 *or*
1 Timothy 6.6-10
Matthew 6.25-33

### Joel 2.21-27

*'... be satisfied, and praise the name of the Lord' (v.26)*

God's heart is set on restoration. Cuts heal themselves. We don't tell them to; it just happens. Leaves that fell last autumn have broken down into their elemental goodness and enriched the ground to produce the harvest for which we are thanking God this weekend. Until it reaches breaking point, planet Earth remains determined to undo the harm that is done to it.

So God promises to those who had experienced the environmental catastrophe of a plague of locusts: 'I will repay you'.

God does not just recycle nature; he recycles experiences as well. If we allow him to, he can recycle our mistakes to produce wisdom that enriches our lives. He can recycle sadness to produce compassion for others. He can recycle good fortune to produce generosity. Nothing need ever be wasted. Everything is leading us on to the great day of resurrection, the day of total healing.

Today we raise our prayers for the lands where the harvest has failed, asking that God's mercy will drive out people's fear. We cry for a change of heart for those who damage this beautiful earth at a more selfish pace than God has set it to repair. And we pray for people who have tipped hours of work into projects that have come to nothing, confident that our recycling God will repay them for the years the locusts have eaten.

*Reflection by* **Peter Graystone**

**Harvest Thanksgiving**

Joel 2.21-27
Psalm 126
**I Timothy 2.1-7** *or*
I Timothy 6.6-10
Matthew 6.25-33

### 1 Timothy 2.1-7

*'... a quiet and peaceable life in all godliness and dignity'*
*(v.2)*

Paul leaps with surprising alacrity from political and military power and its effect on our capacity to get on with our lives undisturbed, to reflection on the salvation found through Jesus Christ alone. More than that, he seems to say that such socio-economic stability reflects the saving purposes of God.

Democracy, human rights and the pursuit of a moral rule of law, as we know them today, hardly reflect Paul's experience of kings and rulers. Yet he is clearly not tempted to see politics and religion as separate spheres of life, as so many argue today. He rather sees himself as herald and apostle of the greater truth of God's salvation mediated in Jesus Christ for all humanity, which means every area of life and action – politics included.

This can help us in our appreciation of what harvest can mean, when so few of us are directly involved in the production of food. The gospel is not just for the life of heaven, 'pie in the sky when we die' but also 'steak (or cake, if you prefer!) on the plate while we wait'. Whenever we share God's salvation and proclaim his truth, we should expect to find it taking concrete expression in just structures and practices of society, which find expression in the flourishing 'life of abundance' that Jesus came to bring (John 10.10). This may not mean worldly riches, but certainly God's productive harvest of dignified, godly lives.

*Reflection by* **Sarah Rowland Jones**

Joel 2.21-27
Psalm 126
1 Timothy 2.1-7 *or*
**1 Timothy 6.6-10**
Matthew 6.25-33

## Harvest Thanksgiving

### 1 Timothy 6.6-10

*'... there is great gain in godliness combined with contentment' (v.6)*

This passage contains one of the most (mis-)quoted verses of the Bible: 'For the love of money is a root of all kinds of evil'. But what should we do about it?

I once worked as a youth worker in an inner London club staffed in part by Cambridge graduates – a rich if strange combination. One night, we were discussing what difference becoming a Christian had made to our lives. We listened to several cerebral, but not unmoving, accounts of deep existential change. Then one of the local young people said: 'I don't skip the barriers on the Underground any more.' Tangible honesty as fruit of conversion.

This is a very tangible passage. We are reminded to be content with the food and clothing we have, not least because we can't take it with us when we go ... These tangible blessings are gifts from God for us to enjoy, though we (the rich) are not to get hooked on them.

Harvest Thanksgiving is a tangible day, especially if we see our church filled with the fruits of the soil. Therefore, we can be thankful for God's tangible gifts as part of his good creation – 'God hates nothing that he has made' – but also be brutally honest with ourselves about what good we have actually done with our money today.

*Reflection by* **Alan Bartlett**

## Harvest Thanksgiving

Joel 2.21-27
Psalm 126
1 Timothy 2.1-7 *or*
1 Timothy 6.6-10
**Matthew 6.25-33**

### Matthew 6.25-33

*'... why do you worry?' (v.28)*

Do you find this question of Jesus rather impractical? Isn't the answer obvious? Doesn't he know how stressing life can be? Do sparrows need school uniforms for their young or have a mortgage to pay?

Jesus is not saying that planning our lives responsibly is wrong; he is asking us to reflect on why this makes us worry so much. The word 'worry' shares the same root as the word to 'choke'. When we are worried, we get up tight. When worries and anxieties drive our pursuit of even the most practical needs of life, nothing we manage to achieve or provide is ever enough. Worry is a symptom of insecurity. The harvest is never enough.

The Ignatian spiritual tradition teaches an approach it calls 'active indifference'. In the desert tradition of prayer, it is called 'detachment'. We are active in the sense of being fully, responsibly, involved in the tasks of living. But we are to be indifferent in not being attached to food, clothes or reputation for our identity, security or fulfilment, which those things simply cannot provide for us anyway. It is not what they are for, so we should not be surprised if they sell us short.

It is all about where our heart is. Worry is a symptom of a heart seeking security in the wrong things.

*Reflection by* **David Runcorn**

# REFLECTIONS FOR DAILY PRAYER

If you enjoyed *Reflections for Sundays (Year B)*, why not consider enhancing your spiritual journey through the rich landscape of the Church's year with *Reflections for Daily Prayer*, the Church of England's popular daily prayer companion.

Covering Monday to Saturday each week, *Reflections for Daily Prayer* offers stimulating and accessible reflections on a Bible reading from the lectionary for *Common Worship: Morning Prayer*. Thousands of readers value the creative insights, scholarship and pastoral wisdom offered by our team of experienced writers.

Each day includes:

- full lectionary details for Morning Prayer
- a reflection on one of the Bible readings
- a Collect for the day.

This book also contains:

- a simple form of Morning Prayer, with seasonal variations, for use throughout the year
- a short form of Night Prayer (also known as Compline)
- a guide to the practice of daily prayer by Rachel Treweek.

Each annual volume contains reflections for an entire year starting in Advent and is published each year in the preceding May.

**For more information about Reflections for Daily Prayer, visit our website:**
**www.dailyprayer.org.uk**

# REFLECTIONS FOR DAILY PRAYER
## App

Make Bible study and reflection a part of your routine wherever you go with the Reflections for Daily Prayer App for Apple and Android devices.

Download the app for free from the App Store (Apple devices) or Google Play (Android devices) and receive a week's worth of reflections free. Then purchase a monthly, three-monthly or annual subscription to receive up-to-date content.

# REFLECTIONS ON THE PSALMS

*Reflections on the Psalms* provides original and insightful meditations on each of the Bible's 150 Psalms, from the same experienced team of distinguished writers that have made *Reflections for Daily Prayer* so successful. The author team comprises:

Ian Adams
Christopher Cocksworth
Joanna Collicutt
Gillian Cooper
Steven Croft
Paula Gooder
Peter Graystone
Malcolm Guite
Helen-Ann Hartley
Barbara Mosse
Mark Oakley
Martyn Percy
John Pritchard
Ben Quash
John Sentamu
Angela Tilby
Lucy Winkett
Jeremy Worthen

Each reflection is accompanied by its corresponding Psalm refrain and prayer from the *Common Worship Psalter*, making this a valuable resource for personal or devotional use. Specially written introductions by Paula Gooder and Steven Croft explore the Psalms and the Bible and the Psalms in the life of the Church.

**£14.99** • 192 pages
ISBN 978 0 7151 4490 9

**Also available in Kindle and epub formats**